Reading the Tapestry

Studies in Biblical Literature

Hemchand Gossai
General Editor

Vol. 14

PETER LANG
New York • Washington, D.C./Baltimore • Boston • Bern
Frankfurt am Main • Berlin • Brussels • Vienna • Oxford

Larry Darnell George

Reading the Tapestry

A Literary-Rhetorical Analysis of the Johannine Resurrection Narrative (John 20–21)

PETER LANG
New York • Washington, D.C./Baltimore • Boston • Bern
Frankfurt am Main • Berlin • Brussels • Vienna • Oxford

Library of Congress Cataloging-in-Publication Data

George, Larry Darnell.
Reading the tapestry: a literary-rhetorical analysis of the Johannine
Resurrection narrative (John 20–21) / Larry Darnell George.
p. cm. — (Studies in biblical literature; v. 14)
Includes bibliographical references and index.
1. Bible. N.T. John XX–XXI—Criticism, interpretation, etc. I. Title. II. Series.
BS2615.2.G485   226.5′066—dc21   98-53609
ISBN 0-8204-4444-8
ISSN 1089-0645

Die Deutsche Bibliothek-CIP-Einheitsaufnahme

George, Larry Darnell:
Reading the tapestry: a literary-rhetorical analysis of the Johannine
resurrection narrative (John 20–21) / Larry Darnell George.
–New York; Washington, D.C./Baltimore; Boston; Bern;
Frankfurt am Main; Berlin; Brussels; Vienna; Oxford: Lang.
(Studies in biblical literature; Vol. 14)
ISBN 0-8204-4444-8

In Loving and Continuing Memory of
Leonard George, Sr.
(1908-1990)

TABLE OF CONTENTS

EDITOR'S PREFACE

More than ever the horizons in biblical literature are being expanded beyond that which is immediately imagined; important new methodological, theological, and hermeneutical directions are being explored, often resulting in significant contributions to the world of biblical scholarship. It is an exciting time for the academy as engagement in biblical studies continues to be heightened.

This series seeks to make available to scholars and institutions, scholarship of a higher order, and which will make a significant contribution to the on going biblical discourse. This series includes established and innovative directions, covering general and particular areas in biblical study. For every volume considered for this series, we explore the question as to whether the study will push the horizons of biblical scholarship. The answer must be *yes* for inclusion.

In this volume Larry D. George undertakes an extensive study of a literary-rhetorical reading of the Fourth Gospel. He argues and concludes that the Gospel of John is a unified and coherent whole as it presently stands. Focusing on John 20-21, George proposes a temporal reading from the perspective of the implied author and implied reader. This volume will certainly be an important addition to the already established volumes on the Study of John.

The horizon has been expanded.

Hemchand Gossai
General Editor

ACKNOWLEDGMENTS

This project was successfully completed thanks to many persons who helped me at various stages of this study and in various ways encouraged me along the way to read the bright, front side of the sacred garment. First, I wish to express my appreciation to Dr. Fernando F. Segovia who, as my advisor and one who I deeply admire for not only his impeccable scholarship but also for his congeniality, provided critical reading and sensitive and careful editing of this project. Second, I am also grateful to my other outstanding committee members: Drs. Daniel Patte, Douglas Knight, Susan Wiltshire, and David Buttrick, who provided helpful advice and support when I was in need. The success of this research effort is directly attributable to the support and cooperation of the Religion Department professors, students, and leaders. Three particular friends at Vanderbilt University deserve special mention, Dr. Lewis Baldwin, Mrs. Betty Ford (d. 1995), Graduate Department of Religion Secretary, and Mrs. Anne Womack, Divinity Librarian, who offered me open ears, assuring words, and helpful ideas. I owe thanks to three professors of San Francisco Theological Seminary, who stood by me as mentors during this scholarly journey: Drs. Eugene Farlough (d. 1996) Robert Coote, and Herman Waetjen. As long as I live, I shall never be able to articulate fully the contribution that Herman continues to make for my life and scholarship. He is not only a colleague and friend, but I will always remember the mentoring sessions that we held together for two years, from two to three hours every week! Finally, on the production of this work, I thank Dr. Hemchand Gossai, Ph.D.,General editor for Peter Lang Publishing, Inc., and Ms. Jacqueline Pavlovic, Production Supervisor, Peter Lang Publishing, Inc., for their thorough and detailed review of this work towards its final production.

There are so many people that contributed not only by providing me financial support but also emotional, spiritual, and psychological encouragement, which translates into my notion of true friends who will never give up on me, completely: Ms. Arvetta Downs, my (adopted) mom, a strong, steady supportive voice in my life, Dr. Ephraim Williams, pastor of St. Paul's Missionary Baptist Church (the church where I received my calling to the Gospel Ministry), Mr. and Mrs. Sandy and Lamont Harris, Rev. Johnny Collins, Rev. Benny Ellis, Dr. Obery M. Hendricks, president of Payne Theological Seminary, Dr. Solomon Avotri, Assistant Professor of Biblical Studies at Payne, and Ms. Wilma Lane, a strong motivational source for my life, who gave me the inspiration and the encouragement to bring closure to this project. I thank her for being in my life and for walking with me during the final steps of this journey. Without her support, this project may have not been possible.

From the very beginning of this life journey, my family stood by patiently and persistently, pushing me towards the completion of my studies at Vanderbilt Graduate School of Religion. I thank my mother, Lillie Mae Prater, and my stepfather, Willie Lee Prater, who taught me valuable lessons about life that has brought me this far in my personal, scholarly, and religious journey. I thank my sister, Linda Mae George, and brothers, Leonard George, Jr. and Maurice George, for their confidence that this study would someday be finished. Moreover, most importantly, I thank the Lord and Savior of my life, who answered all of my prayers and led me by grace to the goal and the completion of the Ph.D.

As noted, the work is dedicated to the continuing memory of Leonard George, Sr. (1908-1990), who inspired me to believe in myself and led me safely with wisdom and advice to the first semester of this program and then died, leaving me a legacy—a love, peace, and work ethic—to face all of life's storms. Moreover, at the end of my father's eulogy, I promised my family that I would dedicate this work to him. I pray that his rest—until the great resurrection of the dead—will be peaceful. Thanks be to God for my father's collegiality and faithful companionship to our entire family during his life.

Larry Darnell George, Ph.D.
Dayton, Ohio

ABBREVIATIONS

ABD	*Anchor Bible Dictionary*
ABR	*Australian Biblical Review*
ABS	Anchor Bible Series
AnBib	Analecta biblica
ANRW	*Aufstieg und Niedergang der römischen Welt*
B&LS	Bible and Literature Series
BEST	*Bulletin of the Evangelical Theological Society*
BETL	Bibliotheca ephemeridum theologicarum lovaniensium
Bib	*Biblica*
BibTo	*The Bible Today*
BMMLA	*Bulletin of the Midwest Modern Language Association*
BT	*The Biblical Translator*
BTB	*Biblical Theological Bulletin*
C&L	*Christianity and Literature*
CBQ	*Catholic Biblical Quarterly*
CCC	*College Composition and Communication*
Cent	*Centrum*
CI	*Critical Inquiry*
CJT	*Canadian Journal of Theology*
ColLit	*College Literature*
ConBNT	Coniectanea biblica, New Testament
CQR	*Church Quarterly Review*
CS	*Chicago Studies*
CT	*Critical Texts*
CW	*Classical Weekly*
Diacritics	*Diacritics*
DoR	*Downside Review*
ELT	*Ephemerides Theologicae Lovanienses*
ExpTim	*Expository Times*
FBBS	Facet Books, Biblical Series

Genre	*Genre*
H&T	*History and Theory*
HDB	*Harvard Divinity Bulletin*
ICNTS	*International Congress on New Testament Studies*
Int	*Interpretation*
IRT	Issues in Religion and Theology
ITQ	*Irish Theological Quarterly*
JAAR	*Journal of the American Academy of Religion*
JBL	*Journal of Biblical Literature*
JES	*Journal of Ecumenical Studies*
JLit&Th	*Journal of Literature and Theology*
JLS	*Journal of Literary Studies*
JNT	*The Journal of Narrative Technique*
JR	*Journal of Religion*
JRT	*Journal of Religious Thought*
JSNT	*Journal for the Study of the New Testament*
JSNTSup	Journal for the Study of the New Testament—Supplement Series
JSOT	*Journal for the Study of the Old Testament*
JSOTSup	Journal for the Study of the Old Testament—Supplement Series
JThSoAfrica	*Journal of Theology for Southern Africa*
L'Esprit	*L'Esprit Createur*
LTP	*Laval Theologique et Philosophique*
LuthThJ	*Lutheran Theological Journal*
Neophil	*Neophilologus*
Neotest	*Neotestamentica*
NLH	*New Literary History*
Nov	*Novel*
NovT	*Novum Testamentum*
NovTSup	Novum Testamentum Supplements
NTS	*New Testament Studies*
PerRelSt	*Perspectives in Religious Studies*
Ph & Rh	*Philosophy and Rhetoric*
Poetics	*Poetics*
PoT	*Poetics Today*
Prooftexts	*Prooftexts*
PTMS	Pittsburgh Theological Monograph Series

RQ	*Restoration Quarterly*
Sal	*Salesianum*
SBL	Society of Biblical Literature
SBLDS	Society of Biblical Literature Dissertation Series
SBLSP	SBL Seminar Papers
SE	*Studia Evangelica*
Sem	*Semitica*
Semeia	*Semeia*
SJT	*Scottish Journal of Theology*
SNT	Studien zum Neuen Testament
SNTSMS	Society for New Testament Studies Monograph Series
SR	*Studies in Religion/Sciences Religieues*
ST	*Studia Theologica*
TB	*Tyndale Bulletin*
TS	*Theological Studies*
TSR	*Trinity Seminary Review*
TToday	*Theology Today*
VT	*Vetus Testamentum*
WUNT	Wissenschaftliche Untersuchungen zum Neuen Testament
ZNW	*Zeitschrift für die Neutestamentliche Wissenschaft*

CHAPTER ONE

Setting the Context for Reading the Fourth Gospel's Resurrection Narrative

Introduction

Despite the long standing New Testament scholarly consensus on John 20-21, where chapter 21 represents an addition of some sort to the Gospel (see below), this body of work argues that, as it now stands, the Fourth Gospel's resurrection narrative (John 20-21) represents a unified, coherent narrative text on its own terms—a finely woven *tapestry*.[1]

---

[1] For historical reviews on the entire Gospel of John, see J. Ashton, *Understanding the Fourth Gospel* (Oxford: Clarendon Press, 1991) 1-117; B. Bacon, *The Fourth Gospel in Research and Debate: A Series of Essays on Problems Concerning the Origin and Value of the Anonymous Writings Attributed to the Apostle John* (New Haven: Yale University Press, 1908); G. van Belle, ed., *Johannine Bibliography 1966-1985: A Cumulative Bibliography on the Fourth Gospel* (Lueven: University Press, 1988); D. Carson, "Selected Recent Studies of the Fourth Gospel," *Themelios* 14 (January-February 1989) 57-64; R. Fortna, *The Fourth Gospel and its Predecessor* (Edinburgh: T. & T. Clark, 1989); D. Moody Smith, "Johannine Studies," in *The New Testament and Its Modern Interpreters*, ed. E. J. Epps and G. W. McRae (Philadelphia: Fortress Press, 1989) 271-296; and R. Kysar, "The Fourth Gospel: A Report on Recent Research," in *ANRW* 25.3 (1972) 2389-2480. Kysar correctly observes: "At the center of those efforts to do studies of the literary character of the FG stands a complex of problems. They may be summarized briefly in terms of the question of the literary unity of the document. Many have seen evidence that the gospel *as it stands* does not constitute a unified piece of work. There are numerous aporias in the narrative which raise the question of whether or not we are dealing here

Though this view of the literary work is not novel, it nonetheless accurately depicts the notion that there exists at least three purposes in which one may study or read a text: (1) for the history behind the text (historical and sociological criticisms), (2) for an understanding of the linguistic codes on the material (philology, textual criticism, and structuralism), (3) for the purpose of appreciating the literary function of the writing as a work of art (literary criticism, ideological criticism, cultural criticism, rhetorical criticism, and to some extent composition criticism).

From a literary-rhetorical perspective, I shall focus primarily on the textual interaction between the implied author and the implied reader constructed on pages as text.[2] In other words, by employing a literary-

---

with a document which is whole or which reflects its original order" (emphasis mine) 2391. With a contrary view on the unity of the gospel narratives, S. Moore asserts: "In the 1980s narrative criticism has replaced structuralism in North America as the prevalent way of doing narrative analysis of the gospels. A central assertion of narrative criticism is that the gospels are unified narratives. I feel that this assertion/assumption may be a blind spot in narrative criticism..." S. Moore, "Are the Gospels Unified Narratives?" in SBLSP, ed. by K. Richards (Atlanta: Scholars Press, 1987) 443.

The phrase "on its own terms" means that this resurrection narrative will not be read in terms of other sources, such as the Signs Source, the Synoptic Gospels (Matthew, Mark, and/or Luke), and the like (see below, note 7).

[2] Throughout this work, unless otherwise noted, the writer will use the terms "author" with reference to the implied author, and "reader" with reference to the implied reader in the text. This usage suggests that the writer believes that the implied author or the implied reader inscribed in the text is not specified—either male or female. The argument could be made, however, that the implied author is referred to with the masculine gender and that the implied author addresses the implied reader with the masculine gender.

Concerning the implied reader in the text, W. Iser notes: "Central to the reading of every literary work is the interaction between its structure and its recipient. This is why the phenomenological theory of art has emphatically drawn attention to the fact that the study of a literary work should concern not only the actual text but also, and in equal measure, the actions involved in responding to that text." W. Iser, "Interaction between Text and Reader," in *The Reader in the Text: Essays on Audience and Interpretation*, ed. by S. Suleiman and I. Crosman (Princeton: Princeton University Press, 1980) 106; and see, e.g., W. Iser, *The Act of Reading: A Theory of Aesthetic Response* (Baltimore: Johns Hopkins University Press, 1978) 3-19. See also, E. Freud, *The Return of the Reader: Reader-Response Criticism* (New Accents. London and New York: Methuen, 1987) 1-20, esp. 69-89, 90-111; J.

rhetorical methodology this work seeks to highlight particular narrative strategies encountered during and after the reading process. By employing this temporal or sequential process of reading, this reading seeks to evaluate the author's progressive arrangement of various episodes, scenes, events, narrative techniques and devices, and so forth in order to determine how John 20-21 as a whole is unified and designed to inform and influence—on a cognitive and emotive level—the reader with regard to Jesus' post-resurrection status and nature, viz., the appearances and the progressive development of the narrative that, for example, depict the characters' faith and mission.[3] In short, from a literary-rhetorical perspective, John 20-21 primarily concerns the implied author's narrative or rhetorical arrangement of evidence to inform and convince the implied reader of the narrative unity of Jesus' four resurrection appearances to the disciples.[4]

Correspondingly, from the point of view of the author and reader in the text, this work seeks to construct a literary-rhetorical reading of John 20-21 as a self-contained narrative text regarding its architecture and strategy.[5] To highlight this architecture and strategy, this work advances

---

Tompkins, *Reader-Response Criticism: From Formalism to Post-Structuralism* (Baltimore: Johns Hopkins University Press, 1980) ix-xxvi; S. Fish, *Is There a Text in This Class?: The Authority of Interpretive Communities* (Cambridge: Harvard University Press, 1980) 21-67; and W. Vorster, "The Reader in the Text: Narrative Material." *Semeia* 48 (1989) 21-39. According to Vorster, "The reader is said to be 'in the text' because of his/her/its presence as an image, created by the author, and because of his/her/its encoding in linguistic signs and textual strategies. This image has to be constructed by the real reader." Ibid., 22.

[3] See, e.g., Ibid., 23.

[4] In the Fourth Gospel or in the Synoptic Gospels (or even in the entire New Testament as a whole) there exist no texts that describe the resurrection event proper; in other words, during the early morning hours of Easter Sunday, there is no narrative description of what actually happened to Jesus while he was inside the tomb. This work will generally employ the term "resurrection" instead of "post-resurrection" for the sake of conveyance. For a detailed discussion of the absence of a narrative account regarding the resurrection event, see, e.g., W. Marxsen, *Jesus and Easter: Did God Raise the Historical Jesus from the Dead?* (Trans. V. Furnish. Nashville: Abingdon Press, 1990) 57-74.

[5] Concerning the architecture and strategy, F. Segovia comments: "I now see the farewell speech as both an *artistic and strategic whole*, with *a unified literary structure and development*, as well as unified strategic concerns and aims... The speech is intelligible *as it presently stands. There is no need to search for meaning*

a temporal process of reading John 20-21, presenting this reading in light of other legitimate interpretations of the Fourth Gospel's resurrection narrative.[6] Before proceeding on to the history of scholarship on John 20-21, it is necessary to provide a rationale for such a reading that seems on the surface, in light of the prevailing consensus on the status of chapter 21 in relation to the rest of the Gospel, as an act of belaboring the obvious.[7]

In the last twenty-five years, the focal point of New Testament studies has experienced a paradigm shift.[8] To mention only one such shift, New Testament scholars have redirected their study of gospel narratives from a primary focus on the history behind the text approach to a focus on various strategies engaged while reading narrative texts, more specifically, to a focus on the reader, howsoever defined, on the narrative-rhetorical features and devices concerning the final form of the

---

outside of the text, especially in terms of an excavative approach and by way of literary layers. There is no need to posit a variety of authors in the process of composition and addition of these layers" (emphasis mine). F. Segovia, *The Farewell of the Word: The Johannine Call to Abide* (Minneapolis: Fortress Press, 1991) viii; see, also, Iser, *Act of Reading*, 86-103. These views also hold true for the implied author of the resurrection narrative and represent a central presupposition of this study.

6   For temporal process of reading and its effect on readers, see J. Resseguie, "Reader Response Criticism and the Synoptic Gospels." *JAAR* 52 (1984) 307-324; and J. Staley, *The Print's First Kiss: A Rhetorical Investigation of the Implied Reader in the Fourth Gospel* (SBLDS 82. Atlanta: Scholars Press, 1988) 8-9, esp., n. 14.

7   Though I will not seek to provide a literary-rhetorical reading of the entire Gospel narrative, I will argue that the resurrection narrative (John 20-21, in particular chapter 21) forms a unity with the rest of the Gospel narrative. The project intends to demonstrate that the past scholarship on this narrative is methodologically insufficient to prove or disproved the literary or rhetorical unity or disunity of this chapter. See, e.g., Moore, "Unified Narratives," 446.

8   For the paradigm shift in New Testament and Biblical Studies, see, e.g., F. Segovia, "Toward a New Direction in Johannine Scholarship: The Fourth Gospel from a Literary Perspective." *Semeia* 53 (1991) 1-22, see, esp., 1-3; Carson, "Select Recent Studies," 60-64; Willi Braun, "Resisting John: Ambivalent Redactor and Defensive Reader of the Fourth Gospel." *SR* 19 (1990) 59-61; Adela Collins, "New Testament Perspectives: The Gospel of John." *JSOT* 22 (1982) 47-53; Mary Gerhart, "The Restoration of Biblical Narrative." *Semeia* 46 (1989) 13-15; and W. A. Beardslee, "What is It About?: Reference in New Testament Literary Criticism," in *The New Literary Criticism and the New Testament*, ed. by McKnight, Edgar V. and Elizabeth S. Malbon (Valley Forge: Trinity Press, 1994) 369.

Gospel as a whole and on the various perspectives of the narrative text's reader. With this advent of studying narrative texts from these two perspectives, scholars are aptly equipped with different and various perspectives for temporal reading processes and interpretive principles while engaging narrative texts.[9] In other words, New Testament scholars are currently re-reading narrative texts not only to challenge the prevailing opinions regarding, for instance, the literary-rhetorical relationship between chapter 21 and the rest of the Gospel, but they are also engaging the texts' final form as readers. In other words, several readings of the resurrection narrative seek to introduce different ways of portraying Gospel texts as narrative texts, rather than as mere historical texts that have been viewed as layers of traditions, which are identified by the alleged seams in the text. Thus, this paradigm shift represents not only a change in the various methodological approaches, but it also entails a change in focus and perspective—from historical to literary interests and from fragmentation to the tapestry of the narrative texts.

Concerning the consensus on chapter 21, New Testament scholars generally agree that this chapter forms some sort of an addition to the rest of the Gospel. Despite the lack of textual evidence to support such a conclusion, some scholars continue to overlook the central message of chapter 21 as an essential part of the resurrection narrative and the Gospel as a whole. Rather than providing coherent readings of the entire resurrection narrative, these scholars have proposed fragmented readings of this and other sections of the resurrection narrative, reading it in terms of the Synoptic Gospels and editorializing it in order to excavate it and thus focus on its historical features, which prevent a coherent reading of viewer's side the tapestry of the Gospel in terms of chapters 1-20 from the perspective of the text's reader (see below).

The next part of this chapter presents a history of scholarship concerning the major trends in the classical readings of this text with a review of how scholars have continued to analyze and read John 20-21—

---

[9] See, e.g., E. McKnight, *Postmodern use of the Bible: The Emergence of Reader-Oriented Criticism* (Nashville: Abingdon Press, 1988) 167-267; S. Moore, *Literary Criticism and the Gospels: The Theoretical Challenges* (New Haven: Yale University Press, 1989); and F. Moloney, "Who is 'the Reader' in/of the Fourth Gospel?" *ABR* 40 (1992) 20-33.

the whole and various parts thereof—from traditional historical-critical perspectives.[10] The second part of this section reviews the major trends of literary-rhetorical readings of the resurrection narrative, from a narrative-critical and rhetorical or reader-response perspective, along with an analysis of the proposals regarding the reader of the Gospel.[11]

After presenting the history of scholarship on the resurrection narrative of the Fourth Gospel, the second part of this chapter constructs a literary-rhetorical methodology, which is employed in this work. Finally, this chapter concludes with the plan of this study, a brief overview of the three episodes and twelve scenes of John 20-21, along with a proposal for an analytical representation of these episodes and scenes in John 20-21, foreshadowing the subsequent readings in Chapters Two through Four.

History of Scholarship

Most of the traditional scholarship on the Fourth Gospel's resurrection narrative has been concerned with comparing it with other sources, particularly the Synoptics, and with rearrangement theories that produced fragmented readings of the text, seeking to reveal its compositional style and nature, its authorship, and so forth. On the one hand, form-, redaction-, and tradition-critical scholars continue to focus on historical aspects—looking behind the garment—of John 20-21 in

[10] Primarily, four classical readings have been identified in this section for review: R. Bultmann, *The Gospel of John: A Commentary* (Trans. G. Beasley-Murray, R. Hoare, and J. Riches. Philadelphia: Westminster Press, 1971) 681-718; R. Brown, *The Gospel According to John* (Vol. 29A of *Anchor Bible Series*. Garden City: Doubleday and Co., 1966 and 1970) 965-1132; C. K. Barrett, *The Gospel According to St. John: Introduction with Commentary and Notes on the Greek Text* (2d ed. London: SPCK, 1978) 560-588; and R. Schnackenburg, *The Gospel According to St. John*. Vol. 3, Commentary on Chapters 13-21 (Trans. D. Smith, R. Foley, and G. Kon. New York: Crossroad Publishing Company, 1982) 300-374.

[11] Primarily, three modern literary-rhetorical studies have been considered in this historical review: A. Culpepper, *Anatomy of the Fourth Gospel: A Study in Literary Design* (Philadelphia: Fortress Press, 1983); Staley, *Print's*, 95-118; and F. Segovia, "The Final Farewell of Jesus: A Reading of John 20:30-21:25." *Semeia* 53 (1991) 167-190.

terms of the Synoptic Gospels and with other sources.[12] On the other hand, some modern literary-rhetorical scholars have continued to read this narrative text, borrowing traditional and historical conclusions of the nature of this narrative, along with literary and rhetorical strategies, to read the text as a historical narrative, howsoever defined.[13] Both of these approaches, for the most part fail to consider fully the text on its own terms and as it now stands, but rather these approaches read the text for the history it may contain, as compared with Matthew, Mark, or Luke, reading chapter 20 as a part of the Gospel but continuing to read chapter 21 as an addition to the Gospel (1-20).

Traditional Historical-Critical Scholarship on the Fourth Gospel's Resurrection Narrative

For the most part, traditional historical-critical scholarship on the Fourth Gospel's resurrection narrative has proposed primarily historical (tradition, source, and form) and theological (redaction and composition) readings of John 20-21. As a result, several studies have been concerned with some aspect of the text's composition history, which are mostly fragmented readings of parts of the Fourth Gospel's resurrection story. For example, R. Bultmann claims that the text as it now stands does not make sense,[14] and consequently he proposed a reconstruction of the Gospel based on rearrangement theories (see below). Additionally, scholars have developed a consensus on the literary nature of chapter 21, claiming that it represents a clumsy addition to the rest of the Gospel (i.e., Since John 20:30-31 serves as the formal conclusion to the Gospel,

[12] Some representative studies are: T. Brodie, *The Gospel According to John: A Literary and Theological Commentary* (New York: Oxford University Press, 1993) 556-596; G. Lüdemann, *The Resurrection of Jesus: History, Experience, Theology* (Minneapolis: Fortress Press, 1994) 1-32, esp. 151-171; B. Witherington, III, *John's Wisdom: A Commentary on the Fourth Gospel* (Louisville: Westminster John Knox Press, 1995) 323-361; and L. Morris, *The Gospel According to John: The New International Commentary on the New Testament* (Revised. Grand Rapids: Eerdmans, 1995) 731-777.
[13] For a recent study from this perspective, see, e.g., C. Talbert, *Reading John: A Literary and Theological Commentary on the Fourth Gospel and the Johannine Epistles* (New York: Crossroad, 1992) 248-264.
[14] See Kysar, "Fourth Gospel," 2391.

there is no need to read further, e.g., John 21). Thus, traditional scholars have not sought to consider both the literary and rhetorical features of the Gospel's final form on its own terms, and as such, historical and literary interpretations of John 20-21 fail to consider adequately the author's content and structure as a coherent, unified narrative text.

Most of the traditional scholarship of the Fourth Gospel's resurrection narrative has noted that this section of the Gospel (20-21) does not cohere organically. For example, as mentioned above, even though there is no textual evidence to suggest that chapter 21 ever circulated without the rest of the Gospel, most of the scholarship of the Fourth Gospel has regarded this chapter as a distinct, separate addition to the rest of the Gospel. Nonetheless, a historical and theological consensus have been adapted on the nature of chapter 21, considering it as some sort of a fragmented addition to the Fourth Gospel.[15]

For instance, Bultmann[16] argues that chapter 21 should be considered as a postscript to the Fourth Gospel; in much the same fashion, Brown[17] and Barrett[18] consider this chapter as an epilogue and appendix, respectively; even though Schnackenburg[19] challenges the ways in which these scholars have designated this section, he nonetheless agrees that chapter 21 stands an addition to the Fourth Gospel. Thus, major studies on this chapter regard its relation to the rest of the Gospel as an addition

---

[15] Brodie argues: "For this view, the following reasons are proposed: (1) In 20:30-31 there is a conclusion to the gospel. Consequently, anything which follows it is secondary, added. (2) Chapter 20 pronounces a climactic blessing on those who have not seen (20:29). The author who did that is unlikely to have then gone on to tell of those who did see. (3) The sequence between chaps. 20 (in Jerusalem) and 21 (in Galilee) is awkward. In particular, it is unlikely that the disciples would go from the climactic experience of seeing Jesus and receiving a Spirit-filled commission to the prosaic business of fishing. (4) Chapter 21 has an extraordinary diversity of elements and consequently is sometimes seen as lacking unity. Such diversity may seem to suggest a different author... 'This noteworthy interweaving of different threads in the story, is not otherwise the evangelist's way' (Schnackenburg, 3:342)" Brodie, *John*, 574, for a list of "severe limitations" to these reasons, see, e.g., Brodie, *John*, 574-575.

[16] See, Bultmann, *John*, 700-706.

[17] See, Brown, *John*, 1077-1082.

[18] See, Barrett, *John*, 576-577.

[19] See, Schnackenburg, *John*, 341-345.

of some sort: an appendix, an addendum, an epilogue, a post-script, and the like.[20]

R. Bultmann. Concerning rearrangement theories of the resurrection narrative, Bultmann situates his reading by noting that 20:1-18 is interpolated.[21] In essence, as in many parts of the Gospel as a whole, he refuses to believe that this story is original.[22] One of the difficulties he finds with this section occurs when Mary Magdalene stands at the tomb after the two disciples leave this setting (20:10). Due in large part to the lack of narration, explaining how she arrived back at the tomb, Bultmann identifies these two stories as being drawn from the Evangelist's source. Concerning the nature of these two stories, he concludes: "Obviously then the two stories are not an original unity; whereas the account of Mary is derived from the tradition to which the Synoptics' stories about the grave also belong, the story about Peter and the beloved disciple doubtless goes back to the Evangelist."[23] In short, Bultmann's reading of this pericope (20:1-18) includes several rearrangement theories that represent a historical reading of the text; therefore, he believes that this pericope lacks originality and points to the use of sources. For instance, he finds that what Peter views in the tomb "originally belonged to the story of Mary... (vv. 6f)."[24]

---

[20]   H. Teeple notes: "Ever since Bretschneider questioned the gospel's solidarity, in 1820 the issue of the unity of the book has continued to be debated. Strauss in 1858 opposed the view that the gospel is a 'seamless robe' by declaring that is has been 'patched together out of miscellaneous shreds of diverse materials.'" Teeple continues: "(the metaphor 'seamless robe' was suggested by John 19:23). Both Bretschneider and Strauss encountered tremendous storms of oppositions." H. Teeple, *The Literary Origin of the Gospel of John* (Evanston: Religion and Ethics Institute, Inc., 1974) 18. In his history of scholarship on the literary puzzle and the hindrances to a suitable solution, Teeple concludes with what he finds to be the different kinds of quests, if you will, to solve the problem of authorship and the sources to the Gospel, which stand behind the question of the unity of the Gospel.

[21]   See, Bultmann, *John*, 681.

[22]   Ibid.

[23]   Ibid.

[24]   Ibid., 682.

As in the previous pericope, Bultmann believes that 20:19-23 is drawn from the Evangelist's sources.[25] As in the previous section, he begins each section by examining the pericope with various methodological assumptions, employing form-, source-, and redaction-criticisms. With these methodological perspectives, he asserts that the text is not unified and then proceeds with a commentary on the salient features of the pericope, namely those that would support his conclusion that the text is not unified. For example, he observes that vv. 19-23 is narrated with a missing disciple, with the exception of Judas.[26] Additionally, he argues that there is no connection between what comes before or after vv. 19-23, apart from the editorial juncture in v. 19. Thus, he concludes that vv. 19-23 is "a story complete in itself."[27] He justifies this conclusion by providing a list of what is not mentioned in the narrative, rather than with a reading of what is included in the temporal flow of the narrative.[28] Further, Bultmann believes that vv. 19-23 is a variant of Luke 24:36-49 and Matthew 28:16-20.[29] He claims that both the appearance and the way in which Jesus appeared are recounted in a popular legend format. In such he concludes by noting that although the Fourth Evangelist edited this story, it was taken from his source; he attributes, however, vv. 21-22 to the Fourth Evangelist.[30]

In the next pericope (20:24-29), Bultmann finds no parallels in the Synoptics, but this section, according to him, does reflect the doubt of certain disciples in the Synoptics,[31] who required a physical manifestation in order to remove their doubt. Nonetheless, since a continuation of v. 23 is not presupposed in vv. 24-29, he holds that there could have been a secondary source, along with a primary source employed by the Fourth Evangelist.[32] In short, he also views these verses (vv. 24-29) as a supplement to the Gospel.

---

[25]   Ibid., 689.
[26]   Ibid., 690.
[27]   Ibid.
[28]   Ibid.
[29]   Ibid.
[30]   Ibid.
[31]   See, e.g., Mt. 28:17; Lk. 24:11, 21-25, 37-41; also in Lk. 24:39-41. See, e.g., Ibid., 693.
[32]   Ibid., 693.

Finally, concerning the concluding verses of chapter 20, Bultmann believes that vv. 30-31 is "a clear conclusion to the Gospel (1-20), in which the selective character of the narrative is stressed and its purpose is declared."[33] As in 12:37, the formulation of vv. 30-31 is occasioned by the fact that the Fourth Evangelist is taking over the conclusion to the Signs Source.[34]

Further, Bultmann believes that the Evangelist directly addresses the reader in v. 31.[35] According to Bultmann, in v. 31a the Evangelist does not address a precise circle of readers.[36] He notes, therefore, that it really does not matter how one reads the text critical marks.[37]

In short, for Bultmann, very little of chapter 20 contains unity; most of it, he believes, is from the Fourth Evangelist's sources, either without editing, with revisions, or from some other sources (the Synoptics, a Signs Source, or a supplementary source).

As mentioned above, although there is no textual or manuscript evidence that indicates chapter 21 ever circulated separately from the rest of the Gospel, the literary and historical nature of this section of the Fourth Gospel was formally challenged by Bultmann on a number of fragmented levels. First, he argues that chapter 21 is a postscript because with 20:30-31 the Fourth Gospel had already reached its natural conclusion.[38] Second, he claims that chapter 21 could not have come from the hands of the Evangelist, the original author of chapters 1-20.[39] Finally, he concludes that chapter 21 was not from the Evangelist based on the following stylistic variations in chapter 21 versus the rest of the

---

[33]   Ibid., 697.

[34]   Ibid., 698, n. 2. He comments that 12:37 and 20:30-31 would have stood together. The former comment is interesting since no one has yet to find this so-called Signs Source.

[35]   See also John 19:35.

[36]   See, Bultmann, *John*, 698.

[37]   Namely, he means that it really does not matter how one reads this variant; it could be either to those who believe [πιστεύβητε, present subjunctive] or to those who might believe [πιστεύβσητε, aorist subjunctive]. Ibid., n. 7; and Brown, *John*, 1056. Based on my reading of the resurrection narrative, this work affirms the former view.

[38]   See, Bultmann, *John*, 700.

[39]   See, e.g., Teeple, *Unity*, 28.

Fourth Gospel (1-20):[40] (1) the difference in language and style, (2) the different sentence connectors, (3) the change of vocabulary, (4) the role of the disciples, (5) the question of the appearance of Jesus in Galilee before the disciples, (6) the difference in character and theme, and so on.[41] Moreover, Bultmann questions the unity of the chapter itself by arguing that chapter 21 is divided into two unrelated sections: vv. 1-14 and 15-23.[42]

Concerning vv. 1-14, Bultmann believes that most of these verses were written through many editorial additions. For example, he notes that among these verses: "probably v. 4b, certainly v. 7, and vv. 9b and 13"[43] were inserted by a redactor. He believes that the reference to 153 fish, which had been caught by the disciples with Jesus' assistance, could go back to the redactor.[44]

Regarding the next pericope, Bultmann finds no connection between vv. 15-17 and 18-22. The two sections, according to Bultmann, have no inner connection with each other but give expression to a variety of interests. For example, Bultmann notes: "It is clear therefore that vv. 15-17 are taken from the tradition, perhaps from a written source, whereas vv. 18-23 of course are the author's own composition."[45] Here, the central thrust for Bultmann is to identify the authorship of this postscript. He notes: "That the Evangelist himself added it, and put it after his first conclusion, then to append yet a second concluding statement (vv. 24f.), is extraordinarily improbable."[46]

---

[40]   Teeple notes: "Writers do not agree on the extent of the stylistic unity in John. In Ruckstuhl's opinion there is an overall unity, and the few variations in style are merely a result of the different materials involved: discourses, narrative, and dialogues." Teeple, *Unity*, 21. These differences can be easily accounted for in a narrative rhetoric, where it is a common feature of the storyteller to leave gaps and blanks for the reader to fill-in during or after the process of reading. See, Iser, *Act of Reading*, 165-69. Bultmann, on the other hand, considers stylistic variations and regard them as evidence of sources.

[41]   See, Bultmann, *John*, 700-701.

[42]   Ibid., 702.

[43]   Ibid., 703.

[44]   Ibid., 708-709.

[45]   Ibid., 706.

[46]   Ibid., 700.

In closing, it is clear that Bultmann is seeking to strengthen an already established tradition of interpretation, which can be seen as he commences his historical reading of the resurrection narrative. Rather than, for example, beginning with a close reading of some sort, he begins with a set of presuppositions and claims, which he clarifies in the methodological section and further seeks to prove in the commentary section. He clearly employs several methodological approaches to provide a detailed and exhaustive analysis, comparative study, with text critical comments (mostly in the footnotes) to strengthen or further points already established in the history of scholarship that preceded him. This methodological rigor is what sets Bultmann apart as someone to contend with in the study of the Fourth Gospel.

R. Brown. Unlike Bultmann, Brown is concerned with an attempt to reconstruct the resurrection stories in the New Testament by means of the earliest formulae in I Corinthians and of narratives in the Gospels and Acts in order to attempt a general portrayal of the resurrection of Jesus.[47] Regarding the Gospels' accounts of the resurrection, he considers six texts from the Gospels for this attempted reconstruction: Mark 16:1-8, Mark 16:9-20, Matthew 28, Luke 24, John 20, and John 21.[48]

Further, this attempted reconstruction leads Brown to the consideration of two types of narratives: the post-resurrection appearances and the empty tomb stories. Brown employs textual-, source-, tradition-, and redaction-criticisms to determine if a harmony of the resurrection narratives exists, comparing the accounts in the Fourth Gospel with those found in the Synoptics.[49] In short, he finds that no harmony of these accounts is possible because, "It is quite obvious that the Gospels do not agree as to where and who Jesus appeared after his resurrection."[50]

---

[47] See, Brown, *John*, 966-969.
[48] For the relationship between John 20:1-18 and the Synoptic Gospels, see, e.g., Brown, *John*, 996.
[49] Brown provides a useful chart to illustrate the various gospel accounts, see, Brown, *John*, 968. For a chart on narrative visits of women to the tomb, see Brown, *John*, 974.
[50] Brown, *John*, 969.

Interestingly, from a traditional historical-critical perspective, Brown identifies the Fourth Gospel as a drama, which can be observed from the way in which he delineates the various scenes. For example, Brown's outline of the Fourth Gospel resurrection narrative (chapter 20) consists of two scenes: Scene One: At the Tomb (20:1-18), and Scene Two: Where the Disciples Are Gathered (20:19-29).[51] Scene One consists of two episodes: Episode One: Visits to the empty tomb (vv. 1-10), and Episode Two: Jesus appears to Magdalene. Scene Two also consists of two episodes: Episode One: Jesus appears to the disciples (vv. 19-23), and Episode Two: Jesus appears to Thomas (vv. 24-29).[52] Like Bultmann, despite the present form of the Gospel, Brown considers vv. 30-31 to be the conclusion to the Gospel as a statement of the author's purpose.[53]

Similar to Bultmann's position on the final chapter of the Gospel text, he views John 21 as an addition to the Gospel narrative, which was written by someone other the author of chapters 1-20. Brown, however, considers chapter 21 to be an epilogue, "an added account of a post-resurrectional appearance of Jesus in Galilee, which is used to show how Jesus provided for the needs of the church."[54] He outlines this chapter into three parts: Part A: The Risen Jesus Appears to the Disciples at the Sea of Tiberias (21:1-14); Part B: The Risen Jesus Speaks to Peter (21:15-23); and Part C: The (Second) Conclusion (21:24-25).[55]

Regarding Brown's reading of the resurrection narrative as a whole, his analysis consists of two sections: Notes and Comment. In the "Notes" section, Brown provides a word-by-word, phrase-by-phrase commentary of the various scenes. As in Bultmann's quest, Brown reads the various scenes of the Fourth Gospel resurrection narrative in terms of the sources

---

[51] For the Fourth Gospel as drama, see, e.g., M. Stibbe, ed., *The Gospel of John as Literature: An Anthology of Twentieth-Century Perspectives.* Leiden: E. J. Brill, 1993.

[52] Ibid., 965. For a survey of the structures of the Fourth Gospel as proposed by various scholars, see G. Mlakuzhyil, *The Christocentric Literary Structure of the Fourth Gospel* (AnBib 117. Roma: Editrice Pontificio Istituto Biblico, 1987) 19-85, esp. 79-83.

[53] See, Brown, *John*, 1055.

[54] Ibid., 1063.

[55] Ibid., 1065.

that he believes the author, John, employed in the composition of the Fourth Gospel. For instance, he compares the pericope of Mary Magdalene's trip to the tomb with the Synoptics' accounts, considering the time, the number of women who visit the tomb, the purpose of her trip to the tomb, and so forth.[56]

In the "Comment" section, Brown provides a history of scholarship on the related scene, discussing the structure of each scene, the theories of composition, an additional analysis of the scene in question, and the like. His main concern in this section is to provide an analysis of the central themes in each section from a historical perspective. For instance, concerning the authorship of chapter 21, Brown considers evidence other than those related to the style of the Evangelist to argue for the addition of this chapter to the Fourth Gospel.[57] Further, he explores possibilities that seek to explain why this chapter was added to the original Gospel. He comments:

> In re-editing the Gospel, the evangelist would have been able to smoothly intercalate (if he knew the sequence); a redactor would be more likely to add on. Moreover, even if the evangelist himself added on a new set of appearances, he would have felt free to move or modify his previous conclusion in xx 30-31, whereas a redactor might not wish to tamper with the Gospel that had come down to him.[58]

In short, similar to Bultmann's approach, Brown is mostly concerned with the history behind the text, with a fragmented reading of the scenes, and with a reading of the Fourth Gospel's resurrection narrative in terms of the sources that may lie behind it. Though he considers chapter 20 as a drama, he continues to regard chapter 21 as an addition to the Gospel, and he searches, as Bultmann, for the author or redactor of this final chapter.

C. K. Barrett. At the outset, Barrett covers several related themes in the introduction to his commentary: (1) The Gospel, its Characteristics and Purpose; (2) The Non-Christian Background of the Gospel; (3) The Christian Background of the Gospel; (4) The Theology of the Gospel; (5)

---

[56] See, Ibid., 980-984.
[57] See, Ibid., 1079-1080.
[58] Ibid., 1080.

The Origin and Authority of the Gospel; and (6) The Text.[59] This outline in the introduction indicates the focus and approach of Barrett's commentary, which is to comment on the historicity of the Fourth Gospel. For example, in the first section of the introduction, Barrett points out: "the purpose of an introduction to any ancient book is that its environment may shed light upon the work under consideration, and that in turn the book may be used to illuminate its environment."[60] This opening statement seems to reflect the critical, scholarly currents of the time. Wherein, for example, Bultmann harshly criticizes scholars, like C. H. Dodd, in his review of Dodd's commentary, for not taking into consideration some of the most essential elements that were being discussed during this period.[61] Hence, Barrett, following Bultmann and Brown, begins his discussion with some of the environmental concerns or social and historical problems concerning the Fourth Gospel, which was the state of scholarship during this era.

Further, in the second section Barrett compares the literary characteristics (word and vocabulary motifs) and structure of the Fourth Gospel with the Synoptics. Here, he concludes that the Fourth Gospel is "a highly individual Gospel; it resembles the style or vocabulary of the epistles of John."[62] He says that the Greek is neither good nor bad, according to the Greek of that day. Regarding the style of the Gospel, he observes that the style is clear, the vocabulary small, yet most of the most frequently used words occur comparatively rarely in the Synoptics.[63] Finally, he considers the style of the Fourth Gospel in an examination of a number of characteristic expressions and usage.[64]

Unlike Bultmann, Barrett considers six sources to have influenced the Fourth Gospel: (1) the Synoptics, (2) material similar to the Synoptic

---

[59] See, Barrett, *John*, 3-146.

[60] Barrett, *John*, 3.

[61] For Bultmann's review of C. Dodd's commentary, *The Interpretation of the Fourth Gospel*, see R. Bultmann, "Rudolf Bultmann's Review of C. H. Dodd: *The Interpretation of the Fourth Gospel.*" Trans. W. Robinson, reprinted from *HDB* 27, 2 (1963) 9-10 (original review: *NTS* 1 (1954/55) 77-91.

[62] See, Barrett, *John*, 5.

[63] Ibid., 5-6.

[64] Ibid., 7-10.

Gospel tradition, (3) a Signs Source, (4) the discourses,[65] (5) a Judaean Source, and (6) the Passion Narrative.[66]

Despite the practice of displacement and redaction theories, the Fourth Gospel, according to Barrett, is as Strauss states, "a seamless robe."[67] Now, let us turn to Barrett's reading of the Fourth Gospel's resurrection narrative.

Regarding the methodological location of Barrett's reading, he seems to be following Bultmann and Brown's position without too many variations. In fact, Barrett begins his reading with similar assertions of Bultmann and Brown, namely that the early traditions of the resurrection of Jesus took two forms: the resurrection appearances to various disciples and the traditions of the discovery of the empty tomb. Further, Barrett refers to Brown's latest edition, which covers these traditions in detail, in the form of charts.[68]

Generally speaking, like Bultmann and Brown, the first section of Barrett's commentary is on various methodological and theoretical issues concerning the resurrection traditions, sources, influences, and the like. The second section is devoted, unlike Bultmann, to an evaluation of the phrases or words that are central to the text, covering most of the words or phrases, if not all, in his word-by-word and phrase-by-phrase commentary on the Greek text. In this section, Barrett refers to other studies and text critical comments in the text. In some places, Barrett differs from Bultmann and Brown, but for the most part, he follows their analysis and comments with slight variation in perspective. Unlike Bultmann, Barrett feels that v. 31 should be translated as it is in the text, namely, "that you may continue to believe, be confirmed in your faith" (present subjunctive).[69]

[65] Here, he rejects Bultmann's Revelation Discourses. Actually, he feels that both the use of a Discourse Source and a Signs Source are unreliable. Thus, these sources, listed here in this section, are merely employed as a grid to test or argue for the most likely sources that the Fourth Gospel employs. See, Ibid., 20-21.

[66] Ibid., 21. Here, Barrett takes the view that the passion narrative is an edited version of the Markan narrative, into which the Fourth Evangelist has introduced some fresh material.

[67] Ibid., 26.

[68] See note 49, above.

[69] Ibid., 575.

Regarding chapter 21, Barrett refers to scholars who challenge the consensus, for example, S. S. Smalley,[70] but he concludes that Smalley's arguments are not convincing. Concerning stylistic and vocabulary considerations, Barrett again refers to Bultmann as the best collection of evidence.

In conclusion, Barrett's method of reading this text is similar to Bultmann and Brown's approaches in the order and type of questions considered. The style of his commentary is different in the analysis section, but it is for the most part the same as that of Bultmann and Brown in their observation sections. Regarding chapter 21, Barrett takes a much stronger stance than Bultmann and Brown regarding the literary nature of this chapter, claiming that it seems necessary to detach the whole of chapter 21 from the main body of the Gospel; hence it should be considered as an appendix to the Gospel.[71]

R. Schnackenburg. Schnackenburg approaches the Fourth Gospel's resurrection narrative from a literary-, tradition- and redaction-critical perspective, seeking the evangelist's intentions in the report of the appearance stories. He seems unsure, however, what to call the "appearance" stories; he believes that the Fourth Evangelist sought to construct his own version of the empty tomb and the story of the appearances. Though he uses the literary terminology, "a narrative point of view," his sense of it is particularly from a source-, redaction-, and tradition-critical perspective.[72] On the one hand, Schnackenburg claims that the Fourth Evangelist used traditions and "certainly traditional material."[73] He believes that the Fourth Evangelist has "a strong

---

[70] See, S. Smalley, "The Signs in John XXI." *NTS* 20 (1974) 275-288.

[71] See, Barrett, *John*, 576. Teeple comments: "Even if there is some stylistic unity, Johannine scholars disagree on its cause... The evangelist may have used sources, rewriting the material in his own style... Or he may have used sources and imitated their style when he composed his own portions of the gospel... Another possible cause of stylistic unity is that a redactor may have revised the gospel later and impressed his own style on the book. Finally, a redactor may have adjusted his own style to that of the gospel... a redactor produced the stylist unity by imitating the evangelist's style." Teeple, *Unity*, 21.

[72] See, Schnackenburg, *John*, 300.

[73] Ibid., 300.

individual composition, however, from the first to be reckoned with."[74]
On the other hand, Schnackenburg claims that chapter 20, though written
to believers, is not unified. Thus, he observes several ways in which
20:1-18 and the entire resurrection narrative may be read.[75]

Regarding the structure of chapter 20, he relies on Brown's analysis,
which breaks chapters 20-21 into scenes and episodes. For
Schnackenburg, the scene is defined as events occurring in one particular
or primary setting. As such, he delineates chapter 20 into two scenes: the
empty tomb and the place of the gathering of the disciples. The first
scene has two episodes: Chap. 20:1-10 and chap. 20:11-18. The second
scene also has two episodes: 20:19-23 and 20:24-29. Though
Schnackenburg regards chapter 21 as an addition, he believes that the
editors weave various themes into the appearance narratives.[76] During
this process, Schnackenburg believes that the editors sought to retain the
unity between chapter 21 and the rest of the Gospel.[77] In such
Schnackenburg contends that Jesus' appearance to Thomas, along with
20:30-31, the Gospel is a self-contained entity, requiring nothing further
to complete the Gospel, such as an additional appearance in chapter 21.[78]
Therefore, unlike that of Bultmann, Brown, and Barrett, Schnackenburg
challenges the traditional characterizations of this final chapter, which he
believes was written by editors. Schnackenburg comments: "The editors
presuppose that and direct the evangelist's message to the Church
(ecclesiastical and pastoral interest)."[79] He argues, despite the prevailing
consensus, for the unity of chapter 21 with the rest of the Gospel
narrative. For example, he argues:

> If that is correct, then it has to be asked how this editorial chapter is to be
> characterized in relation to Jn 20 and to the entire gospel: is it a 'postscript'

---

[74] Ibid.

[75] Ibid., 302-303.

[76] See, Ibid., 343-344.

[77] See, Ibid., 343.

[78] Schnackenburg observes: "The evangelist did not need or intend any such
continuation as is found in Chapter 21, not even as 'Postscript'. After the words to
Thomas (20:29) and the concluding words in 20:30f, the new appearance before the
disciples has the effect of being rather unsuited and disturbing for his presentation."
Ibid., 343.

[79] Ibid., 344.

[Bultmann], an 'appendix" [Barrett], or an 'epilogue' [Brown]? None of these designations fully applies. It is not a postscript because there is really nothing more to be said; 'appendix' is to see it too much from an external point of view not corresponding to the inner importance given to this chapter by the editors; 'epilogue' sounds (at least in German) again too inconsiderable to be just in respect of the function for the readers in the Church of those days. For us, it also has a certain key-position for the better understanding of the evangelist's work in its historical circumstances; for by means of it, it is recognizable that, and in that way, it is shared by a rather large circle of disciples and friends and received by the Church. If the explanation proposed in this commentary of the secondary 'farewell addresses' in Chapters 15-16 (and possibly of the prayer in Chapter 17) is correct, that namely, they are continuations and applications of the farewell address in Chapter 14 for the life of the Church(es), the analogy for the relationship of Chapter 21 to Chapter 20 forces itself upon us: in a similar way and with similar intention the editors have worked here as there. But that does not have to mean that we are dealing with the same compilers; for, the rest, the differences remain considerable between the shape of those addresses and the narrative material in Chapter 21.[80]

In other words, though Schnackenburg argues for the unity of chapter 21 with chapter 20 and the rest of the Gospel, he nonetheless believes that it is an addition of some sort to the Gospel narrative added by editors (1-20).

In short, Schnackenburg's approach to this Gospel, unlike Bultmann, Brown, and Barrett, seeks to stay as close to the text as possible. Though he still compares chapters 20-21 with the Synoptics, Schnackenburg first considers 21:1-23 on its own terms, comparing it with chapters 1-20,[81] and then, as the others, he studies the traditional historical-critical riddle in search of a suitable solution.[82]

Since Bultmann's commentary on the Fourth Gospel, several scholars have accepted, with slight variations, Bultmann's theory of the composition of chapter 21, as being an addition of some kind to the Gospel.[83] Recently, several scholars have challenged this consensus from

---

[80] Ibid.

[81] See, Ibid., 341.

[82] Ibid., 344-351, 375-388.

[83] See, Neirynck, "John 21." *NTS* 36 (1990) 321-336.

a historical-critical perspective.[84] For example, Smalley's article, based on the signs in the Fourth Gospel, argues that the theme of chapter 21 is different enough to account for a change in the vocabulary from chapters 1-20; thus, according to Smalley, chapter 21 should not be considered as coming from the hands of a redactor.[85] He then proceeds to confront Bultmann's other claims concerning the nature of the relationship between chapter 21 and the rest of the Gospel, employing a historical approach. Further, Paul Minear's article challenges the consensus with the claim that 20:29-31 concludes chapter 20 and not the entire Gospel, which he sees as the function of chapter 21.[86] Minear observes many connections between chapter 21 and the rest of the Gospel.[87] Finally, Peter Ellis, using composition and narrative criticism, argues that the entire Gospel is from the hand of one author and that its unity can be demonstrated according to the laws of chiastic parallelism rather than the laws of narrative.[88] Thus, for Ellis and others using this approach,[89] the literary and historical nature of this chapter has again gained scholarly attention.

Regarding the practice of reading narrative texts as historical documents, historical-critical scholars have searched for alleged seams or gaps to identify sources and real, flesh-and-blood authors in order to reveal the various historical or compositional layers behind the text and the writer(s) or editors responsible for such texts, rather than viewing these elements in the narrative text as rhetorical strategies employed by

[84] Some earlier representative studies are: E. Hoskyns, *The Fourth Gospel* (2d ed. London: Faber and Faber, 1947) 550; and M. Lagrange, *L'Evangile selon Saint Jean* (Paris: Gabalda, 1948) 520-21.

[85] See, Smalley, "Signs," 275-288.

[86] See, Paul Minear, "The Original Function of Jn. 21." *JBL* 102 (1983) 85-98.

[87] Ibid., 96-97.

[88] See, P. Ellis, *The Genius of John: A Composition-Critical Commentary on the Fourth Gospel* (Collegeville: Liturgical Press, 1984) 280-312.

[89] Some representative studies are: B. Barnhart, *The Good Wine: Reading John from the Center* (New York: Paulist Press, 1993) 216-290; Talbert, *Reading John*, 248-264; F. Moloney, *The Gospel of John* (Collegeville: The Liturgical Press, 1998) and *Glory not Dishonor: Reading John 13-21* (Minneapolis: Fortress Press, 1998); and B. Olsson, *Structure and Meaning in the Fourth Gospel: A Text Linguistic Analysis of John 2:1-11 and 4:1-42* (Trans. J. Gray. ConBNT 6. Lund: Gleerup, 1974) 1-17.

an implied author.[90] Because biblical texts have been variously
investigated for the history behind the text or lack thereof, which have
been gleaned from the text's compositional history along with the
various approaches for reading texts for possible sources, scholars have
faced certain limitations in that they have neglected to consider each text
as a narrative text on its own terms and as its now stands—as unified,
coherent narrative texts. That is, scholars have not considered how real
authors create implied authors to address implied readers in narrative
texts, which can be re-constructed with certain theoretical constructs, for
example, with a temporal process of reading of narratives, focusing on
the implied reader's reactions to the literary strategies of the implied
author.

   Concerning the literary nature of the narrative text, another limitation
that further weakens traditional historical scholars' readings is their
attempt to employ historical-critical methodologies to answer literary
questions, which are outside the scope of their methodological and
theoretical apparatus. This weakness, which investigates narrative texts
as historical texts and traverses beyond the methodological boundaries of
the historical-critical approach, resulted, in part, in the failure to reach an
adequate consensus regarding various issues, particularly the unity of
John 20-21 and specifically the literary characterization of chapter 21 in
terms of the rest of the Gospel. Moreover, limitations such as these were
presented as scientific, objective quests for the history behind the text,
rather than as mere readings that may contribute to the overall meaning
of the text—historical- and narrative-critical, or otherwise.[91]

---

[90] See, Iser, *Reading*, 22, 165-169, 171-172, 174, 179, and 225.
[91] This discussion naturally proceeds in the direction that necessitates my dependence
     on some of the presuppositions of New Criticism. R. Detweiler notes: "What was
     new about the New Criticism was its focus on the literary text as the object of
     scrutiny in terms of its formal properties of texture and structure, in contrast to the
     'old' criticism that concerned itself with the cultural, historical, moral, and other
     dimensions of the literary work." R. Detweiler, "After the New Criticism:
     Contemporary Methods of Literary Interpretation," in *Orientation by Disorientation:
     Studies in Literary Criticism and Biblical Literary Criticism in Honor of William A.
     Beardslee* (ed. by Richard A. Spencer. PTMS 35. Pittsburgh: Pickwick, 1980) 3.
     Vincent Leitch lists five distinguishing characteristics of the Formalist School: "First,
     New Criticism separates *literary* criticism from the study of sources, social

Narrative-Rhetorical Scholarship on the
Fourth Gospel's Resurrection Narrative

Though some literary-critical Johannine scholars have assumed from the outset that chapter 21 is a part of the Fourth Gospel as a whole, for the most part their readings fail to illustrate explicitly how this narrative section is a unified narrative text from a literary-rhetorical perspective on its own terms and as it now stands.[92] Employing literary-rhetorical approaches, other scholars continue to borrow the conclusions of traditional historical-critical studies, neglecting to deal with chapter 21 as a unified narrative text. In other words, though the literary-rhetorical approach assumes from the outset that texts contain unity, some modern narrative-critical scholars continue to read the resurrection narrative as a fragmented text. Moreover, most of these scholars combine historical

---

background, history of ideas, politics, and social effects, seeking both to purify poetic criticism from such 'extrinsic' concerns and to focus attention squarely on the 'literary object' itself. Second, New Criticism explores the structure of a work, not the minds of authors or reactions of readers. Third, New Criticism champions an 'organic' theory of literature rather than a dualistic conception of form and matter; it focuses on the words of the text in relation to the full context of the work: each word contributes to a unique context and derives its precise meaning from its place in the poetic context. Fourth, New Criticism practices close reading of individual works, attending scrupulously to nuances of words, rhetorical figures, and shades of meaning as it attempts to specify the contextual unity and meaning of the work in hand. Fifth, New Criticism distinguishes literature from both religion and morality mainly because many of its adherents have definite religious views and seek no substitutes for religion, morality, or literature" (author's emphasis). V. Leitch, *American Literary Criticism from the Thirties to the Eighties* (New York: Columbia University Press, 1988) 26-27. Unless otherwise noted, this work subscribes to most of these characteristics of New Criticism. However, at the outset, it signals a firm rejection of the fifth point due to the nature of the literature being studied herein.

[92] For example, F. Moloney is in the process of writing a commentary on the Fourth Gospel from a literary-rhetorical perspective. His first volume is complete, covering chapters 1-4, and he proposes to write two additional volumes to include chapters 5-12 and 13-20, which excludes chapter 21 from his analysis. He says, "In this study the *text itself* is at the center of my analysis. I consistently direct my reading of John 1-4 toward a discovery of the emerging implied reader, created as the text unfolds. This heuristic device can only be traced through close attention to the text. It must not simply reflect the experience of a contemporary reader" (emphasis mine). F. Moloney, *Belief in the Word. Reading the Fourth Gospel: John 1-4* (Minneapolis: Fortress Press, 1993) x-xi.

approaches with their narrative methods, comparing the Fourth Gospel's resurrection narrative with the Synoptic Gospels.[93]

In addition to focusing on the narrative text as it now stands and on its own terms, this work concerns two other constructs: the implied author and the implied reader in the text. In such the following section on narrative-rhetorical scholarship of the Fourth Gospel's resurrection narrative evaluates the major trends of reader-constructs employed by contemporary Johannine scholars regarding this section of the Gospel.

A. Culpepper. In *Anatomy of the Fourth Gospel: A Study in Literary Design,* Culpepper primarily employs narrative criticism, supporting it with various literary theories borrowed from outside New Testament studies.[94] His approach dissects the Fourth Gospel in order to reveal various literary-rhetorical features, narrative devices, and constructs of the Gospel, considering, for example: the implied author and implied reader, narrator and narratee, narrative and story time, explicit and implicit commentary, events, setting, characters, and so forth. Culpepper proposes essentially four analytical literary perspectives, but he only provides an analytical section or chapter on three of these perspectives, which consist of: (1) real author and real reader;[95] (2) the implied author

---

[93] See, e.g., M. Stibbe, *John as Storyteller: Narrative Criticism and the Fourth Gospel* (Cambridge: Cambridge University Press, 1992) 1-2, 67-92. This narrative commentary on the Fourth Gospel argues that there are several editors at work in the compositional-structure of the gospel. Even though Stibbe believes that this work in its final form contains editorial layers, he employs a narrative-critical perspective from a synchronic and diachronic perspective to present the unity of chapter 21 with the rest of the gospel. See also, M. Stibbe, *John* (England: JSOT Press, 1993) 198-215.

[94] Some of the representative studies are: S. Chatman, *Story and Discourse: Narrative Structure in Fiction and Film* (Ithaca: Cornell University Press, 1978); B. Uspensky, *A Poetics of Composition: The Structure of the Artistic Text and Typology of a Compositional Form* (Trans. V. Zavarin and S. Wittig. Berkeley: University of California Press, 1973); M. Sternberg, *Expositional Modes and Temporal Ordering in Fiction* (Baltimore and London: Johns Hopkins University, 1978); G. Genette, *Narrative Discourse: An Essay in Method* (Trans. J. Lewin. New York: Cornell University Press, 1980); and W. Booth, *The Rhetoric of Fiction* (2d ed. Chicago: The University of Chicago Press, 1983).

[95] For his construct of the real author and real reader, see Culpepper, *Anatomy,* 15 and 265, which lists the other pages that consider various readers and includes the implied

and the implied reader:[96] here Culpepper presents two views which portray the communication between the implied author and the implied reader: (a) explicit commentary[97] and (b) implicit commentary;[98] (3) the narrator and narratee;[99] and (4) the story or message or code, which consists of: (a) events,[100] (b) characters, which are further delineated into two sections: action and dialogue,[101] (c) setting or scene.[102] Further, Culpepper presents two chapters not specifically mentioned above that provide a part of the theoretical framework for his study: Chapter One "Narrator and Point of View,"[103] and Chapter Three, "Narrative Time."[104] Culpepper, however, devotes a considerable amount of his work to a consideration of these features without explaining explicitly how these literary devices may help to illustrate the unity of the resurrection narrative or the Gospel as a whole.

In what follows, the section considers the reading process that Culpepper employs, in *Anatomy of the Fourth Gospel*, to define and later to construct his notion of the implied reader. This analysis focuses particular attention to sources, benefits, aims, limitations, and in the end, how he reads and engages the real reader in the act of reading. That is, two questions will be addressed: How does one read through the eyes of

---

reader, the first reader, the contemporary reader, as well as the flesh-and-blood, real reader.

[96] For the implied author and implied reader, see, e.g., Ibid., 15-16; 205-227.

[97] For explicit commentary, see, e.g., Ibid., 7, 17, 19, 206, 208, 224, 225, and 234. Culpepper does not provide an analytical chapter on explicit commentary.

[98] For implicit commentary, see, e.g., Ibid., 6, 7, 151-202, 233, and 234. In Chapter Six, regarding implicit commentary, Culpepper discusses three concepts: misunderstanding, irony, and symbolism as types of implicit commentary between the implied author and the implied reader. These types have been referred to as the communication that occurs on the dialogue or discourse level of the narrative. See also, e.g., Chapman, *Story*, 196-262.

[99] For types of commentary that also exist between the narrator and narratee, see notes 97 and 98, above.

[100] For plot, see Culpepper, *Anatomy*, 79-98.

[101] For characters, see, e.g., Ibid., 101-148.

[102] For setting and scene, see, e.g., Ibid., 19, 20, 30, 31, 61, 71, 72, 74, 87, 106, and 234, as well as the name of cities, etc., in Culpepper's Index.

[103] Ibid., 15-49.

[104] Ibid., 53-75.

Culpepper's implied reader? Moreover, How may readers employ Culpepper's implied reader to read the narrative text?

Culpepper's reader is first pointed out in a diagram,[105] in which Culpepper locates the implied reader inside the narrative text in relation to the implied author, who communicates to the implied reader through explicit and implicit commentary, which is defined by Culpepper as misunderstanding, irony, and symbolism. More specifically, Culpepper says: "The implied reader is defined by the text as the one who performs all the mental moves required to enter into the narrative world and respond to it as the implied author intends."[106]

More significant is Culpepper's notion of how the implied reader is constructed. He comments:

> ... a narrative inevitably projects a picture of the reader for which it was intended. When an explanation is offered, for example, the intended reader would not have understood that point without it. On the other hand, when characters, places, and terms are not explained, the interpreter can assume that the intended reader was capable of understanding them without any explanation from the narrator. By systematically collecting and analyzing such data one can construct a portrait of the gospel's implied reader. In John the implied reader is scarcely distinguishable for the narratee, just as the implied author can hardly be separated from the narrator.[107]

In other words, in order to construct a portrait of Culpepper's implied reader, one would first collect data regarding the narrator's comments to the so-called intended reader.[108] Next, one would analyze this data in order to ascertain what kind of information the narrator

---

[105] Ibid., 6.
[106] Ibid., 7.
[107] Ibid., 7-8.
[108] Culpepper states: "The narrator's commentary is a major source of definition for the reader's identity" Ibid., 206. I would add: the order of the text, the information provided by the characters about themselves, other characters, and so forth assist in the construct of the implied reader. Here, according to S. Rimmon-Kenen, a character analysis can be depicted on a scale represented by three literary devices: surface action only (outside) vs. the penetration into the character's inner life; no development, which indicates a function beyond itself or the character, vs. development; complex, with at least one dominate trait, with a few secondary traits, vs. simple, i.e., a single trait. See, S. Rimmon-Kenan, *Narrative Fiction: Contemporary Poetics* (New York: Methuen, 1983) 41-42.

assumes that the reader knows and does not know, according to the information given in the text and the information not provided in the text. Lastly, this information would be systematically analyzed to develop a portrait of the implied reader of the Gospel.

Regarding the construct of the reader, Culpepper begins by listing the various types of readers: "intended readers, implied readers, historical readers, model readers, mock readers, ideal readers, and an equal number of narratees."[109] He believes the reason for so many different types of readers is that different narrative texts create their own readers.[110] That narratives create their own readers is hardly the case since the real reader determines how she or he will read a particular text. Rather, the various kinds of readers are in part due to the demands or needs of the various critics and readers who study texts for different reasons.[111]

Second, Culpepper's study on the implied reader is informed by the vast literature on reading. Culpepper notes:

> Within the growing literature on readers one discerns the pursuit of answers to two fundamental questions: Who is the reader? And, what must the reader do to read a text? A great deal of what has been put in earlier chapters of this book is related to what the reader of the Fourth Gospel must do to read it successfully.[112]

The only question, although Culpepper seems to avoid it, is what does he mean by "What a reader must *do*... to read it [the text] *successfully*?" I think that what a reader must first do is read, charting his or her reactions during the temporal process of reading. In order for a reader to read successfully, he or she must enter and engage the narrative world of the text and experience the narrative as the implied author has designed it; in the case of the Fourth Gospel's resurrection narrative, the

---

[109] Culpepper, *Anatomy*, 205.

[110] Here, Culpepper is following Booth. See, Ibid., 205-206, esp. n. 3.

[111] See, e.g., F. Segovia, "Reading Readers of the Fourth Gospel and Their Readings: An Exercise in Intercultural Criticism," in *"What is John?": Readers and Readings of the Fourth Gospel* (ed. by F. Segovia; Symposium Series, SBL; Atlanta: Scholars Press, 1996) 237-277.

[112] Culpepper, *Anatomy*, 205.

reader must leave the reading experience with a conviction and a corresponding level of belief or faith.[113]

Third, in order to distinguish between the various types of audiences or readers, Culpepper employs Peter J. Rabinowitz's model, which posits at least four audiences in any narrative text.[114] Following Rabinowitz's model, Culpepper identifies the type of audience required to make sense of the Fourth Gospel: the type of audience required by the implied author.[115]

Finally, Culpepper concludes with his process for constructing the ideal audience of the Fourth Gospel. He states:

> In John the ideal narrative audience adopts the narrator's ideological point of view, penetrates the misunderstandings, appreciates the irony, and is moved to fresh appreciation of transcendent mystery through the Gospel's symbolism. The Gospel is, ostensibly at least, entirely realistic. The narrative audience merges with the authorial audience, but the authorial audience is culturally, historically, and philosophically distant from the contemporary actual audience. We can concentrate, therefore, on the gospel's definition of its authorial audience and the work of the contemporary reader in adopting the perspective of that audience.[116]

What I initially find problematic in this procedure is that one's systematic analysis, along with its results, will be different from one reader to another. What Culpepper refuses to admit here is that what he is constructing is precisely a "portrait" of the implied reader, namely a construct, a construct that is precisely of the one who is in the act of reading.

---

[113] See, Ibid.

[114] According to Rabinowitz, the four types of readers or audiences are: "(1) The actual audience, (2) The authorial audience, (3) the narrative audience, and the ideal narrative audience." Quoted in Ibid., 206. Culpepper claims: "The possibility remains, however, that by studying the authorial audience implied in the gospel a clearer picture may emerge of the audience for which the evangelist intended to write." Ibid., 207. This audience still exists for those who read the Bible from a pre-critical perspective. Booth describes two of these readers in *Rhetoric*, 89-116, 424.

[115] See, e.g., Culpepper, *Anatomy*, 207-208.

[116] Ibid., 208.

This process of constructing the implied reader further presupposes a construct that will be made at the end of the reading process.[117] Could not another possibility be to construct the implied reader during the reading process, which would assure the critic of the fact that the data that is being analyzed will not be taken out of context? *Reading the Tapestry* takes seriously this method of constructing the implied reader.

Additionally, what Culpepper fails to realize is that the implied reader is a construct of the implied author or narrator, which are also considered to be constructs of the real, flesh and blood author.[118] The purpose of such constructs is to conceive of a recipient during the act of reading. The implied reader, in the narrative text, serves as a guide for the real, flesh-and-blood reader during the temporal flow of reading. The sole purpose of creating a reader—who would have followed the implied author into and through the narrative world of the text—is the necessary first step towards fully engaging the narrative text, namely by a close reading or unpacking of the narrative text (see below).

In the end, Culpepper does suggest, in a piecemeal fashion, from both a synchronic and a diachronic perspective,[119] that the Fourth Gospel is more unified and coherent than most studies in the past have demonstrated. He believes that the unity of the Gospel can be illustrated in a study of the plot development, the thematic development of characters, the work of the narrator, and the narrative and rhetorical structure.[120] Besides, as traditional historical scholars, he believes that chapter 21 was composed by another hand, and he believes that chapter 21 forms some sort of an addition to the Gospel. Yet, he includes some of the features and perspectives from chapter 21 into his analysis of the Gospel as a whole.[121]

---

[117] Culpepper further defines the implied reader near the end of his book, which may be due to his presupposition of how one should construct the implied reader. See, e.g., Ibid., 205-227.

[118] See, e.g., Booth, *Rhetoric*, 118, 397-398.

[119] On mixing synchronic, Formalist Studies, and diachronic studies, and historical critical concerns: form, source, and redaction criticism, see Staley, *Print's*, 12.

[120] See, Culpepper, *Anatomy*, 45-46

[121] Ibid., 66, 121, 180, and 197.

Only a few Fourth Gospel literary-rhetorical studies have demonstrated that chapters 20 and 21 are explicitly unified. Two of these studies are considered below with a focus both on their process of reading and their perspective on the nature of the final chapter, chapter 21.[122]

J. L. Staley. In *The Print's First Kiss: A Rhetorical Investigation of the Implied Reader in the Fourth Gospel*, J. Staley focuses on the rhetorical interrelationship between the text of John (the print) and the reader (the kiss), with the underlying theme of orality, which Staley borrows from Walter Ong.[123] Staley claims, following Ong, that a great difference occurs in the thinking process between an aural society and a society which internalizes the written text, that is in an oral society a greater dynamic of speaking and hearing occurs due in part to the intertextuality of the spoken word.

The theoretical foundation of his study project, according to Staley, "will adopt much of the terminology of Reader Response Criticism—an approach in contemporary literary criticism which deals primarily with the analysis of the modern novel."[124] Reader Response Criticism also focuses on the reader or the audience. The method of this study employs rhetorical strategies, along with Reader-Response Criticism and theories of Narratology. One of the major goals of this work is to apply the canons of Reader Response Criticism to the Fourth Gospel and to focus attention on the temporal reading process and its rhetorical effects.[125]

Staley's analysis focuses on the narrative levels or voices in the Fourth Gospel. In his treatment of 21:24, he notes that the confusion of authorship can be resolved by recognizing the shift in narrative voices. As such, given the shift in the narrative voices in 21:24, he claims that there should be no confusion over the number of authors and insists that

---

[122] See, e.g., Staley, *Print's*, 111-118; and Segovia, "Final Farewell," 167-190. See, e.g., Stibbe, *John*, 198-215.

[123] W. Ong, *Orality and Literacy: The Technologizing of the Word* (London: Methuen Co., 1982).

[124] Staley, *Print's*, 4.

[125] Ibid., 9.

an implied author with different focalizations, borrowing from Genette,[126] can be seen at work.

In studying different constructs of the implied reader, Staley's construct of the implied reader differs from Culpepper's construct in *Anatomy of the Fourth Gospel*, which tends to confuse the implied reader with the real first-century, first-reader, and the narratee.[127] In Staley's construct of the implied reader, he assumes wrongly that the implied reader is victimized by the implied author in chapter 21, where he concludes that the implied reader is on the same level as Peter when the narrative is concluded.[128]

Basically speaking, on the one hand, Culpepper believes that the implied reader can be reconstructed based on the information that the narrator provides to the narratee and implied reader, that is what the narrator provides or does not provide can be used to construct an overall "portrait" of the implied reader. On the other hand, here Staley's construct is a bit more descriptive than Culpepper's construct of the implied reader in that he believes that the implied reader, not to be confused with the narratee, can be reconstructed from: "The interaction of narrative's various levels, the manipulation of narrative temporality, and the evocative role of narrative's linguistic signifiers and medium will all work together to form the text's implied reader and create the text's rhetorical power."[129] Staley, however, only uses the information provided in the text and not that which the critic assumes to be known by the narratee: this is an assumption which he does seem to be aware of in the theoretical section of his book; however, in the final chapter of his work

---

[126]   See, Genette, *Narrative Discourse*, 185-210.

[127]   W. Booth describes the implied reader in terms of an author who "creates… an image of himself and another image of his reader; he makes his reader, as he makes his second self, and the most successful reading is one in which the created selves, author and reader, can find complete agreement." Quoted in Staley, *Print's*, 7 n. 7. W. Iser writes, "the term 'implied reader'… incorporates both the prestructuring of the potential meaning by the text, and reader's actualization of the potential through the reading process." Quoted in Ibid.

[128]   Staley notes: "But upon a close reading one discovers that he [Culpepper] often confuses narrator/implied author with editor/author, while at the other end he confuses narratee/implied reader with the first reader." Staley, *Print's*, 12.

[129]   Ibid., 49.

he does not take this assumed information into account. Thus, he focuses only on one half of Culpepper's basic formula for constructing the implied reader from the text.

In short, both Staley's and Culpepper's constructs seem to be somewhat limited. The weakness in Staley's construct is the fact that he does not posit an implied reader who can fully understand the narrative text. Rather, what he offers is an analysis of the second level of narration, the implied author and the implied reader, rather than allowing the implied reader to interact with the characters in the story-world.[130]

F. F. Segovia. In "The Final Farewell of Jesus: A Reading of John 20:30-21:25,"[131] Segovia studies the compositional structure and unity of 20:30-21:25 from a literary-rhetorical perspective, arguing that this section is a coherent and meaningful narrative scene. In fact, Segovia approaches this study as a continuation of his work on the Fourth Gospel with the same literary-rhetorical methodology as he employed in *Farewell of the Word: The Johannine Call to Abide.*[132] Segovia's literary-rhetorical approach consists of two perspectives. First, the literary aspect refers to the way in which he synchronically analyzes the genre, the structure of the text (e.g., the chiastic pattern to differentiate the beginning and end of each section), and the technique or pattern of repetition in ancient narrative of the section in question.[133] Finally, with a rhetorical approach he not only employs reader-response theories, with a focus on flesh-and-blood readers (from his own social location),[134] as an

---

[130] B. Olsson's 1974 dissertation *Structure and Meaning in the Fourth Gospel* employ the term "ideal receiver." His discussion of the "ideal reader" becomes a description of the hypothetical original reader because, according to Staley, "his critical method does not provide him with the tools to clearly distinguish between the inter- and intratextual relationships, nor with the sensitivity to enunciate clearly between discourse and story order, the rhetorical power of the narrative's temporality and of its inter/intratextual relations are often missed." Quoted in Ibid., 11.

[131] See, Segovia, "Final Farewell," 167-190.

[132] For Segovia's methodology, see Segovia, *Farewell of the Word*, 48-58.

[133] See, Segovia, "Final Farewell," 169-172; and Segovia, *Farewell of the Word*, 49-54.

[134] See, F. Segovia, "Toward a Hermeneutics of the Diaspora: A Hermeneutics of Otherness and Engagement," in *Reading from this Place: Social Location and Biblical Interpretation in the United States*, Vol. 1. ed. by F. Segovia, and M. Tolbert (Minneapolis, Fortress Press, 1995) 57-73; and Segovia, "Final Farewell," 168-169.

important pole in his reading strategy and as a negotiation between text and reader in the construction of meaning, but also he studies the rhetorical function of the narrative, employing the following five types: admonitory, exhortative, didactic, consolatory, and polemical as descriptions of the type of rhetoric employed by the implied author.[135]

He studies the Gospel's narrative features—patterns of repetition and recurrence in ancient narrative, and common type-scene—in the farewell scene in ancient narratives to suggest explicitly that this section of the Gospel serves as a conclusion to this scene (18:1-21:25) and the final form of resurrection appearances (20:1-21:25).[136] His work clearly focuses on the unity of the final narrative section (20:30-21:25) of the Fourth Gospel from a literary-rhetorical perspective, using the generic classification of ancient narratives, as a way of reading the Gospel as a whole.

Borrowing his initial insight from R. Alter,[137] Segovia analyzes narrative conventions to accomplish two objectives: (1) to focus on the work from a narrative perspective to enable the critic to observe the basic conventions of narrative texts, with clarity and precision; that is the way in which a work has been artistically composed; (2) to focus on the reader or the audience from a rhetorical perspective to enable the reader to perceive the "complex communication," which a work of art has on the reader.[138] More specifically, he borrows from Alter the study of repetition in biblical narrative, which leads him (Alter) to the recognition of a compositional pattern of the "type-scene."[139] With the perspective of

---

[135] See, Segovia, "Final Farewell," 168, 172-173; and Segovia, *Farewell of the Word*, 55-56.

[136] See, Segovia, "Final Farewell," 170.

[137] The pattern of type-scenes need not be the same. Segovia concludes: "Indeed, it becomes clear from Alter's own analysis of one of these biblical type-scenes that the distinctive character of each example is also related in a direct and fundamental way to the character of the narrative within which the type-scene is located, thus involving a detailed focus on such matters as narrative development, characterization, literary structure and development, and overall thematic concerns. Only then, through this search for the artistic uniqueness of each example, can the reader come to understand with some degree of accuracy what the author was trying to communicate to the intended audience." Segovia, *Farewell of the Word*, 2.

[138] Segovia, "Final Farewell," 184-185.

[139] Ibid., 170-171.

genre criticism, such a type-scene could be studied for the pattern of repetition of the same story with different characters to compare the compositional features of the work in question. From this general notion of a type-scene, Segovia lists several of such narratives, from which he focuses on the testament or farewell of a dying hero. He notes: "All of these type-scenes are dependent on the use of a fixed number of predetermined motifs."[140]

Though Staley and Segovia focus on the unity of this section of the Gospel, their works lack a thorough analysis of chapters 20-21 as a whole. From a literary-rhetorical perspective, their works, however, were not concerned with this type of reading. Their works concerned only certain sections of the resurrection narrative. Thus, to this point in my research, I have not found a work from this perspective that reads the resurrection narrative as whole, chapters 20-21.

Scope and Methodology:
A Literary-Rhetorical Approach

This work proposes a literary-rhetorical, synchronic reading on the unity of John 20-21 in and of itself and as a unified and coherent narrative. Since little or no attention has been given to a literary analysis

---

[140] Segovia, *Farewell of the Word*, 1. Concerning the farewell type-scenes and their motifs, Segovia searches within Jewish and Greco-Roman literature as well as biblical narratives for common features of the type-scene of farewell or the last words of great men. In footnote note 2 (p. 5), he lists the various works which deals with this genre. In this section of the chapter, he relies on various studies (German works, French works, dictionaries, and so forth) in order to glean from the results to construct his final approach, which will also led him into a particular methodological approach at the close of the chapter. For example, as a point of departure, he observes E. Stauffer (1950) use and development of this tradition in four different bodies of material (Greco-Roman, the Hebrew Bible and extra-biblical Jewish material, the New Testament, and later Christian literature). Segovia then breaks down each of the four categories listed above into the ways in which this genre of type-scene could be distinguished by different kinds of speakers in question; for example, in Greco-Roman literature, he finds: (1) famous men at the end of their lives, (2) divine men before their transfiguration and ascent, and (3) gods in human disguise prior to their homeward departure. See, e.g., Ibid., 5-7.

of John 20-21 as a coherent, unified narrative text from this perspective, this reading does attempt to investigate explicitly how John 20-21 might contain certain literary or narrative characteristics that might lead the implied reader in the text to respond to the narrative as multiple conclusions or summaries to the Gospel. For instance, what has been considered as the appropriate conclusion to the Gospel, 20:30-31 could be read as a summary of the events at the tomb and at the house where the disciples were gathered, that is it could be considered as a conclusion to chapter 20.[141] Additionally, the final verses of chapter 21 (vv. 24-25) could be read as a conclusion to the resurrection narrative and to the Gospel as a whole and therefore could narrate to its implied reader a unified, coherent interpretation of the resurrection appearances of Jesus.

Although this work considers how John 20-21 forms a unity with the rest of the Fourth Gospel, it is not the intention of this project to illustrate explicitly the unity of the entire Fourth Gospel. This section primarily concerns a literary-rhetorical methodology for reading John 20-21, suggesting an approach to the unity and coherence of this narrative in and of itself.

From a literary perspective, this method employs a formalist, close-reading tactic, borrowing New Critics' presuppositions, that is, that texts contain meaning, that meaning is located in the structure of the text, and that narrative text forms a coherent, self-contained whole.[142] On the other hand, unlike the New Critics' presupposition that says that one must determine the meaning of texts apart from so-called external factors, for example, political, social, cultural, economic, author or reader, and so forth, the rhetorical or reader-response side of this methodology suggests that narrative texts need implied readers in as much as implied readers need narrative texts. This rhetorical emphasis not only seeks to determine the so-called rhetoric of the Johannine resurrection narrative, but it also seeks to determine the extent to which the implied readers are informed and persuaded by this narrative and the various functions that these rhetorical devices and techniques have in producing certain responses in the implied readers, that is, how a reading that includes chapter 21 as a

[141] See, e.g., T. Wiarda, "John 21:1-23: Narrative Unity and its Implication." *JSNT* 46 (1992) 53-71.
[142] See note 90, above.

part of the resurrection narrative can offer the implied reader additional rhetorical possibilities. In short, these two approaches together allow room for the narrative critic to consider seriously the narrative text as well as the various rhetorical responses of the implied reader in the text, negotiating with the text.

Literary-Rhetorical Methodology and
The Plan of the Present Study

The first chapter of this study has provided a history of scholarship regarding historical-critical and literary-rhetorical readings on the Fourth Gospel's resurrection narrative, with a special emphasis on how scholars have perceived and studied the nature of chapters 20 and 21 in comparison to the rest of the Fourth Gospel.

This first chapter has also included a literary-rhetorical framework for studying the resurrection narrative on both the narrative and rhetorical level.[143] This framework focuses on the story-level and the rhetorical-level, which are integrated and developed during the temporal process of reading. Each of the following chapters (Two through Four)

---

[143] For representative studies on gospel narratives from this perspectives are: J. Anderson and S. Moore, eds., *Mark and Method: New Approaches in Biblical Studies* (Minneapolis: Fortress Press, 1992); E. Best, *Mark: The Gospel as Story* (Edinburgh: T. & T. Clark, 1983); R. M. Fowler, *Let the Reader Understand: Reader-Response Criticism and the Gospel of Mark* (Minneapolis: Fortress Press, 1991); J. Heil, *The Gospel of Mark as a Model for Action: A Reader-Response Commentary* (Mahwah: Paulist Press, 1992); W. Kelber, *Mark's Story of Jesus* (Philadelphia: Fortress Press, 1979); J. Kingsbury, *Matthew as Story* (Philadelphia: Fortress Press, 1986); W. Kurz, *Reading Luke-Acts: Dynamics of Biblical Narrative* (Louisville: Westminster/John Knox Press, 1993); D. Rhoads and D. Michie, *Mark as Story: An Introduction to the Narrative of a Gospel* (Philadelphia: Fortress Press, 1982); C. Talbert, *The Narrative Unity of Luke-Acts*, vol. I, (Philadelphia: Fortress Press, 1986); M. Tolbert, *Sowing the Gospel: Mark's World in Literary-Historical Perspective* (Minneapolis: Fortress Press, 1989); B. van Iersel, *Reading Mark.* (Translated by W. H. Bisscheroux. Collegeville: The Liturgical Press, 1988); and H. Waetjen, *A Reordering of Power: A Socio-Political Reading of Mark's Gospel* (Minneapolis: Fortress Press, 1989).

includes the following sections: (1) an English translation,[144] (2) a delineation of the episodes and scenes, according to the immediate context or literary units:[145] here the study argues that the narrative text as it now stands represents an organic, sustained whole,[146] (3) a temporal process of reading, wherein the temporal- and spatial-settings, the events, narrative devices and techniques, an analysis of the characters, and so forth are integrated in the temporal process of reading from the perspective of the implied reader.[147] This work proposes a literary-rhetorical reading by employing a narrative-critical perspective.[148] Moreover, the work proposes a reading that is strategically designed as a negotiation between its implied author and its implied reader—both on the narrative level and on the rhetorical level—which contributes to the architectural unity of the resurrection narrative as a whole from the standpoint of a delineation of the various episodes and scenes and from a temporal process of reading.[149] (4) Conclusion, where due consideration

---

[144] Throughout this study, I have based my English translation on, K. Aland, M. Black, C. Martini, B. Metzger, and A. Wikgren, eds., *Novum Testamentum Graece* (27th ed. Stuttgart: Deutsche Bibelstiftung, 1993).

[145] For a thorough discussion on criteria for the delineation of structure, see Mlakuzhyil, *Christocentric*, 112-121.

[146] J. Bailey and L. Broek note: "Organic form refers to a unique structure or organization of a piece of literature, that which is invented or fashioned by the author to best communicate the desired meaning. In organic form, the structures are as diverse as the ideas expressed, as diverse as the author's whims. Almost every piece of literature has some structure, some organic form that the reader can discern." J. Bailey and L. Broek, *Literary Forms in the New Testament: A Handbook* (Louisville: Westminster/John Knox Press, 1992) 13.

[147] For temporal process of reading, see note 6, above.

[148] For the narrative-critical perspective employed in this study, see, e.g., Rimmon-Kenan, *Narrative Fiction*, 1-117.

[149] For reader-response theory, see, e.g., Iser, *Act of Reading*, 107-134; and Fish, *Is There a Text*, 21-67. Some representative studies on the reading process are: W. Braun, "Resisting John: Ambivalent Redactor and Defensive Reader of the Fourth Gospel." *SR* 19 (1990) 59-71; R. Crosman, "How Readers Make Meaning." *ColLit* 9 (1982) 207-215; R. Fowler, "Who is the 'Reader' in Reader-Response Criticism." *Semeia* 31 (1985) 5-23; P. Kotze, "John and Reader's Response." *Neotest* 19 (1985) 50-63; W. Kurz, "The Beloved Disciple and Implied Reader." *BTB* 19, 3 (1989) 100-107; B. Lategan, "Introduction: Coming to Grips with the Reader in Biblical Literature," *Semeia* 49 (1989) 3-20; and Rimmon-Kenan, *Narrative Fiction*, 117-129.

is given to the overall rhetorical design of the narrative from the standpoint of the implied author and implied reader, recording a summary of the temporal process of reading.[150]

In short, this literary-rhetorical reading intends to illustrate and describe how each of these literary-rhetorical elements within each episode and scene is logically connected, constituting a unified and coherent narrative text. With a focus on the overall thematic thrust of the resurrection narrative, the conclusion seeks to determine how the various elements in the narrative function to persuade the implied reader of the central objective of the protagonist, Jesus, and of the strategic design of the resurrection narrative from the standpoint of the implied author and implied reader. On the rhetorical level, this project will employ the following construct of the implied reader: (1) a sequential, temporal process of reading, that is, an implied reader who is presupposed by the text itself—the implied reader is expected to respond to the narrative text as it unfolds; (2) An implied reader, that is, one who possesses knowledge of the narrative text and interprets every level of the narrative text.[151] This construct of the implied reader is necessary to detect the rhetorical, affective, and narrative aspects of the implied author's work in this section of the Fourth Gospel.

The resurrection narrative represents the work of an implied author, who is the construct of a real, flesh-and-blood author, and who has produced this resurrection narrative as an artistic creation, a creation for an implied reader in the text. The implied author is responsible for the overall design of the narrative, the order, or repertoire in which it was recorded.[152] As such, this study also focuses on the effect that the resurrection narrative has on the implied reader, viz., the implied author's design of the complete artistic whole; that is the implied author creates a sense of unity for the real reader's perception of the work,

---

[150] See, e.g., Moloney, *Belief*, 1-22; Stibbe, *John*, 9-19, 198-215; Culpepper, *Anatomy*, 15-49.

[151] One assumption that I will have to make is that the implied reader knows what has transpired before the twentieth chapter begins. But my ultimate focus is the resurrection narrative itself.

[152] For repertoire, see Iser, *Act of Reading*, 53-85.

including even the gap-filling process, seeking to show how the implied author achieves unity—a finely woven tapestry—for the implied reader.

In Chapters Two, Three, and Four this study provides a literary-rhetorical reading of John 20 (Chapters Two through Three) and 21 (Chapter Four). With the integration of these two methods (narrative criticism and reader-response criticism), this project offers a reading of John 20 and 21 as a unified, coherent narrative text. The final chapter, Chapter Five, provides the conclusion to this work as a whole.

The resurrection narrative, of the situations surrounding the four appearances of Jesus,[153] consists of three unified episodes[154] that transpire in three central locations: the sites in and around the tomb (John 20:1-18);[155] the house where the disciples were gathered (20:19-29);[156] and the sites on and by the sea of Tiberias (21:1-23).[157] Two of these episodes occur in Jerusalem, and the final episode takes place in Galilee.

---

[153] Jesus appears only once in the first episode, twice in the second, and finally once in the last episode. In 21:14 the implied author reports to the implied reader that Jesus appears in the final episode for the third time. The implied author, however, is referring only of Jesus' appearances to the male disciples. See, e.g., Barrett, *John*, 582. Here, Barrett believes that Mary Magdalene "is not counted because she was not a *mathetes*." For a discussion on Mary's status in the Fourth Gospel, see G. O'Day, "John," in *The Women's Bible Commentary*, ed. by C. Newsom and S. Ridge (London: SPCK and Louisville: Westminster/John Knox Press, 1992) 300-302; and S. Schneiders, "Women in the Fourth Gospel." *BTB* 12 (1982) 25-45.

[154] What historical-critical scholars generally call a "pericope," this study refers to it, roughly speaking, as an "episode." The basis for this usage is the central location or site of the events that transpire. See G. Prince, *A Dictionary of Narratology* (Lincoln and London: University of Nebraska Press, 1987) 27. Barrett, *John*, 965, refer to my episodes as "scenes."

[155] See, e.g., Bultmann, *John*, 681-689; Brown, *John*, 979-1017; Barrett, *John*, 560-566; and Schnackenburg, *John*, 302-321.

[156] See, e.g., Barrett, *John*, 965.

[157] Several historical scholars divide this chapter into two pericopes: 21:1-14 and 15-23. The structure of this chapter will be analyzed according to criteria established, above. Below, I argue that the events of chapter 21 occur on and by the Sea of Tiberias, see Chapter Four. See Brown, *John*, 1082: "All of the action of chap. xxi is localized in the course of one encounter with the risen Jesus on the shore of Tiberias." Brown delineates chapter 21 into two scenes (episodes).

These three episodes will be further delineated into twelve scenes that will be studied to illustrate the unity and coherence of the resurrection narrative:[158]

(1) The tomb episode (Chapter Two) consist of four scenes: in scene one Mary Magdalene visits the tomb and reports to two disciples (20:1-2); in scene two Peter and the Beloved Disciple race to the tomb, inspect it, and return to their home (20:3-10); in scene three Mary and the two angels meet briefly (20:11-13); and in scene four, Jesus appears to Mary and commissions her to report back to the disciples (20:11-18).

(2) The house episode (Chapter Three) includes three scenes: in scene five Jesus appears to the disciples, breathes the Holy Spirit upon them, and gives them the authority to remit or forgive sins (20:19-23); in scene six the disciples report on their meeting with Jesus to Thomas, and he does not believe but rather states his conditions in order to believe (20:24-25); and in scene seven Jesus appears to the disciples with Thomas and shows him his wounds: Thomas replies with a high Christological statement, and Jesus rebukes him and offers a beatitude on the benefit of believing without seeing (20:26-29). A summary statement (20:30-31) by the implied author is strategically inserted as a summary to chapter 20, standing between the house and sea of Tiberias episode.

(3) The episode on and by the sea of Tiberias (Chapter Four) contains five scenes: in scene eight the disciples decide to go fishing at Peter's request—the disciples fish all night without success (21:1-3); in scene nine Jesus appears to the disciples and instructs them of where to locate fish—they haul in a large number of fish (21:4-9); in scene ten the disciples haul in the fish and Jesus has breakfast with them—the implied author reports in this scene that this is Jesus' third appearance to the disciples (21:9-14); in scene eleven Jesus questions Peter in a direct dialogue on love and predicts the way in which Peter would glorify God (21:15-19a); in scene twelve Peter becomes concerned about the fate of the Beloved Disciple and Jesus responds by commanding Peter again to follow him—the implied author employs this scene to dispel a rumor concerning the fate of the Beloved Disciple (21:19b-23). Finally, the

---

[158] Each of the following scenes is delineated after the translation of the text in Chapters Two through Four.

implied author ends the resurrection narrative proper and the Gospel narrative as a whole with a concluding statement and hyperbole (21:24-25).

CHAPTER TWO

Episode Number One:
At the Tomb—
Jesus' First Appearance
To Mary Magdalene, John 20:1-18

Introduction

In episode number one, the implied author presents the first post-resurrection appearance of Jesus in the Fourth Gospel narrative. It commences with the appearance stories' first major complication,[1] which results from Mary's glance at the tomb. As she departs from the tomb and reports to the disciples her supposition regarding Jesus' body being removed from the tomb (20:1-2), the author suspends Jesus' first appearance in this narrative until the final scene of this episode, scene four (vv. 14-18).

Concerning the story-world of this first episode, the author situates the reader within the atmosphere of the narrative, with certain events, with the temporal- and spatial-settings, and with a relatively small amount of dialogue in comparison to the amount of narrator's asides, comments, and footnotes.[2] With such action and with a minimum amount of direct discourse, the author allows the reader to experience—with the

---

[1] For a discussion on the complexity in narratives, see, e.g., W. Booth, *Rhetoric*, 50, 124, 301-304; and Rimmon-Kenan, *Narrative Fiction*, 41-42.

[2] For "telling" versus "showing" in narration, see, e.g., Booth, *Rhetoric*, 3-20.

characters in the story-world—the events as they unfold. Further, the author saturates this episode with suspense and drama, centering it on the question concerning the status of Jesus' body, which is presumed to be missing until scene four. With such a complication, the author also employs literary devices in the narrative—action, minimum direct discourse, suspense and drama, and so forth—keeping the reader in suspense until scene four. While employing these strategies and devices as rhetorical tactics, the author causes the reader to empathize to a certain extent with the characters in the story-world, using the characters, events, and temporal- and spatial-settings to convince the reader of Jesus' status after his crucifixion.

Furthermore, the author constructs an episode that is self-contained, occurring in one principal site, in and around the tomb where Jesus was placed, which consists of four scenes. In scene one, 20:1-2, on the first day of the week, while it was still dark, Mary Magdalene makes an early morning trip to the tomb of Jesus, expecting to mourn his death. The author, however, does not specify the purpose of this trip, but since his body had already been prepared for burial (19:38-40), the reader can presume that her purpose was to mourn Jesus' death. When she arrives at the tomb, however, she notices that the stone had been removed. She immediately runs to report on her findings to the two disciples, Peter and the Beloved Disciple.

In scene two, 20:3-10, Peter and the Beloved Disciple race to the tomb in order to investigate Mary's report. Upon arriving at the tomb first, the Beloved Disciple sees the linen clothes; however, at this point in the narrative, he does not enter the tomb. Then Peter arrives and immediately enters the tomb. While inside the tomb Peter notices the linen wrappings and the head clothe. At this point, the Beloved Disciple enters the tomb, sees the contents in the tomb, and believes. Their reaction to the same information is mixed: on the one hand, Peter wonders what could have happened to Jesus' body; on the other hand, the Beloved Disciple believes that Jesus had risen from the dead. The author notes, however, that they did not understand the Scriptures regarding this event, and finally they return to their homes.

Scene three, 20:11-13, involves a brief exchange between Mary Magdalene and two angels. The scene begins with Mary standing and weeping outside the tomb. After bending over to look inside the tomb, she notices two angels dressed in white, sitting, one at the foot and the other at the head, where Jesus had lain. The angels ask Mary why was she weeping, and she replies by saying that someone had removed the body of Jesus and that she did not know where they had taken him.

Scene four, 20:14-18, contains Jesus' first post-resurrection appearance to Mary Magdalene after she had engaged in a brief exchange with the two angels. After she told the two angels of her plight, she turns around and sees Jesus standing behind her. At first, she did not recognize him, presuming him to be the gardener. Jesus asks her two questions: Woman, why arc you weeping? Moreover, whom are you seeking? Again, Mary explains her plight to the stranger, without recognizing that it was Jesus. Finally, Jesus calls her by name, and immediately she recognizes and holds onto him, worshipping him. Because he had not yet risen to the Father, Jesus tells her to stop holding onto him. He then commissions her to deliver a message to the disciples. Scene four and episode number one end after Mary reports to the disciples for the second time, which prepares the reader for episode number two. In the next two sections, episode number one is outlined and differentiated from the previous (19:38-42) and following episode (20:19-31) in order to establish settings for episode number one.

Outline of Episode Number One

I.   Episodes at the Tomb, John 20:1-18.
   A.   Scene One: Mary Magdalene Visits the Tomb and Reports to the Two Disciples, 20:1-2.
   B.   Scene Two: Two Disciples' Race to and Inspection of the Tomb; Their Reaction and Return to Their Homes, 20:3-10.
   C.   Scene Three: Mary Magdalene's Brief Meeting with Two Angels, 20:11-13.
   D.   Scene Four: Jesus' First Appearance to and Commission of Mary Magdalene; Mary Reports to the Disciples, 20:14-18.

Delineation of Episode Number One

Concerning Mary Magdalene's visit to the tomb, the author thematically connects episode number one to the last scene of chapter nineteen (19:38-42). In fact, the author introduces the scene with the temporal- and spatial-settings, which are sequentially presented in relation to the events in chapter 19 (20:1-18). Further, the author places the major conflict first in this episode, along with a brief introduction of the conflict with which this episode will be concerned.

In the last part of chapter 19 (19:38-42), the author also situates the spatial-setting of episode number one, the tomb where the body of Jesus was placed. Scene one of chapter 20 marks the initial period in which this narrative begins—in the early morning before dawn. The author rapidly develops the episode in this setting to result in a resolution of Mary's plight, which eventually results in Jesus' first appearance to Mary Magdalene (20:14-18). That is, within the burial scene (19:38-42), the author prepares the reader for the resurrection narrative, providing the manner in which the body was prepared for burial, a brief description and location of the tomb—the location where the body of Jesus was placed and last seen by Mary Magdalene and others (19:41-42). Spatially, then, in episode number one the author situates the reader at the main site of the resurrection narrative, the tomb where Jesus was placed at the end of chapter 19, in Joseph of Arimathea's new unused tomb.

As episode number one develops, the author progressively alters the situation within the tomb, providing an *inclusio* (beginning with the situation at the end of chapter 19): at the end of chapter 19 the tomb contains the body of Jesus (19:41-42); in scene one the tomb is implicitly empty, as reported by Mary Magdalene (20:1-2); in scene two, first the Beloved Disciple sees only the linen clothes and then Peter and the Beloved Disciple respond differently to Jesus' head cloth and linen wrappings, which were placed on his body in 19:40 and are now lying alone inside the tomb (20:3-10); in scene four it is occupied by two angels (20:11-14); and in scene four Mary stands outside of the tomb and turns around to see Jesus, who had been placed in the tomb at the end of chapter 19:42 (20:15-18).

In episode number two (20:19-31, however, the principal site becomes the house where the disciples were gathered. Thus, the spatial-setting suggests the differentiation of this episode from the subsequent episodes, numbers two and three, which occur at the house where the disciples were gathered on and around the Sea of Tiberias, respectively.

Scene One: Mary Magdalene Visits the Tomb and Reports to Two Disciples, 20:1-2

Translation of John 20:1-2

1. Now on the first day of the week, Mary Magdalene comes to the tomb early, while it was still dark, and she sees the stone removed from the tomb. 2. Therefore, she runs and comes to Simon Peter and to the other disciple, whom Jesus loves, and she says to them: "They have taken the Lord away from the tomb, and we do not know where they have placed him."

Introduction

It is in this first scene that the author introduces and begins to develop the first major complication of the resurrection narrative. With the setting of the tomb established in 19:38-42, the author arranges the introductory section of the narrative with three events: (1) Mary visits the tomb (20:1a-b); (2) she sees the stone removed from the tomb (20:1c); (3) she runs and reports the absence of Jesus' body to the two disciples— Simon Peter and the other disciple, whom Jesus loves—who were gathered in an unspecified location (20:2). With the events the author employs the narrative device of dramatic irony,[3] that is, the author reports on a situation wherein the reader, at this point, does not suspect that Jesus is risen from the dead but believes Mary's report that Jesus' body was stolen. The function of this literary device is to create suspense. The use of this device also allows the author to draw the reader

---

[3]   For dramatic irony, see, e.g., P. Duke, *Irony in the Fourth Gospel* (Atlanta: John Knox Press, 1985) 107. Here, commenting on this scene, Duke labels this type of irony as "symbolic imagery."

into the flow of the narrative, following and accepting Mary's preliminary observations.[4]

Additionally, the author depicts the spatial-setting of this first scene in such a way that it invokes the reader to supply the missing information. In other words, the author does not inform the reader that Mary actually looked inside of the tomb, and, as a result, the reader has to wait until more information is provided to detect a problem with Mary's report.

Finally, in this scene Mary's report to the disciples constitutes the only direct discourse by a disciple up until scene six (20:24-25). With her direct discourse, the author composes a situation wherein the reader wonders and awaits complete resolution. Moreover, with this discovery approach of narrating, the author impedes, for the reader, the resolution of Mary's plight, thus creating both drama and suspense.

Delineation of Scene One

By noting differences in the events, characters, and temporal- and spatial-settings between John 19:38-42 and 20:1-2, the author suggests the differentiation of scene one (20:1-2) from the last scene of chapter 19 (19:38-42). Moreover, the author uses the beginning of scene one to connect thematically a narration of the resurrection with the previous scene, the narration of the death (19:28-30) and burial of Jesus (19:38-42). In chapter 19, the author reports concerning the events surrounding the death of Jesus and the burial of his body in Joseph's new tomb. The author then develops the narrative with an initial progression that eventually moves from the burial of Jesus in the last scene of chapter 19 to a search for his body in episode number one.

Further, concerning the four events in 19:38-42, over and against those narrated in 20:1-2, the author indicates the division of these two scenes. With four events in 19:38-42, the author develops the theme of burial and establishes the purpose for the following scene (scene one,

---

[4]   See, e.g., Culpepper, *Anatomy*, 165-180; Duke, *Irony*, 41: "It must be remembered, however, that irony is usually not the manner of outright ridicule. There remains in irony, if not always the hope of correction, at least a touch of identification with the victim, and so quite often an element of sorrow. From the mixture of mirth and sadness can stem a degree of redemption."

20:1-2): (1) Joseph requests Jesus' corpse (19:38a-e); (2) Pilate allows him to take the corpse (19:38f); (3) Nicodemus prepares Jesus' corpse for burial (19:39-40); (4) Joseph and Nicodemus place Jesus' corpse in the tomb (19:41-42). Thus, the author records 19:38-42 to function as the initial confirmation of Jesus' burial before the Jewish day of Preparation (19:42).[5]

Conversely, the author's use of three events in 20:1-2 consist of a new situation and purpose: (1) Mary visits the tomb of Jesus (20:1a); (2) she observes the stone removed from the tomb's opening (20:1c); (3) she runs to where Peter and the Beloved Disciple were staying and reports her findings to them (20:2). Thus, in 20:1-2 the author creates the beginning of a new situation, the partial discovery of the empty tomb and the search for Jesus' missing corpse, which arise out of the events narrated in 19:38-42.

The characters present in the last scene of chapter 19 differ from the characters mentioned at the beginning of episode number one (20:1-2). In 19:38-42 the author presents Joseph of Arimathea and Nicodemus to serve as the principal characters in the burial scene. The last scene of chapter 19 indicates how Joseph and Nicodemus had prepared the body of Jesus for burial.[6]

Further, the author describes how Jesus' corpse was prepared for burial; it was treated lavishly by Nicodemus, who applied an excessive amount of spices and ointments to preserve the body of Jesus (19:39).[7] Thus, these two scenes (19:38-42 and 20:1-2) are thematically connected but are to be treated separately, where the latter scene sequentially and thematically follows the former, in the same vicinity, the tomb where Jesus' body was placed (19:41).

Concerning the delineation of scene one from scene two (20:3-10), the author provides several factors, such as the change of characters and events, to suggest a transition in reading between these two scenes.[8] In scene one of chapter 20, the author reintroduces Mary Magdalene into

5 See, e.g., Schnackenburg, *St. John*, 295-296. For the Jewish day of Preparation, see, e.g., Bultmann, *John*, 680.
6 For the Jewish custom of burial, see, e.g., Bultmann, *John*, 680, n. 6.
7 See, e.g., Ibid., 680, n. 4; and Barrett, *St. John*, 559.
8 Cf. Mlakuzhyil, *Christocentric Literary*, 103.

the narrative (cf. John 19:25). In 20:1-2 Mary is the principal character, who alone visits the tomb of Jesus. In 20:2c-d, however, a brief transition occurs between scene one and scene two, where Mary provides a report to the two disciples, shortly changing the site of the narrative. The author indicates a transition from one spatial-setting to another; this transition occurs between the tomb and the house where the disciples were staying. The author inserts this transition (20:2), however, as a part of scene one, involving primarily the main character in this scene, Mary Magdalene. The author includes her direct discourse and advances the plot of the episode and narrative.

In scene two (20:3-10) the author re-introduces into the narrative two new characters, Peter and the Beloved Disciple: the last reference to Peter was in 18:27 (the denial scene) and the last reference to the Beloved Disciple was possibly in 18:15-16. To advance the plot of this episode, the author introduces two new characters but retains the initial theme of scene one, the search for the body of Jesus with new events in 20:3-10, consisting of six movements: (1) the two disciples race to the tomb (20:3-4a-b); (2) the Beloved Disciple runs ahead of Peter (20:4c-d); (3) the Beloved Disciple reaches the tomb first; he looks inside the tomb, sees only the linen clothes, but remains at the opening of the tomb (20:4c); (4) then Peter arrives at the tomb and enters it; while inside of the tomb he inspects the linen clothes, and the cloth that was placed on Jesus' head (20:6-7); (5) the Beloved Disciple then enters the tomb (20:8a-b); and, (6) the author reports on the faith experience of the Beloved Disciple (20:8c) and finally mentions the disciples' return to their home. Thus, the author employs the second scene to develop the two previous scenes (19:38-42 and 20:1-2), with these two disciples' inspections of the tomb to investigate Mary's report.

Therefore, the author employs events of scene two to connect sequentially—temporally and spatially—to the previous scene (19:38-42). First, in the last scene of chapter 19 the body of Jesus is placed in the tomb. Second, in scene one (20:1-2) the body of Jesus is assumed to be taken away. Finally, in scene two (20:3-10) the tomb and its contents are noticed by the two disciples.

Temporal Process of Reading Scene One

Though one of the functions of temporal markers is to indicate in part a change in scenes, the author also employs it here symbolically to establish the atmosphere of the scene.[9] The reader is led to connect the symbolic darkness of this scene with the previous scene's reference to time; that is, it stands in sequence with the day in which Jesus was crucified and buried.[10] To develop the mood of the scene, the author inserts two temporal markers in 20:1: (a) "the first day of the week" and (b) "early, while it was still dark." The author's use of temporal symbolism seems to suggest that a significant happening or event is about to occur. The reference to the first day of the week indicates that the events, which are to follow, would also represent something mythical or symbolic for the reader. These markings are signals to the reader of a new reality bursting forth in the story-world. On the one hand, the reader would expect, from the day of the week, that an event would be of great significance for the faith community. On the other hand, for the reader, the darkness in which Mary moves, early on the first day of the week, expresses her own condition of grief and unbelief. In this temporal context, a new beginning is emerging; she will eventually participate in a situation that could be viewed symbolically by the reader. In other words, this scene would end according to the atmosphere of the scene.[11]

The second temporal marker indicates the time of day, "early, while it was still dark." The motif of darkness may also indicate the emotional or spiritual state of Mary Magdalene (cf. John 3:2, the meeting between Jesus and Nicodemus). The reader, however, anticipates a positive experience to result from the temporal-settings, in terms of how Mary's faith or belief would be tested. The condition for this testing is confirmed in part within this atmosphere.

Overall, these temporal markers reflect Mary's mood, regarding the situation of Jesus' missing body. On the one hand, the atmosphere of this scene—referred to here as the first day of the week—points the reader

---

[9]   Ibid., 112-113.

[10] For light and darkness in the Fourth Gospel, see, e.g., C. Koester, *Symbolism in the Fourth Gospel: Meaning, Mystery, Community* (Minneapolis: Fortress Press, 1995) 123-152.

[11] Ibid., 7, 151, esp. 10.

back to a positive experience of remembrance, which Jesus spoke of earlier in the narrative, regarding his rising on the third day (cf. 2:19-22, 14:1-14, 18-24). On the other hand, the atmosphere of this scene depicts the condition of Mary's faith, as she approached this unexpected situation. Thus, the atmosphere indicates boundaries that this scene establishes for the reader; for example, either Mary will find Jesus' corpse or she will encounter a realization of the resurrection.

As mentioned above, the author situates the reader with three events to establish the narrative's major complication. When Mary came to the tomb, she noticed that the stone was removed from the entrance. From this brief observation, she concludes, apparently without even a glance into the tomb, that the body of Jesus was stolen. The author reports only that she saw that the stone had been removed.[12]

The spatial-settings mentioned in this scene consist of two locations: the "tomb," which is outdoors and of a specific design, and an unspecified location where Mary reports to the disciples. This tomb site is described further in the reference to Mary's observation of the stone having been removed: "the stone was rolled away from the tomb" (20:1c). Here, the reader is initially confronted with the reality of an opened tomb. In 19:42 it was explicitly stated that the tomb was shut. No mention is made, however, of her entering or stooping down to look inside of the tomb.

The next event provides for the reader a somewhat expected yet surprising situation. When Mary Magdalene arrives at the tomb, she sees that the stone was removed. Here, the author creates a level of suspense and surprise. In order to address the question regarding the possible reconstruction of the events in this scene, the reader has to conclude that something significant has taken place in this setting.

The transition part of this scene (20:2a) includes Mary's trip from the tomb to the place where the disciples were gathered. No mention is made of the distance traveled between the tomb and the disciples' home. In addition, no narration is presented—direct or indirect or otherwise—of Mary's thoughts while she was in transit to the tomb or to the house.

---

[12] Later in the narrative, the author depicts the type of tomb where Jesus was placed, implying that an observer had at least to bend over to observe the place where Jesus was placed (cf. 20:5, 11).

When she arrives at the disciples' house, however, the author includes direct discourse on her report, which includes her cursory findings, regarding the absent body of Jesus. Thus, this transition scene holds the reader in suspense, anticipating the events that are forthcoming in the narrative.

In this scene, within the framework of direct discourse, the author employs two possible devices toward a preliminary characterization of Mary, regarding two personal pronouns a part of the verbs employed by her: ἦραν (they took) and οἴδαμεν (we do [not] know; 20:2). The first personal pronoun, "they," is indefinite: It refers to the ones that Mary had suspected of removing the body of Jesus from the tomb. The only development of this "they" is in reference to the persons that Mary thought was responsible for the absence of Jesus' body. It could not refer to the disciples; rather, she seems to be referring to someone outside of the Christian community, possibly to the antagonists—the Jews (certain ruling officials) or the Roman officials. The author does not provide this information; therefore, the function of this reference is beyond the simple reference to their presence, at this point. It seems, however, to function as a narrative device to build towards a climax regarding the appearance of Jesus.

The author does not provide names or a description of the "we" in this scene, either here or later in the narrative. In fact, later in the narrative (20:13c), Mary uses the first person singular pronoun in the place of this first person plural pronoun. The use of this plural pronoun could refer to the common language of the period; that is, it was common to use the first person plural "we" to indicate a sense of respect or humility. This usage, however, does not refer, according to the context, to a group of women who visited the tomb with Mary Magdalene.

The temporal-, spatial-settings, and events of this scene also assist the reader with an initial characterization of Mary Magdalene, which will be supplemented further in scene three and completed in scene four. The author does not specify why she makes this trip alone. In this scene, her trip to the tomb is without a stated purpose or intent. The author without certain literary devices develops her situation: no inner dialogue, no other characters involved (except when she reports to the disciples), and no meetings or incidents with other characters along the way. Nonetheless, the setting of this scene indicates a sad, dark moment in

Mary's life, a trip that must be made. From this information, the reader suspects that she goes to the tomb to grieve.

In this first scene, there is also no explicit description of Mary Magdalene, physical or otherwise. Can one assume here that the setting of the text provides a characterization that points only to her function in the narrative? Moreover, since no development of Mary is provided, at this point, is her function in this scene employed to point beyond her? To answer these questions, the reader has to anticipate how the author will present her later in the narrative.

Conclusion

In scene one, along with the previous scene (19:38-42), the author provides strategic events to introduce one of the resurrection narrative major complications. In 19:38-42 the request for Jesus' body, the preparation of his body for burial, and his burial in a new tomb, are events reported with some details by the author. These events are connected to but stand in contrast with those that occur in scene one (20:1-2).

In this first scene the author includes Mary's trip to the tomb, the brief, cursory glance at the tomb, and her report to the disciples on her speculations concerning the body of Jesus. The brief narration of these events creates suspense for the reader. As such, the author creates conflicts in the narrative, which functions to introduce one of the major conflicts in the narrative and to draw the reader into the narrative of the resurrection appearances.

In the first scene the author portrays to the reader the circumstances surrounding Mary's ambiguity ironically. First, the author presents this trip with uncertain and unclear narration. The author does not provide any internal or explicit commentary on the purpose of her trip to the tomb. The reader, however, suspects that she is going to the tomb to grieve. Second, the author does not provide any textual clues or commentary on the details of Mary's emotional experience at the tomb. Here, the reader perceives that Mary is speculating and creating a scenario for the supposed missing corpse of Jesus. Third, the reader does not know that the body of Jesus was actually taken from the tomb, and that Jesus has already risen. The author, however, allows the reader to possess certain information, which is not supplied to the characters in the story-world. Finally, the reader must move along with the narrative, without the end in view, with an insufficient knowledge or understanding of how Jesus' resurrected body will be manifested.

Additionally, in this first scene, in light of the last scene in chapter 19, several important factors emerge. First, in connection with the previous chapter (19:28-30; 38-42), where the death of Jesus is confirmed, his body is prepared for burial, and his body is placed in the tomb, the author implicitly indicates that these events were necessary for the confirmation of Jesus' death and burial.

Second, in scene one (20:1-2), both the temporal- and spatial-settings point beyond a mere representation of a location and a chronological happening. This atmosphere, however, sets the mood and tone for Mary Magdalene's experience at the tomb and prepares the reader for her subsequent report to the disciples. Moreover, the atmosphere suggests the nature of the resurrection proper, whereby it introduces, along with the previous scene in 19:38-42, additional proof of Jesus' death, burial, and subsequent absent body from the tomb, which was briefly observed and hastily inspected by Mary. The conditions during her inspection, however, suggest that what she concluded and reported should only be regarded as a mere supposition, but as a matter that necessitates further verification. Thus, the atmosphere depicts the nature of the conflict to be resolved and points to an initial characterization of Mary's faith.

Third, the events further suggest that Mary's role in this scene serve as a foil to present one of the major complications in the narrative. Subsequent events indicate that she had only speculated that Jesus' body had been removed and taken away from the tomb and that she did not know where his body had been taken because none of her findings were adequately tested by her. Thus, Mary's experience represents dramatic irony for the reader, as it relates to the major complication of Jesus' death and his alleged missing corpse.

Finally, the reader, therefore, is led to conclude, at this point in the narrative, that Mary's suspicion is in fact correct and must await further narration to confirm or deny her report. In other words, at this point of the narrative, the reader does not know that Jesus has risen from the dead. The author provides the reader with minor details of Mary's experience. The reader, therefore, anticipates what the author has to offer before any resolutions or conclusions are made regarding the nature of

Jesus, after his death and burial—a resolution to the major complication introduced in the last scene of chapter 19 and brought to light here in this first scene of episode number one. The reader only suspects that this Mary's plight will offer some details on the significance of this phenomenon, which will be provided in the next scene wherein the two disciples race to the tomb in order to investigate her report (20:3-10).

In retrospect, Mary's cursory inspection of the tomb took place in a dark, obscure setting. She immediately runs to tell the disciples that someone had stolen the body of Jesus and that she did not know where they had placed him. Here, there are several problems with her report, all of these problems are based upon Mary's inability to verify or carefully inspect the tomb under these temporal and spatial circumstances. Due to the darkness and her position outside the tomb, the reader would recognize the difficulty with which she would be unable to view the contents in the tomb from the outside; in other words, she could not perform a careful inspection of the tomb, which is not indicated at this point in the narrative (see, e.g., 20:5, 11).

Finally, Mary's report that the body of Jesus was taken from the tomb requires further verification. Mary's report also indicates that she did not know where the body of Jesus was taken; the author only reports to the reader that she immediately ran to the disciples to report on her supposition, which implicitly suggests her lack of searching for the body of Jesus. From the previous narration provided the reader suspects that Jesus will rise from the dead. On the contrary, concerning Mary's inspection of the tomb from the outside in the dark, the reader is led to believe that someone took the body of Jesus from the tomb.

In short, in scene one the author reports to the reader three events: the trip, the inspection, and the report. A brief description of the temporal- and spatial-setting creates a dramatic setting for the unveiling of the Easter event. The reader is briefly allowed to experience the trip to the tomb, which is in the darkness of the morning. Not only does this scene depict a certain situation in which these events occurred, but it also links this scene with previous scenes in the narrative; for example, the events which occurred in the darkness over and against those which occurred during the day (see, e.g., John 3:1-15, 4:1-38, and 9:1-41). Thus, with these devices and techniques, the author connects this scene (scene one) with the last scene of chapter 19, providing unity between the narration of Jesus' death and the narration of the resurrection event, which is not narrated. The next scene involves the inspection of the tomb by Peter and the Beloved Disciple, continuing the theme presented in scene one—the status or whereabouts of Jesus' body.

Scene Two: Two Disciples' Race to and Inspection of the Tomb; Their Reactions and Return to Their Homes, 20:3-10

Translation of John 20:3-10

3. Therefore, Peter and the other disciple came out, and they were going to the tomb. 4. Now, the two were running together. But, the other disciple ran ahead faster than Peter and came to the tomb first. 5. And having stooped down, he sees the linen cloths lying, however, he did not enter. 6. Then came also Simon Peter following him, and he entered the tomb, and he views the linen cloths lying, 7. and the face cloth, which was on his head, not lying with the linen cloths, but folded up apart in one place. 8. So then, the other disciple, the one having come to the tomb first, also enters and he sees and believes. 9. But, they did not yet know the Scripture that it was necessary for him to rise from the dead. 10. Therefore, the disciples went away to their homes.

Introduction

In scene two the author employs a number of literary devices to show the reader the actions, observations, responses, and internal knowledge of Peter and the Beloved Disciple (20:3-10), which lacks direct dialogue from these two disciples. To this point in the resurrection narrative, the author has only included the direct discourse of Mary Magdalene, who reports to the two disciples. From this point on the author presents to the reader several events in sequence and thereby presents not only an initial portrait of these two disciples, but also the necessary evidence to confirm Mary's report.

Initially, the reader is drawn into the story-world with the author's report from Mary, which is placed at the end of scene one. The reader is further drawn into the narrative with the actions of Peter and the Beloved Disciple. The situation itself warrants action and confirmation; the reader is able to anticipate the confirmation or denial of Mary's report from the action of the two disciples. The author makes it clear that a distinction should be made between Peter and the Beloved Disciple, concerning not only the race to the tomb but also in terms of what happens at and inside the tomb.

In this scene the tomb is inspected from the inside by the two disciples. One of the disciples believes and the other does not. In the end, the author provides more suspense in the narrative for the reader by reporting that the disciples return to their homes in Jerusalem, the place in which they had begun, really without resolving the major complication of the narrative, which was to locate the body of Jesus.

In scene two Peter and the Beloved Disciple are presented in a contrasting fashion with a literary device that focuses on the action of these disciples rather than on direct dialogue or character interaction, with information that is necessary for the development of these characters. For example, there are two events in the course of the scene that move progressively towards the development of characterization: the race to and the inspection of the tomb. For instance, the transition of Peter and the Beloved Disciple to the tomb appears on the surface as a race, in and of itself. When one considers the scenes that follow, however, a contrast between them begins to emerge (see Chapter Four, 21:4-8; 20-23).

At this point in the narrative, it is difficult to argue persuasively on the point or intent of such a contrast. Rather, the reader could posit some observations that occur and keep in mind that something more than reporting is taking place here. The questions the reader could raise regarding characterization is: "How is this race relevant to the story as a whole?" and, "What, if any, are the elements that contribute to the formulation of these characters?"

In short, scene two provides a response to the report of Mary, a contrast between these two disciples. More importantly, it describes the first reactions to the evidence in the empty tomb; that is, after a close examination of the contents, Peter does not believe and the Beloved Disciple believes. Using the temporal- and spatial-settings the author highlights the contrast between Peter and the Beloved Disciple; in other words, the atmosphere sets the boundaries for their contrast and hence their faith.

Delineation of Scene Two

In scene two (20:3-10), with a change in characters and with a slight change in the spatial-setting, the author inserts the two disciples' transition or race from their homes to the tomb and differentiates this scene from the previous scene. In the previous scene, the author concludes with Mary's transition from the tomb to report to the disciples: "They have taken the Lord out of the tomb, and we do not know where they have laid him" (20:2c-d). As mentioned above, this verse serves as a transitional scene between scene one and scene two. It also signals the theme of scene two, namely the disciples' inspection of the tomb to confirm Mary's report.

The characters reintroduced in the narrative are Peter and an unnamed disciple, referred to as "the disciple whom Jesus loved" [τὸν μαθητὴν ὅν ἐφίλει Ἰησοῦς] (v. 2a). By definition, this change in characters formally constitutes a new scene. Thus, the scene begins with the transition of the two disciples' race to the tomb (20:3-4), which is dramatically described in more detail than Mary's trip to the tomb or her trip to report to the two disciples.

In scene two the author constructs an *inclusio* (A-B-A): the disciples at home (20:3a); a race to and inspection of the tomb by the two disciples (20:3b-9), and the disciples returning to their homes (20:10). At the center of this *inclusio* ("B"), the author continues to focus primarily on the site of the tomb—to this point in the narrative, the principal location of the tomb remains the central location of episode number one (20:1-18). In 20:1-2 the author's focus concerns a cursory inspection of the empty tomb by Mary, with a subsequent report to the disciples. In 20:3-10 the author situates the events, which are principally focused at the tomb, where the two disciples, in part, confirm Mary's report, that is, they discover that the body of Jesus was missing, but from their observations, the reader infers that the robbery of the body was unlikely, since the clothes were neatly folded in their places. The Beloved Disciple, however, believes that the resurrection of Jesus has taken place. The intensity and drama of scene two are increased and focused more on the contents of the tomb than the tomb itself. Thus, the purpose and function of scene two naturally and reasonably flow from and build upon the events of scene one. The spatial-setting also constitutes a chiastic

pattern: "A-B-A" (home—tomb—home). According to this chiasm, the
primary event occurs at the tomb, both on the outside and inside.

First, while outside the tomb the Beloved Disciple looks in and sees
the linen clothes, which adds specificity to the setting in this scene, the
contents inside the tomb. Second, when Peter arrives at the tomb, he
immediately enters the tomb and inspects the contents, with no reported
response. Finally, the Beloved Disciple enters the tomb, presumably
while Peter was still inside the tomb, and while inside the tomb the
Beloved Disciple sees and believes.

While outside the tomb, the Beloved Disciple inspects the situation
by stooping down and looking inside of the tomb, seeing only the linen
clothe. Afterwards, Peter arrives at the tomb and enters the tomb, sees
the linen clothing and the head cloth within the tomb, but without any
consequence or conclusion to his faith. Then finally, the Beloved
Disciple enters the tomb, looks, and believes.

What is the point of the author in presenting these two characters in
this contrasting fashion? One of the ways to address this situation is
merely to note the contrasts until other similar or like situations can be
used to construct adequately a comparison between these two disciples.

The Beloved Disciple believes, and Peter at this point does not.
Neither one of them, however, understood the Scripture that reveals the
truth of Jesus' necessity to rise from the dead. This contrast will be
addressed in other sections to establish this pattern (see Chapter Four).

Therefore, with a change in the characters and with the amplification
of events to confirm her report, scene two (20:3-10) is delineated from
scene one and scene three, where Mary reappears at the tomb standing
and weeping.

Temporal Process of Reading Scene Two

The initial events in scene two were prompted by Mary's report to
the two disciples (20:2c-d) and focus on the following: the race (20:3-
6c), the arrival (20:4c-5, 6a-c), and the inspection of the tomb by the two
disciples (20:5b, 6d-7, and 8c), the narrator's summary (20:9), and the
disciples' return to their homes (20:10), which are reported in a
continuous, progressive fashion.

There is one significant temporal marker in this scene, namely, the
inferential conjunction οὖν (then), indicating the moment in which Peter

and the Beloved Disciple respond to the report of Mary, and it marks the start of the race to the tomb (20:3). This marker also suggests that practically no time had elapsed between the report and the race; therefore, it depicts a degree of urgency in the situation that prompted immediate action.

The scene immediately commences with the race between Peter and the Beloved Disciple. They leave their house, running together to the tomb (20:3). This race scene involves a transition from the house to the tomb. The reader is informed that the Beloved Disciple runs ahead of Peter and comes first to the tomb. In essence, this race symbolically functions as a contrast between Peter and the Beloved Disciple, which ends in the favor of the Beloved Disciple.

After the Beloved Disciple outruns Peter and arrives at the tomb first (20:4), for whatever reason he stops at the opening of the tomb and, while stooping to look inside of the tomb, he inspects the inside.[13] He sees (βλέπει) the linen clothes lying (τὰ ὀθόνια κείμενα), but he did not enter the tomb (20:5). Peter then arrives at the tomb and enters without hesitation. After he enters the tomb, he observes (θεωρεῖ) both the linen clothes (τὰ ὀθόνια) and the head cloth (τό σουδάριον), both of which were lying neatly apart from each other (20:6-7).

After Peter investigates the clothing, the Beloved Disciple, who was standing outside, enters the tomb, sees (εἶδεν), and believes (20:8). Here, the narrator's aside provides omniscient information to the reader and indicates that the two disciples did not know the Scriptures, particularly the one which says that Jesus would rise from the dead (20:9). Without direct discourse, the author informs the reader, by way of action only, that both of the disciples observed the contents of the tomb. In other words, Peter curiously looks (θεωρεῖ), while the Beloved Disciple sees the situation in light of his experience or his faith, which is indicated in the verb εἶδεν.

At end of the scene the author does not include any information that would indicate that Peter believes that there is enough evidence to

---

[13] For a contrast between this scene and the resuscitation of Lazarus, see, e.g., D. Carson, *The Gospel According to John* (Grand Rapids: William B. Eerdmans Publishing Company, 1991) 637-638.

warrant belief; he only observed the clothes; whereas, the Beloved Disciple sees the same evidence and believes. The narrator's footnote records their different responses, both of which occur with a lack of knowledge of the Scripture (20:9). In the narrator's report, the author provides omniscient information to the reader; thus, it has no effect on the temporal-setting inside of the story-world. The scene ends with the disciples leaving the tomb and returning to their homes (20:10).

The author's reporting of these events functions to show the race and inspection that occurred in response to Mary's report; therefore, the narration of the events also function to illustrate a contrast between the action and the corresponding response of the two disciples in their attempt to investigate the report of Mary. The inspection, action, and response of the two disciples confirm Mary's report to the reader that the body of Jesus was in fact missing, as well as provide a contrast between the two disciples.

Furthermore, the author reports on the internal knowledge of Peter and the Beloved Disciple: neither one of them knew the Scripture. From this contrast, the reader favors and identifies with the Beloved Disciple.

In the conclusion to this scene, the author reports that they went home, without an indication of the time during which these events took place. Therefore, the reader assumes that this event likely occurred immediately following Mary's report. Thus, the temporal markers represent a temporal succession of the events; that is, one event follows immediately after the other. After the tomb is thoroughly inspected by the two disciples, again with more specificity than that which is presented in scene one with Mary Magdalene (20:1c), they return to their homes: "ἀπῆλθον οὖν πάλιν πρὸς αὐτοὺς οἱ μαθηταί" (literary: "then the disciples return again to their own [places]" 20:10).[14] The

---

[14] This note confirms the fact that the reference to their home is not a reference to their homes in Galilee because they are still in Jerusalem. Though no details are provided on where their homes were located, one can infer that the way in which the race is narrated the distance could not have been too far, e.g., in Galilee, assuming that the time of narration equals the story time. If this is the case, the implied reader could roughly estimate the amount of time it took to narrate these events and thereby estimate the distance between their homes and the tomb.

purpose of their trip was solely to inspect the tomb, and after they failed to confirm completely Mary's report, they return to their homes.

Conclusion

In this scene the author provides additional evidence to the reader on the resurrection of Jesus, but a question still remains: "What happened to Jesus' body?" Peter and the Beloved Disciple confirm Mary's report that Jesus' body is missing, after viewing the contents of the tomb and reaching different conclusions. Further, the author includes a contrasting portrait between Peter and the Beloved Disciple, creating an initial characterization of them. With the repertoire of the race and the inspection, the author initiates a comparison between these two disciples, which will continue in chapter 21. The central thrust of this scene, however, is not the two disciples' ability or inability to believe, but its central thrust is to provide evidence to the reader regarding these two disciples' perception of the evidence in the empty tomb.

The author expects the reader, as the Beloved Disciple, to gather this evidence and believe, without a sign of Jesus' presence. The author provides several repetitions of the clothing in the tomb—the clothing and where it was lying—to indicate that with this information the reader should also believe. In fact, the author omits information on the object of the Beloved Disciple's belief. That is, the reader has to supply the missing information that this belief was in the resurrection of Jesus. The author's summary, however, is quite telling in that neither one of them knew the Scripture, which says that Jesus must rise from the dead. Is this to be taken to mean that the Beloved Disciple believed without the knowledge of the Scripture? Indeed, the reader could readily make the connection, since this is a belief of the highest type, believing that Jesus rose in and of itself. Although this information remains vague and incomplete, the reader identifies with the Beloved Disciple's propensity to believe, despite the insufficient amount of evidence.[15]

---

[15] For the levels of belief expected in this episode and in episode number two, see below. Is the reader intended to identify with Peter or with the Beloved Disciple? The reader already knows the previous narrative and suspects that Jesus will be raised from the dead, again the question for the reader concerns the way in which this information will be communicated and revealed. In other words, the reader is

Thus, the function of this scene is to provide evidence for the resurrection, short of the body of Jesus, to present a contrast between Peter and the Beloved Disciple and to explain the setting in which the Beloved Disciple was the first one to believe after Jesus' resurrection and before his appearances.

In short, scene two builds upon the information in scene one; however, there is still no definite resolution regarding the body of Jesus. This resolution will have to wait until the following scenes. In terms of the overall theme of the narrative, up to this point, the reader is beginning to form a picture of the resurrection event from the evidence provided by the author, who omits information pertaining to the resurrection event. Thus, the final chapter (chapter 21) of the Fourth Gospel is imperative to continue the characterization of the Beloved Disciple and Peter, which is introduced in this scene and continued in the final chapter of the Gospel. In the next scene (scene three), Mary returns to the tomb and sees two angels inside the tomb.

Scene Three: Mary Magdalene's Brief Meeting with Two Angels, 20:11-13

Translation of John 20:11-13

11. But, Mary stood at the tomb weeping outside. Then, while she was weeping, she stooped to look into the tomb. 12. And, she sees two angels in white sitting where the body of Jesus was lying, one at the head and one at the feet. 13. And they said to her, "Woman, why are you weeping?" She said to them, "Because they have taken away my Lord, and I do not know where they have laid him."

---

intended to identify with the Beloved Disciple and not with Mary because the evidence leads the reader to do so, but also it seems to be the point of view of the author of which the reader must accept in order to enter into the story-world. The race to and the events at the tomb indicate the point of view of the author that the Beloved Disciple is the one to identify with in this scene. Nevertheless, the reader identifies with the Beloved Disciple, over and against Peter, due to the Beloved Disciple's belief without a sign, which was established earlier in narrative and will be further developed as the narrative unfolds.

Introduction

After the disciples leave the tomb, at the end of scene two, the author reports that Mary Magdalene stood weeping outside the tomb. In the previous scene, the two disciples visited the tomb and inspected its contents, and, after they had completed their inspection, they returned to their homes. The transition between scenes two and three is marked with a continuative, contrasting conjunction (δὲ), which indicates that Mary stood at the tomb, refusing to leave until some resolution takes place. She re-enters the narrative standing and weeping at the tomb (20:11). There is no narration or communication between Mary and the two disciples concerning their findings and responses while inside the tomb.

Scene three involves a brief meeting or exchange between Mary and the two angels, consisting of a unified scene with a specific function: to report on Mary's inspection of the tomb and meeting with two angels. This exchange is in a question-and-answer format, focusing again of the major complication of this episode. While Mary stands outside the tomb in a grief-stricken state, she stoops and looks inside the tomb and sees two angels, who question her plight. She responds to their question, after which the scene immediately shifts to scene four, the first resurrection appearance of Jesus.

Delineation of Scene Three

Scene three (20:11-13) is differentiated from the previous scene with a change of characters, which begins with the reintroduction of Mary Magdalene, who first appeared in scene one (20:1-2) and with the introduction of two angels (20:11-13).

The location of this scene remains the tomb where Jesus was placed. Since there are no temporal markers to mark specifically the period of the events in scene three, the time of the scene is assumed to follow that of the previous scene, after the two disciples depart from the tomb.

A brief transition occurs between scenes three and four, from a discussion with the two angels on the inside the tomb (scene three) to an encounter with Jesus standing outside the tomb (scene four). Thus, this scene will be treated separately from 20:14-18, rather than reading it as one scene.

After she answers their question, she then turns and sees Jesus; however, at this point, she does not recognize that it is Jesus. Even though the two angels do not play a major role in the narrative, a change of focalization and events does occur.[16] Scene three, 20:11-13, is self-contained, and scene four comprises 20:14-18, which will be discussed in the next section.

Temporal Process of Reading Scene Three

On the same day of the week, the author composes these events within the same time-frame—occurring during the early morning period—scene one took place early, while it was still dark, and scene two's events happened in a relatively short period of time thereafter. As mentioned above, with the exception of the brief period that had elapsed between the disciples' departure and Mary's return to the tomb, there is no report on the precise time in which these events happened; therefore, these events are narrated in a continuous fashion, with no major temporal gaps, from the beginning of Mary's trip to this point in the narrative.

This brief period seemingly occurs in narrative time, wherein the author does not narrate or mention how or when Mary actually returned to the tomb, nor if she could have been following the part of the race of the two disciples. The reader, however, can assume that she was trailing immediately behind or at some distance from the two disciples. Since the author excludes any dialogue that could have possibly occurred between her and the two disciples—that is, after these two disciples had completed their inspection of the tomb—the reader is not informed of an interaction between Mary and the two disciples before they returned to their homes. Thus, the reader is called upon here in this scene to account for or fill-in this temporal gap. Nonetheless, additional time has to be allocated for Mary's trip back to the tomb, which would explain why there was no interaction between them at the tomb, along with the period in which she stood weeping outside the tomb before her inspection.

The spatial setting of this scene remains the tomb, with action and narration occurring both outside and inside the tomb. While outside the tomb, Mary stands weeping. Later she stoops to look inside the tomb. No reference or narration is provided to indicate that she actually entered the tomb. The two angels are inside the tomb, one at the head and the other

---

[16] For types of focalization, see, e.g., Rimmon-Kenan, *Narrative Fiction*, 43, 71, 74-79.

at the foot where Jesus had laid. Again, there is no narration to indicate that Mary or the angels noticed Jesus' clothes; only the two disciples notice these items. The reader is required to fill in this information, which would explain the absence of the clothing in scene three and conversely the absence of the angels in scene two. In other words, the angels in this scene occupy the head and foot positions of Jesus' body while in the tomb: representing a change in the content inside of the tomb beginning at the end of chapter 19, where the body of Jesus was placed in the tomb. In scene one the body is reported as missing. In scene two the clothing is in place inside of the tomb. Finally, in scene three the angels now occupy the place where the body of Jesus was placed. In other words, there is no narration of the removal of the clothes in scene two, and there is also no narration indicating that the disciples had seen angels inside the tomb in scene two.

Scene three consists of four related events: (1) Mary stands and weeps outside the tomb (20:11a); (2) She looks inside of the tomb, where she views (θεωρεῖ) two angels dressed in white (ἐν λευκοῖς, 20:11b-12); (3) Two angels engage her in a brief exchange—with a specific question and with her corresponding response (20:13). The first event in this scene continues the mood of scene one: The author portrays Mary as one who is deeply concerned and grief-stricken regarding the whereabouts of Jesus' body. The repetition of Mary's situation is designed to invoke a concern of the reader regarding her inability to respond with faith to this situation.

Immediately after the disciples return to their homes, Mary appears standing at the tomb. She followed them back to the tomb, which is not narrated. Apparently, before they return to their homes, the two disciples do not share their findings with her. The following narrative indicates that Mary did not weep passively, but she was still searching for the body of Jesus, who she thought was dead and his body being taken away from the tomb.

Remembering scene one, the reader recalls that, while it was still dark, Mary saw the stone removed from the tomb and without mentioning her looking inside the tomb, she hastily runs to report to the disciples, (20:2). Here, in this scene, however, the reader is informed that she took time to stoop and look into the tomb (20:11d). As the Beloved Disciple, who at first does not enter the tomb, she does not enter into the tomb; rather, she inspects the tomb from the opening. The tomb is not empty because now there are two angels inside (20:12).

The angels were wearing white, one was sitting in the place where Jesus head had lain, and the other was where his feet were positioned. The author does not indicate why the two angels were in such positions, but the reader can assume that their positions allude to the only other mention of angels in the Gospel, where Jesus says: "Truly, truly, I say to you, you will see heaven opened, and *the angels of God ascending and descending upon the Son of man*" (emphasis mine, 1:51). In 20:13, after Mary sees the two angels, they asked her a question, to which she responds.

After Mary sees the two angels, the third event of this scene unfolds into a brief dialogue between the two angels and Mary, a question by the two angels (20:13a-b) and a personal response by Mary (20:13c-e). Although the author does indicate the fact that she sees two angels, there is no indication that she actually recognizes them as such. Since they are a part of Mary's and the reader's world-view, she is not startled by the angels' appearance, nor does her response to their question vary much from the report that she gave to the disciples at the close of scene one.

As the author notes, the two angels question her: "Woman, why are you weeping?" The full implication of their question is unclear. They could have known that Jesus was alive and was standing behind her outside the tomb, which could explain why she turned after her response, but this is only a speculation. Nonetheless, the angels must have known more than what is presented here in the narrative. They phrase their question to show concern for her plight and thus produce a slightly different response to her plight than that which is narrated in scene one (cf. 20:2).

Mary's response to the angels is the fourth and final event in this scene. Her response to the angels' question is modified slightly from her report to the two disciples at the end of the first scene. She modifies her response by specifically addressing the two angels' question with the words "because," (ὅτι) and instead of using the third person plural pronoun, "we," her response is modified to the first person singular pronoun, "I" (οὐκ οἶδα; literally, I do not know). Why does she modify her answer? In the second instance, she seeks to pose her question as a direct response to the angels' question. In scene one Mary's statement is an unsolicited report to the disciples, whereas in this scene she adds the word *because* to show cause for *her* weeping. In scene one Mary employs a different pronominal case to show respect to the disciples by employing an editorial "we." Conversely, in scene three she personalizes her response to the angels' inquiry, "Woman, why are you weeping?"

More specifically, Mary's response indicates two personal reasons for her sorrow: (1) her Lord is missing; (2) she does not know where he has been placed. This repetition with slight variation suggests that the theme from scene one be continued and still is a matter to be resolved: the problem of Jesus' absence from the tomb and the situation of the body's location. Mary is characterized in terms of continued weeping and intense sorrow, which functions to solicit the reader's concern and sympathy. In the following scene (scene four), Mary will continue to search desperately to achieve her goal—namely, to locate the corpse of Jesus, which of course the reader suspects will not be found as such (see below).

Conclusion

In this brief scene, the author includes more information toward a characterization of Mary Magdalene. Here again, she is still grief-stricken, desperately searching for the body of Jesus. The author inserts two angels to convince the reader of Mary's sorrow and of her determination to find the body of Jesus. Concerning the angels' position inside the tomb, the reader would compare this scene with a scene earlier in the Gospel (cf. Jn. 1:51). This reference is the only mention of angels in the Gospel, which the reader would not overlook in this allusion the reference to angels and their location. Clearly, given their limited role in the scene, it seems that the angels' function does not proceed far beyond that of intensifying the drama.

Because of these allusions or clues, the reader wonders why Mary fails to believe at this point, as the Beloved Disciple who believes upon entering the tomb. This short scene, therefore, does not merely function as a transition scene. Rather, it functions to inform the reader of the depth and determination of Mary's grief and sorrow, which caused her to pursue desperately the body of Jesus. As such, this scene further illustrates Mary's relentless search for Jesus' body.

To this point in the episode, the author not only contrasts the two disciples—Peter and the Beloved Disciple—but also presents another contrast between Mary and the two disciples. With the adversative conjunction, "but," (δὲ) the author emphasizes Mary's persistence over and against the two disciples, who return to their homes after they sought to confirm her report.

Unlike scene one, where Mary carelessly inspects the tomb and hastily reports her speculations to the disciples, in this scene the reader notices that she pursues this matter more closely; as the Beloved Disciple, she bends over and looks into the tomb. To the reader's surprise, she observes something quite different from the two disciples: the reader is surprised because the reader was informed of the two disciples' finding and response (scene two). The reader, being confronted with conflicting stories, is led to conclude that her persistence caused her to receive more proof than the disciples. Thus, the events concerning Mary at the tomb function to contrast or compare her with the two disciples, and the events with the two angels function to convince the reader that Mary needed the physical corpse of Jesus in order to believe; thus, she required a sign in which Jesus himself would have to appear in order for her to believe.

In scene one the reader was presented a snapshot of Mary Magdalene, but not enough to develop a complete portrait of her. In that scene the reader was given information concerning her sorrow, which apparently led her out into the darkness to visit the tomb of Jesus.

In this scene, scene three, Mary is still stricken with sorrow, but this time the author allows her to tell the angels the causes or reasons for her sorrow: "because they have taken away my Lord, and I do not know where they laid him" (20:13b). From these two reasons, the reader is led to identify with her sorrow.

Nonetheless, despite the fact that she inspects the tomb from the outside and despite the fact that she sees two angels, she recounts essentially the same report to the two angels, which she first made to the two disciples (cf. 20:2). In other words, Mary still believes that the body of Jesus had been taken away or stolen and placed in an unknown location (20:13 d-e). Though she evidently possesses more information than Peter and the Beloved Disciple, namely she sees two angels; yet, as Peter, she still does not believe at this point. Thus, the author provides unity between scenes two and three with the continuation of the theme and with the lack of resolution to Mary's plight, which will be resolved in the next scene, scene four.

Scene Four: Jesus' First Appearance to and Commission of Mary Magdalene; Mary's Report to the Disciples, 20:14-18

Translation of John 20:14-18

14. After she said these things, she turned to the back, and she views Jesus standing, but she did not know that it was Jesus. 15. Jesus said to her: "Woman, why are you weeping? Whom do you seek?" Supposing that he was the gardener, she said to him, "Lord, if you have carried him away, tell me where you have taken him, and I will take him." 16. Jesus said to her, "Mary." She turned and said to him in Hebrew, "*Rabbouni!*" (which means teacher). 17. Jesus said to her, "Stop touching me, for I have not yet ascended to the Father, but go to my brothers and tell them, I am ascending to my Father and your Father and to my God and to your God." 18. Mary Magdalene went announcing to the disciples, "I have seen the Lord," and she told them that he had said these things to her.

Introduction

During scene four the author brings closure to a major complication in episode number one, the end of Mary's search for the body of Jesus, a search that ironically comes to fruition at first with Mary's inability to recognize Jesus, who she mistakes to be a gardener. After Jesus questions her regarding her plight, Mary responds to his query, explaining her desperate situation without recognizing the person that she was addressing. It is only after Jesus calls her by name that she recognizes him as such, and then she precedes to hold on to him, worshipping him. Jesus then forbids her from continuing to hold on to him and proceeds to commission her to report to the disciples.

In this last scene of episode number one the author's primary purpose shifts from non-recognition to recognition to worship and finally to Jesus' specific commission of her to report his words to the disciples. Herein lies the first resurrection appearance of Jesus to a disciple, Mary

Magdalene.[17] As such, after the actual recognition occurs, the purpose of
the scene is continued but enlarged, preparing the reader for the next
episode, where the second resurrection appearance of Jesus occurs
behind closed doors to the male disciples.

Delineation of Scene Four

Scene four commences immediately after Mary responds to the
angels' question, when she turns her head around and sees Jesus standing
behind her, but she does not recognize him (20:14). The brief change in
characters, from Mary and the two angels to Jesus and Mary, primarily
constitutes the criterion for considering scene four as a unified scene.

As in the previous scenes, the spatial-setting for scene four remains
in the same vicinity of the tomb. This fourth scene consists of 20:14-18,[18]
which is signaled primarily with a focus inside the tomb to an eventual
recognition of Jesus in front of the tomb.

This scene provides the resolution to the major conflict of the
narrative that was introduced in 20:1-2. The spatial setting—exhibited by
Mary's bodily positions—shows the progression of the theme from non-
recognition to recognition.

The author employs a number of devices and techniques in this scene
to privilege the reader with information not available to Mary. The use of
dramatic irony and misunderstanding functions to reveal the nature of
Jesus in his pre-ascended state, which in the end reveals her inability to
believe despite Jesus being in plain sight, and it also reveals the
prohibition of Jesus' direct dialogue to Mary, causing the reader to
wonder what Jesus' physical state was after the resurrection.

The events of this scene are composed of action, narrator's asides,
and direct dialogue, a dialogue that results in Mary's commission. These
events function to present the nature and character of Jesus in his post-

[17] For women disciples and women in the four Gospels, see, e.g., C. Ricci, *Mary
Magdalene and Many Others: Women who Followed Jesus* (Translated from the
Italian by Paul Burns. Minneapolis: Fortress Press, 1994) 42-43; 61-72; R. Brown,
"Roles of Women in the Fourth Gospel." *TS* 36 (1975) 688-699; and S. Schneiders,
"Women in the Fourth Gospel." *BTB* 12 (1982) 25-45.
[18] Traditionally, 20:11-18 has been studied as a unit, but the unit is differentiated into
two scenes due to a change in characters.

resurrection, pre-ascension state. Mary's role in the resurrection narrative ends not only with a resolution of her sorrow but also with the task to deliver the first Easter proclamation to the disciples.

Temporal Process of Reading Scene Four

Immediately after Mary Magdalene responds to the angels' question, the author changes characters, from the two angels and Mary to Jesus and Mary. She turns around (ἐστράφη εἰς τὰ ὀπίσω; literally she turned back around) and sees Jesus standing behind her, but at this point, she does not recognize him. The author omits narration both on why she turned around in such a fashion and on why she was unable to recognize him (20:14).

As stated earlier there are two directional changes, representing Mary Magdalene's spatial positions, which symbolically suggest a movement from non-recognition to recognition. For example, the scene begins with Mary in a stooping position, looking toward her rear over her shoulder. Here, the reader can visualize the initial spatial positions with which Mary progressively turns as she begins to recognize Jesus. Later in this scene, she turns completely around after Jesus calls her by name (see below).

Concerning the way in which the author moves Mary from non-recognition to recognition, several events are arranged to privilege the reader with information that is not a part of the story-world; that is, the reader possesses information that Mary does not. First, Mary turns toward Jesus, but she does not recognize him (20:14c). Because Jesus was standing behind Mary—saying nothing at this point—the reader wonders what led Mary to turn to her back (ἐστράφη). In addition, upon seeing Jesus, the reader is told that Jesus had been standing there (ἑστῶτα, literally, having stood), but the author reveals to the reader that Mary does not recognize him. Thus, this scene represents the beginning of a recognition scene, in which the reader is given information that the characters do not possess, which is a situation of dramatic irony.

Second, Jesus asks Mary two questions (20:14a-c). The first question repeats the two angels' question: "woman, why are you weeping [γύναι, τί κλαίεις;...]?" Not only does the reader sense in this repetition

Jesus' concern, but also the reader recognizes the irony of the situation. Here, the author gives the reader information that Mary does not possess. Thus, while Jesus is standing behind her in plain sight, at this point the reader does not sympathize with her situation.

The second question, "Whom do you seek?" (τίνα ζετεῖς...), intensifies the dramatic irony. It not only shows why Mary's sorrow is unnecessary, since Jesus is standing in her presence, it also points to him since he is the one who she seeks. These two questions not only present a situation of dramatic irony; they also present a situation where misunderstandings exist. For instance, Mary misunderstands that the man to whom she is speaking is Jesus and not the gardener; in reality the reader knows and understands—because of the author's aside—that Jesus is not dead, yet she does not recognize what seems to be obvious. Thus, the author allows the reader to recognize Jesus before the characters in the story-world.

Regarding these two questions, not only does the author suggest Jesus' concern for her in this scene, but also Jesus' questions serve as one of the themes of the Gospel, "whom do you seek?" (Cf. John 1, etc.) The first question directly indicates Jesus' concern for her. The second question, found in a slightly different form in other parts of the Gospel (cf. 18:4), demonstrates his concern for Mary, since it seeks to direct her attention directly to the cause of her sorrow. Jesus empathizes with her sorrow,[19] and the reader senses Jesus' concern for her by way of the author's direct discourse, particularly when he initially addresses her in this scene.

Third, Mary confuses Jesus to be the gardener, and as such she makes a specific, unrealistic request to him, supposing that he knew where the body has been taken and that she would be able alone to take it (the body) away (20:15e-g). In 20:15d the author informs the reader that Mary thought that Jesus was the gardener. Accordingly, Mary addresses Jesus with a first-class conditional statement. In the protasis, 20:15f, when she states "If you [the gardener] have carried him away," she wrongly assumes that Jesus is a gardener. Her failure to see will become

---

[19]   There exist three moments in this narrative where Jesus expresses his concern for others: 20:15a-b, 20:16b, and 20:17d-f.

clear as the narrative develops. Mary's response to Jesus' questions further establishes her inability to understand. The fact that she thinks that he is someone who he is not, namely the gardener, causes her to proceed with a question that is based on a wrong assumption, as if he knew something about the corpse and, if so, would or could tell her where he had placed it. Since Mary perceives that the man she is speaking to is somehow responsible for the missing body, she addresses him in such a way as to request that he tell her where the body was, if he had in fact removed it, so that she could take it away. This request is problematic in several ways: (1) why would Mary suppose that this man was responsible for the missing corpse? (2) Why should the gardener simply tell her where the body was? These questions preclude any motive for taking the body on the part of this so-called gardener. (3) If he did take it and if he chose to tell Mary, where it was, then how could Mary take it away alone? This information could only lead to further problems, since Mary would have to leave the body and go search for help, while in the meantime the body could again presumably end up missing.

The irony that the reader perceives now becomes nonsensical to a point; that is, why does she not she recognize him? Not only does the reader wonder why Mary does not recognize Jesus, but also why she still thinks that he is dead and that she can move the body alone.

Fourth, Jesus calls Mary by her name (20:16a-b). When Jesus calls her name, only then is she able to recognize him. Perhaps, it is at this point that Jesus allows himself to be known. When Jesus calls her name and then she recognizes him, the reader recalls an early scene in Gospel (10:1-6). In v. 16b Jesus says "Mary," which indicates implicitly in the Gospel (cf. 10:3) that Mary is one of his sheep. Even though Mary seemingly exhibits a state of blindness, which could be depicted by her sorrow and grief, Jesus still considers and addresses her as one of his own.

Fifth, she turns—presumably, in the earlier part of this scene, she only turned her head, but now she turns her whole body—and addresses Jesus (20:16b). The reader is somewhat surprised by the Christological title that Mary uses to refer to Jesus because the reader knows that this role constituted his ministry prior to his death and that higher titles have been given to Jesus earlier in the narrative (cf. John 1). Nonetheless, the reader does anticipate some form of worship since Mary's speculations and false expectations have been reversed.

Sixth, Jesus forbids Mary from continuing to hold onto him because he has not yet to ascend to the Father (20:17a). In other words, while she is holding onto him, Jesus forbids her. Here, in this scene, Jesus could not be detained because he needed first to ascend to the Father.

Seventh, Jesus commissions Mary to go to the disciples (brethren) and proclaim to them a new relationship (20:17b). In v. 17 although Jesus did not allow Mary to keep on holding him, he provides a reason why she could not continue to do so and proceeds immediately to commission her, showing his concern toward the disciples by establishing a new relationship with them. In this commission, Jesus identifies his Father as their Father and his God as their God. Despite the fact that the disciples were absent and had abandoned Jesus, the reader perceives Jesus' continued concern for them. Even before he had ascended, he instructs Mary to report a new relationship with the disciples (his brethren). The reader observes this first reference to the disciples within a message to be delivered by Mary Magdalene, a theme reminiscent of Jesus' farewell address (cf. chapter 17).

Finally, Mary reports to the disciples (20:18), which serves as a fulfillment of her commission. Here, the reader perceives Mary's role in the narrative as now resolved. At the end of this scene, as in scene one, Mary proceeds to report to the disciples, but this time she bears good news, "I have seen the Lord," as a part of the message from her Lord. The spatial location is not given specifically, but this location is seemingly a house, probably a house where the disciples gathered frequently. This spatial location—inside of a house—is the location of several informal and formal events, and at this point in the narrative, it is where Mary traveled to report to the disciples (see episode number two).

Conclusion

The author employs this scene to establish three central goals: to move Mary and the reader from non-recognition to recognition; to commission Mary with the first Easter proclamation to the disciples; and to announce a new relationship between Jesus and the disciples that existed before his death, which was necessary due to their desertion, with the exception of the Beloved Disciple (cf. 19:26-27).

As evident by now, the author places several resolutions before the reader in this scene, the conclusion to episode number one. This scene resolves a long awaited event that was anticipated from the very beginning of the resurrection narrative, namely, the question of the whereabouts of Jesus' body. This question is addressed and resolved in a way that creates more questions that the reader cannot answer with certainty at this point in the narrative. For example, although Jesus appears for the first time in the resurrection narrative, the reader is not quite sure what to make of Jesus' new physical state.

Concerning the assumption with which Mary proceeds to respond to Jesus' questions, the author reports to the reader that Mary supposed, or thought that he was the gardener. Why did Mary think that he was the gardener? Again, the reader could speculate on a number of reasons, but this is not the point of this section. Mary replies to Jesus' query with her supposition in mind. Thus, the scene's main thrust focuses on a non-recognition to recognition motif, in other words the duration of this scene takes up most of the narrative time, including descriptions, direct dialogue, and action.

The author establishes the development of non-recognition to recognition with the devices of dramatic irony and misunderstanding in two stages of Mary's inability to recognize Jesus. After scene three, where the two angels' role in the narrative point to Jesus by addressing Mary's weeping with a rhetorical question, the misunderstanding occurred when Mary mistakes Jesus to be the gardener. The misunderstanding is intensified with the repetition of Jesus' two questions, which are designed to establish this misunderstanding episode, privileging the reader with knowledge of Jesus' status.

Further, the reader notes a misunderstanding device when Mary employs an old Christological title to address Jesus as *Rabbouni*. This misunderstanding causes the reader to wonder about the nature of Jesus, due to his forbidding her to hold onto him. The author, by way of direct discourse, informs Mary and the reader of the reason for this prohibition, namely that Jesus has not yet ascended to the Father. Thus, in part, this scene functions to establish the nature of Jesus in his post-resurrection, pre-ascended state.

After the disciples' desertion before Jesus' death (with the exception of the Beloved Disciple), Mary's message also functions as the first

Easter proclamation and as an encouraging report that brings good news, regarding the status of Jesus after his death and burial. Since there is no mention of praise or activity on the part of the disciples, this omission signals the need for Jesus himself to appear to the disciples.

In short, scene four functions as a whole to present Jesus' first appearance in a post-resurrection, pre-ascension state. This scene resolves the problem of Jesus' bodily absence and establishes, for the reader, the character of Jesus in this state. In this scene Mary's concern is satisfied; she has seen the Lord. What remains is a response from the disciples' encounter with the risen Jesus, which will be developed, in full, in the following episodes.

Further, this scene presents another portrait of Mary, which is developed further and for the final time in the resurrection narrative, a portrait of Jesus, and a characterizing reaction of the disciples. In what follows first a final characterization of Mary will be presented in light of the other scenes where she appears, and then a preliminary characterization of Jesus and the disciples will be presented.

Although Mary appears in three scenes—one, three, and here in four—her character can be depicted with a single main trait and several minor traits; namely, as a sorrowful, emotional, grief-stricken person who is not only concerned about the location of Jesus' corpse, but who is also quite persistent in her search for it. One ambivalent main trait concerns her inability to believe in the resurrection of Jesus before his addressing her by name, a belief that requires Jesus' assistance, as the disciples in the final episode, during the fishing and recognition scenes (cf. 21:1-14).

Mary's grief-stricken state is portrayed by way of the author's asides, the author's description of these actions, and direct discourse. In scene one the author presents the setting and direct discourse of Mary's first trip to the tomb, in which she is depicted in terms of sorrow and disappointment concerning the status of Jesus' body. Her cursory inspection of the tomb requires further inspection and verification by the two disciples to confirm her suspicions that the body was in fact missing. The two disciples did not confirm her claim that someone had removed the body or corpse from the tomb and placed it elsewhere. Rather, their inspection merely confirmed the fact that the body was missing. Thus, in scene one the author presents her as one who is concerned and who reports her speculation to the disciples.

In scene three, concerning Mary's brief meeting with the two angels, the author further depicts Mary's emotional state with description and direct discourse (question-and-answer) narrative devices. The two angels' question and their role in the narrative function to identify Mary's reason for weeping and possibly to point her towards Jesus. Mary's answer further identifies the cause of her sorrow, which is twofold: "they have taken away my Lord," and "I do not know where they have laid him." Thus, the conflict of Jesus' missing corpse serves to illuminate Mary's dilemma and determination to locate Jesus' corpse because there is not the slightest hint in the narrative that she thinks that Jesus has been raised from the dead.

In scene four Mary's sorrow causes her further grief and sorrow, upon which Jesus repeats the angels' question to her. Yet, she overlooks the possibility of Jesus' resurrection. Though she searches for him for a period, she does not recognize him when she meets him, but rather she mistakenly confuses him to be the gardener, either because of her emotional state or because of Jesus' different, quasi-physical nature. In other words, Mary's grief and sorrow, which are described by her weeping, cause her to miss several clues, thus indicating a type of spiritual blindness. This lack of perception indicates her state at this point in the narrative. Her blindness further indicates her inability to believe. When Jesus addresses her by her name, however, she immediately recognizes him. Mary is evidently one of Jesus' sheep who responds when he calls her by name. Thus, her role in the narrative is ambivalent at best: on the one hand, she is blind and cannot believe without Jesus' assistance; on the other hand, she is identified as one of Jesus' sheep who follow once they hear his voice and are called by their name. Mary complies with his commission by delivering the first Easter proclamation to the disciples.

The nature of Jesus' character in scene four is difficult to describe because the author develops his resurrection character throughout several scenes. The following identify some of the traits that the author introduces in this scene and, as the narrative progresses, some patterns will emerge to characterize his new post-resurrected nature.

Jesus' characterization will be dealt with here as an initial characterization of him throughout the resurrection narrative. This characterization of Jesus will show how the reader may discern Jesus' character in this post-resurrection state. Once this characterization is advanced it could then be compared with the author's portrayal of Jesus in episodes two and three.

In scene four Jesus appears for the first time since his death in chapter 19. His character, in this new state, is developed to a great degree in terms of its complexity and how it permeates into a concern for others: Mary and the disciples. His concern is presented in the direct discourse to Mary and delivered to the disciples by her.

Jesus' quasi-physical, post-resurrected state is addressed, albeit in a pre-ascended state. In this state he can be touched, but he forbids being held onto because he must first ascend to the Father.

Finally, the disciples as a group are referred to here, but they are not developed at this point. Their function at the end of this scene is to hear the report of Mary, where the disciples do not respond to her report. While Jesus is instructing Mary to stop touching him, he proceeds to commission her to proclaim to the disciples a new relationship after his resurrection, when he returns in a post-ascended state. Since Jesus mentioned this kind of relationship earlier in the narrative, it is not necessarily a *new* relationship (cf. chapters 15 and 17). The intent of this report is to re-establish their relationship and to encourage them with regard to an existing and expanding relationship with Jesus and with God as their Father.

This scene brings to a close the events and scenes that precede it. Though resolution is achieved in this scene, many questions remain for the reader, namely the post-ascended activities and future appearance of Jesus to the disciples. This episode is unified and brings resolution to the events at the close of chapter 19. The unity of this scene is represented in the author's use of narrative devices, events, characters, and the reader's responses to the narrative as it unfold. In the next episode, Jesus makes his first and second appearances to the male disciples, who are in seclusion behind closed doors in fear of the Jews.

CHAPTER THREE

Episode Number Two:
The House Where the
Disciples Gathered—
Jesus' First and Second Appearance to the
Male Disciples, John 20:19-31

Introduction

The major complication of episode number one concerns the question of how will the author depict Jesus' two appearances in order to be convincing to the male disciples and the reader. It commences in a new spatial location: the house where the disciples were gathered. It continues, however, the theme introduced in scene four—the narrative accounts of the post-resurrection appearances of Jesus, which are again prompted by Mary Magdalene's report to the disciples, as in scene one. Rather than search for Jesus, in this episode he comes to the disciples who are gathered behind closed doors.

Episode number two (vv. 19-31) includes three scenes in this spatial-setting: scene five (vv. 19-23), scene six (vv. 24-25), scene seven (vv. 26-29), and a narrative summary (vv. 30-31). In the evening of the day on which Jesus rose from the dead, Jesus appears among the disciples in scene five. While the disciples are shut in a secluded location in fear of the Jewish authorities, Jesus greets the disciples and shows them the marks of his crucifixion. After seeing his marks and recognizing him as their Lord, the disciples rejoiced. Jesus greets them again, with the same greeting, "Peace be with you," after which Jesus commissions them with the words, "As the Father has sent me, even so send I you." Along with this commissioning, Jesus breathes on them and bids them to receive the Holy Spirit. Finally, Jesus gives them the authority to forgive or retain the sins of anyone.

In scene six, later that evening on the same day of the week, the author informs the reader that Thomas was not with the disciples when Jesus had appeared to them behind closed doors. Therefore, the disciples, like Mary, render their Easter proclamation to Thomas: "We have seen the Lord." Thomas, however, refused to accept their proclamation and proceeds to convey his conditions for believing, which entailed putting his hands into the marks of Jesus hands and putting his finger into Jesus' side. Unless Thomas is given such physical evidence, he will not believe.

Scene seven occurs one week later when Thomas was present with the disciples; here, Jesus appeared to the male disciples for the second time. While the disciples are still in seclusion in the house where they gathered, Jesus appears among them, as in scene five, with the same words of greeting. After this, Jesus challenges Thomas to confirm his suspicions, instructing him to "Put your fingers here and see my hands, and put out your hands, and put it in my side and do not be faithless, but believing." To this challenge, Thomas responds with a high Christological confession of faith, exclaiming to Jesus: "My Lord and my God." Then Jesus responds with a twofold, gentle rebuke: first Jesus asks a rhetorical question regarding Thomas' belief based on seeing Jesus; finally, Jesus renders a beatitude, which blesses those who believe without seeing him.

Finally, the author provides a narrator's summary to the first two episodes, referring to the other signs that Jesus did in the presence of the disciples, and the purpose of the sign, which suggests that the disciples may continue to believe that Jesus is the Christ, the Son of God. Thus, the major complication of episode number two essentially entails the author's attempt to convince the male disciples and the reader of Jesus' post-ascension, post-resurrection status and purpose.

Outline of Episode Number Two

II. Episode Number Two at the House Where the Disciples Gathered: Jesus' First and Second Appearance to the Male Disciples, John 20:19-31.
  A. Scene Five: Jesus' First Appearance to the Male Disciples, without Thomas: The Appearance and the Disciples' Reactions; Jesus' Commissioning and Bestowing of the Holy Spirit with Authority, 20:19-23.
  B. Scene Six: The Disciples' Brief Report to Thomas; Thomas' Conditions in Order to Believe, 20:24-25.
  C. Scene Seven: The Second Appearance of Jesus: to Thomas with the Disciples Present: Jesus' Challenge to Thomas' Conditions; Thomas' High Christological Response; and Jesus' Reply; Narrative Summary of Chapter 20: The Purpose of the Resurrection Signs in the Presence of the Disciples, 20:26-31.

Delineation of Episode Number Two

Episode number one is differentiated from episode number two with a major change in the temporal- and spatial-settings, with a change in characters, and with a change of purpose. The temporal-setting in the first scene of episode number one occurs during the evening of Jesus' resurrection. In episode number one, however, the events take place during the early morning hours.

The second episode of the resurrection narrative involves a major change in location, from the tomb, which is located outside, to the house, which is an inside, secluded location, where the disciples were gathered. The spatial location of episode number one, scenes one through four (vv. 1-18), was the tomb where Jesus was placed (see 19:38-42), the site where Jesus was desperately searched for by Mary Magdalene, Peter, and the Beloved Disciple (vv. 1-15) and inevitably encountered by Mary Magdalene (vv. 16-18). In episode number two the author includes two appearances of Jesus at the house where the disciples gathered: one in scene five (vv. 19-23) and the other in scene seven (vv. 26-29).

In episode number one Jesus, Mary Magdalene, Peter, and the Beloved Disciple are featured as the principal characters. The only pre-ascended appearance of Jesus, however, was to Mary Magdalene, representing also the only appearance of Jesus in episode number one.

Regarding the change in purpose of episode number two in comparison to episode number one, the events of the first episode focus primarily on events that eventually involve Jesus' pre-ascended appearance to Mary Magdalene. In episode number two the author's purpose now concerns convincing the disciples that Jesus had been raised from the dead. To establish such a phenomenon, the author provides two scene where Jesus offers proof of his resurrection to the disciples, first without Thomas and then the second appearance (to the disciples, all together this is Jesus' third appearance) with Thomas present, to further convince Thomas of Jesus' resurrection. The episode concludes with a narrative summary on the purpose of Jesus' signs in the presence of the disciples.

Episode number one is differentiated from episode number three with a major change in the spatial- and temporal-settings, with a change in characters, and with a change in purpose. This delineation will be provided in the next chapter. Episode number two is differentiated from episodes number one and three, represented in 20:19-31.

Scene Five: Jesus' First Appearance to the Male Disciples, without Thomas: The Appearance and the Disciples' Reactions; Jesus' Commissioning and Bestowing of the Holy Spirit with Authority, 20:19-23

Translation of John 20:19-23

19. Then, in the early evening, on the first day of the week, and the doors were shut where the disciples were, for fear of the Jews, Jesus came and stood among them, and said to them, "Peace be with you." 20. And having said this, he showed them his hands and his side. Then, the disciples rejoiced, when they saw the Lord. 21. Then he said to them again, "Peace be with you. As the Father has sent me, even so I send you." 22. When he had said this, he breathed on them and said to them, "Receive the Holy Spirit. 23. If you forgive the sins of any, they are forgiven; if you retain the sins of any, they are retained."

Introduction

During the first appearance of Jesus to the disciples in scene five, the disciples are addressed as a group, and the meeting takes place without Thomas, after which the disciples meet with Thomas to report on their encounter with Jesus in scene six. Jesus' second appearance to the male disciples occurs in scene seven, which narrates his appearance to Thomas with the other disciples lurking in the background.

This day is full of events that occur from early while it was still dark and continue until "the early evening of that day, the first day of the week" (v. 19a-b). The author makes certain that the reader does not confuse the temporal setting, repeating the day of the week, using a double, temporal reference pointing to "that day" and "the first day of the week." With these two temporal references, the reader again, like in scene one, anticipates a significant event.

Delineation of Scene Five

Scene five forms a complete unit and is differentiated from that which precedes it primarily with a major change in characters and with a major change in the spatial- and temporal-settings (vv. 19-23). These major changes, however, are alluded to in the previous episode, thus connecting this episode with the one that precedes it and providing continuity with the overall theme of the appearances of Jesus to the disciples. The author makes an allusion to the characters and to the spatial- and temporal-settings that are a part of this new episode: (1) The disciples are mentioned throughout episode number one; they are referred to as a group, however, only at the end of the first episode (v. 18); in scene two, Peter and the Beloved Disciple are mentioned specifically and are the principal characters. (2) The house where the disciples were gathered is mentioned twice in episode number one (cf. vv. 2 and 10; see also v. 19, where it is possibly the location of Mary's final report to the disciples); the location is now in a house where the disciples are in seclusion, due to their fear of the Jews; finally, this episode is temporally connected to the previous episode, occurring in the evening of the same day. Thus, the temporal-setting of scene five also occurs on the first day of the week, but now it is in the early evening, and scene five presents the account of Jesus' first appearance to the male disciples, without the presence of Thomas, who is not mentioned until scene six (vv. 24-25).

The disciples encounter the post-resurrected and post-ascended Jesus in scene five. In this scene Jesus is the principal character, who is apparently now in a post-resurrected, post-ascended condition, along with the disciples, who are portrayed as a group. Jesus appears suddenly and without notice among the disciples with a specific purpose and intent: to commission the disciples and to breathe the Holy Spirit upon them. Thus, the change in characters along with a change in the temporal- and spatial-settings constitute the establishment of scene five from scene four.

Concerning the differentiation of scene five from scene six, in 20:23 Jesus grants the disciples the Holy Spirit and gives them the authority to forgive or retain sins. After this brief ceremony, Jesus leaves the scene, and a new scene begins with a meeting between the disciples and Thomas (cf. v. 24). The temporal- and spatial-settings of this meeting, however, are not narrated.

In scene six, after a report from the disciples concerning their encounter with Jesus, Thomas requires further proof in order to believe that Jesus had risen from the dead. Whereas, scene five mainly deals with the disciples' experience with Jesus, scene six includes the disciples' report to Thomas and presents Thomas' doubt regarding how he would come to believe that Jesus had risen from the dead. As such, scene five is differentiation from scene six primarily due to this change in characters and theme, the belated introduction of Thomas and his doubting role, beginning with v. 19 and ending with v. 23.

Temporal Process of Reading Scene Five

The temporal references, "When it was evening on that day" and "the first day of the week," suggest that the order of these events in this scene were presented in a sequential fashion relative to the events of episode number one. While the day of the week is the same, the time of the day changes to early evening.

Apparently, the disciples are in strict seclusion due to their fear of the Jews, which is a motif introduced and developed earlier in the narrative and still a factor to this point (cf. 7:13, 9:22; 10:31-39; 11:8; 11:54-57). It was in this setting that Jesus appeared among the disciples.

His manner of appearance among them suggests that his post-resurrected presence is quasi-physical in nature—his ability to come through closed doors and shows himself standing among the disciples, which is presented without commentary by the author.

Although the doors were shut, "Jesus came and stood among them." The reader suspects that Jesus is able to appear among the disciples through a locked door. Jesus knew where the disciples gathered, and the reader suspects that this site may have been a place where they also gathered before Jesus' death. The reader senses the need for this appearance of Jesus probably due to the lack of response and faith of the disciples at Mary's report, as well as due to the disciples' fear, which necessitated a personal visit from Jesus.

In scene five, though the exact location of the house where the disciples are gathered is not given, the mood of the location is that of fear. The author reports that "the doors being shut where the disciples were" (v. 19c) was due to their fear of the Jews. In this spatial-setting of fear, behind closed doors, Jesus comes and stands among them (v. 19d), offers them words of comfort (v. 19e) and shows them visual proof of his death and resurrection (v. 20b).

Jesus' initial statement reflects the words he proclaimed to Mary Magdalene in 20:17: both statements function to bring comfort to the disciples in this post-resurrection experience. After Jesus provides words of comfort, "Peace be with you," he shows them his hands and side, as proof that it was in fact he and that he was alive. The disciples' reaction of elation verifies this point to the reader (v. 20d). At the end of scene four, the disciples showed no sign either of doubting or of rejoicing; the author concludes the narrative after Mary's report with no reaction from the disciples. Yet, when Jesus shows them his marks, the disciples demonstrate their first indication of joy in the resurrection narrative, which is narrated with indirect discourse by the author.

After Jesus provides words of comfort, the reader receives no report on the disciples' response, indicating that they did not recognize Jesus standing in their presence. Therefore, Jesus shows them his hands and his feet (20:20b), making a direct reference to the crucifixion, confirming that it is the same Jesus who had been crucified. During the crucifixion Jesus' hands and side had been pierced, at least those who stood at the cross witnessed, among whom was the Beloved Disciple (cf. 19:26).

These marks suggested to the disciples that this one among them had the
marks of the one who had been crucified; thus, these marks serve as
evidence that this same person was none other than Jesus. So together
with the report of Mary and with the words of comfort, Jesus' marks
assured the disciples of the risen Jesus and therefore confirmed for the
reader that Jesus was alive and had been raised from the dead.

After the disciples rejoiced, Jesus once again repeats the same words
of comfort, "Peace be with you" (v. 21b), and proceeds to commission
the disciples with the words: "As the Father has sent me, so I send you"
(v. 21c). The Father bases this commissioning on Jesus' own
commission, which is one of the central motifs in the Gospel (cf. John
5:36-37; 6:29, 38-40, 44, 57; 7:16; 8:16; 9:4; 12:44-50; 14:24; 17:3, 18-
25).

After Jesus gives the disciples their commission, Jesus breathes
(ἐνεφυσωσησεν) the Holy Spirit on them in a ceremonial fashion. Jesus'
own breath symbolizes the endowment of the Holy Spirit, which was
rendered in a ritual-like fashion: words of comfort; the commission; a
sign or symbol of his resurrection; the endowment of the Holy Spirit
being given to the disciples; finally, the authority needed to carry on or
perform their commission, namely the authority to forgive (ἀφῆτε) or
retain (κρατῆτε) the sins of any. As such, this scene functions to bring
comfort to the disciples, to commission the disciples, to grant to them the
Holy Spirit and the authority to forgive or retain sins. The reader senses
the need for these words of comfort and assurance ("Jesus said to them,
'Peace be with you'") because of the disciples' fear and lack of response.
Evidently, the disciples were discouraged and disbelieving as can be
detected from the previous scenes (cf. Scene Two, v. 8).

In 20:20c the author records the response of the disciples to the
reader, which was that of gladness because they had seen the Lord. This
revelation was the evidence the disciples required to change their fear
into gladness: "Then the disciples were glad when they saw the Lord" (v.
20c).

With this revelation, the reader's perception of the disciples' delayed
response was indeed correct. The disciples required a physical sign to
demonstrate some sort of response: a report from Mary and the message
from Jesus were not enough to evoke a response, which was designed by

the author to convince the reader of Jesus' physical resurrection. Besides, the disciples' response of gladness still falls short of an adequate faith or belief in Jesus, which is a major theme in the resurrection narrative. In other words, that the disciples required more than a report and words from Jesus suggests a need much more than that of the Beloved Disciple and Mary. What really matters to the reader is that this proof was sufficient for them to verify that it was, in fact, the Lord who they saw. This report of the author, however, is a reliable one nonetheless because it was consistent with the words and actions of Jesus.[1]

In 20:21 the reader perceives this event as necessary since this is the first time Jesus made it. The disciples either were not sure that it was the Lord or they were so startled over the experience of a stranger standing among them that they were hesitant to draw any conclusions.

After the disciples' response, Jesus repeats his initial words of comfort and proceeds to commission them. The basis of this commissioning consists of Jesus' commissioning by the Father. So, regardless of their fear and delayed response, Jesus still commissions them as he had been commissioned. The reader thus weighs this commissioning of the disciple in the same light as they viewed Jesus' commission and ministry.

In 20:22b the reader recognizes the ritualistic nature of Jesus' visit. Early in the narrative breathe or wind serves or functions as a symbol of the Holy Spirit (cf. Jn. 3:8). Jesus' command, "Receive the Holy Spirit" (v. 22c), confirms the reader's speculation that Jesus was formally commissioning the disciples. The reader recalls Jesus' teaching earlier in the narrative (cf. chapter 14 and 16), which suggests that the disciples would receive assistance from the Holy Spirit for their mission. It also suggests that the disciples would have some form of authority, with their reception of the Holy Spirit (cf. Jn. 16:13).

In 20:23 the reader is provided more specificity with regard to their authority, which includes two first class conditional statements: "If you forgive the sins of any, they are forgiven; if you retain the sins of any, they are retained" (v. 23). Not only does Jesus provide the disciples with the Holy Spirit, but also he equips them with the authority to carry out

---

[1] For reliable narration, see e.g., Rimmon-Kenan, *Narrative Fiction*, 94, 100-103.

Jesus' mission. They are endowed with the authority to forgive or retain sins of anyone. This authority places the disciples on a new level, a level above the one that they had experienced during Jesus' earthly mission.

Conclusion

In scene five the narrative progresses along the lines from non-recognition to recognition to gladness to commission to authority. As such, this is the second recognition scene in the resurrection narrative. The first recognition scene involved Mary in scene four. The function of this scene is to provoke recognition of some kind, which is eventually indicated by a response from the disciples. After the recognition is confirmed, Jesus proceeds in a ritual manner, where in the end the disciples are endowed with the Holy Spirit and authority. The structure of this scene evokes much more from the reader than a confirmation of who Jesus is; it also functions to inform the reader of the disciples' new mission.

In this scene the author introduces the major complication: the recognition scene that seems to be the major theme in the last two scenes (four and five; cf. episode number three). Here, the author places the reader in a privileged position. The reader is informed that the person in the scene is Jesus, whereas the characters in the story do not initially possess this information. The author's devices indicate, however, that recognition is not primary. Rather, the author places greater emphasis on the commission and authority of the disciples. In other words, even though the reader recognizes Jesus before the characters, the disciples' commission is the focus of the scene.

The temporal-setting of this scene occurs later in the day at early evening, on the first day of the week, stressing the continued significance of the events on this day. Several events are covered on this day: the discovery of the empty tomb; the inspection of the tomb by Peter and the Beloved Disciple; Mary's brief meeting with two angels inside of the tomb; Mary's recognition of Jesus, Jesus' commissioning of Mary in a post-resurrection, pre-ascended state; an apparent ascension of Jesus to the Father; and Mary's Easter proclamation and report to the disciples. Further, on the evening of the first day of the week, Jesus' post-resurrection, post ascended appearance provides proof of his resurrection to the disciples behind closed doors: Jesus' commissions the disciples, endows them with the Holy Spirit, and grants them authority. Thus, the function of scene five was not only to provide evidence of Jesus' resurrection but also to narrate Jesus' appearance among the disciples and to commission them with the Holy Spirit and authority.

The major complication of these events reaches a climax with Jesus' commissioning of the disciples. Indeed, the risen Jesus is not only concerned about the emotional state of the disciples, but also he grants them the necessary authority to carry out their mission, which is based on Jesus' commission by the Father. Thus, scene five begins a new episode where Jesus appears in a post-resurrection and post-ascension state, in which Jesus' identity has to be established with a sign from Jesus before the disciples respond with gladness.

The house where the disciples were gathered serves as a meeting place for the disciples in Jerusalem. The reader, however, can only speculate that this site was probably where Mary made her reports to the disciples (cf. 20:2, 18); where Peter and the Beloved Disciple begin their race to the tomb and return after they inspected the tomb (cf. vv. 3, 10); and finally where Mary makes the first Easter proclamation to the disciples (20:18). This place is quite likely the one where the two disciples return in 20:10. Here, however, it serves as a place of refuge to hide from the Jewish authority (v. 19c).

Obviously, the Jewish leaders were still a threat to the disciples. "[F]or the fear of the Jews," the disciples remain, for the most part, behind closed doors. Apparently, the disciples' safety is in question because of a possible threat from the Jewish leaders, who sought to persecute the disciples for their allegiance with and following of Jesus. To avoid the Jewish authorities, the disciples remain in fear behind closed, shut doors. This state of fear sends a signal to the reader that the disciples lacked courage or faith to continue the ministry of Jesus Christ, or better it suggests that without Jesus the disciples can do nothing, a theme that will be advanced in episode number three.

The rhetorical emphasis of this passage is to reveal the disciples' new authority. Despite their inability to recognize Jesus immediately, as in Mary's situation, the disciples are still commissioned. Privilege is granted to the reader, a dramatic irony, similar to scene four (without the notion of misunderstanding); however, the ritual of commissioning is new and unexpected by the disciples and the reader. Thus, the rhetorical dimension places the reader and the characters on the same plane of authority and responsibility.

The following deals with characterizations of Jesus, the disciples, and the Holy Spirit will be presented. Concerning the portrayal of Jesus to this point in the narrative, in scene four the reader noticed that Jesus appeared to Mary Magdalene during his first appearance, in a pre-ascended, post-resurrected state. In that scene, he was not immediately recognized. When she recognized him, he forbade her to hold onto him because he had "not yet ascended to the Father" (v. 17). In the following scene (scene five), the reader observes that Jesus appears among the disciples, behind closed doors, in a post-resurrected, post-ascended state. Apparently, Jesus comes through closed doors, and the disciples are unable to recognize him until Jesus shows his marks as proof of his resurrection. This type of appearance seems to resemble Jesus' pre-ascended state, in which he allows others to recognize him, but only after he offers a sign of some sort. The disciples, like Mary, do not immediately recognize him. In fact, once Jesus shows his hands and side, which bore the marks of his crucifixion, the disciples' reaction indicates to the reader that they are now able to recognize who this person is standing among them, which is a pattern that will be addressed in episode number three.

In addition, as in scene four, after Jesus shows concern for the disciples, he then commissions them. First, Jesus assures the disciples of his concern with the words: "Peace be with you." Second, again with a concern for the disciples, Jesus shows them his hands and side, as proof of his resurrection, to which the disciples respond with gladness, "When they saw the Lord." Again, Jesus reassures the disciples with the same words of comfort and commissions them. Lastly, Jesus gives the disciples authority to forgive and to retain sins. Thus, Jesus' role in this scene is to offer words of comfort, offer proof of his resurrection, and commission the disciples with the authority to forgive or retain sins of any person.

Lastly, as in scene four, in scene five Jesus' character is one of showing concern for his own and commissioning them: Mary was to proclaim the first Easter event, and the disciples were commissioned with the Holy Spirit and authority. Twice he offers the same words of comfort, "Peace be with you," to demonstrate his concern for the disciples. In a ritualistic fashion, he comforts, commissions, bestows the Holy Spirit, and grants the disciples authority. Similar to scene four, Jesus provides a double formula to provide the disciples with authority: "My father, your Father; My God, your God" (v. 17d-f); "forgive the sins of any, they are forgiven; retain the sins of any, they are retained" (v. 23). The first formula provides the disciples with a new authority by means of a new relationship with the Father and with God and hence with the resurrected Jesus. In the second formula, with two first-class conditional statements, Jesus gives the disciples authority in a new relationship by means of the ability to forgive or retain the sins of any person. Thus, Jesus places the disciples into the position he once held before his death.

Concerning a portrayal of the disciples as a group, in this scene, as in scenes one, two, and four, the disciples are developed with indirect discourse. They are developed in these scenes with narrator's asides and Jesus' direct discourse. In the previous scenes the disciples are merely referred to in the narrative: (1) in 20:2 Mary reports to Peter and the Beloved Disciples; (2) in 20:3-10 the two disciples race to the tomb, inspect it, and return to their homes; (3) in 20:17 Jesus commissions Mary to go to his brothers; and (4) in 20:18, Mary reports to the disciples, who receive no narration regarding their response.

In scene five the author reports that "then the disciples were glad when they saw the Lord" (v. 20c). Their gladness, however, comes only after Jesus had shown his hands and side. This delayed reaction indicates, as in the previous scene with the exception of the Beloved Disciple, that they were slow to respond and only able to do so with visual, physical evidence.

Despite the disciples' fear and their delayed response, Jesus again greets them with the same words of comfort he offered them in 20:19f. In addition, Jesus grants them the Holy Spirit and authority. Thus, in this scene, three days after Jesus' death and hours since the report of Jesus' resurrection to the disciples, the disciples are depicted by way of the author's asides and the direct discourse of Jesus as: fearful, commissioned, endowed with the Holy Spirit and authority.

Finally, concerning a portrayal of the Holy Spirit, as in the Gospel and in the resurrection narrative, the Holy Spirit remains voiceless, without direct discourse. According to this scene, however, with brief mention of the Holy Spirit with indirect discourse, the following should be noted about the Holy Spirit's role in the resurrection narrative: (1) Jesus grants or bestows (breathes) the Holy Spirit to the disciples, which comes only after the disciples recognize Jesus and respond with joy; (2) the Holy Spirit provides the disciples with the authority to forgive or retain sins. Thus, in this scene the Holy Spirit's role is that of a helper or comforter to the disciples (cf. chaps. 14 and 16).

Scene Six: The Disciples' Brief Report to Thomas and His Conditions in order to Believe, 20:24-25

Translation of John 20:24-25

24. But, Thomas, one of the twelve, called the Twin, was not with them when Jesus came. 25. Then, the other disciples were saying to him, "We have seen the Lord." But, he said to them, "Unless I see the marks of the nails in his hands, and put my finger in the marks of the nails, and put my hand in his side, I will not believe."

Introduction

Scene six occurs sometime after Jesus' first appearance to the male disciples. The disciples after their meeting with Jesus are now informing Thomas, who was not among the disciples when Jesus appeared. Apparently, Jesus departs from the disciples after v. 23; however, the author does not provide narration of his departure.

The mood and tone of this meeting with Thomas are of a different nature from scene five. That is, in scene five the mood of the disciples is established with their fear of the Jews and is transformed into gladness, after they recognize Jesus. The temporal setting occurs during the late evening, and the spatial-setting is possibly in the house where the disciples were gathered.

In scene six the mood remains that of gladness, but it changes into one of doubt and suspicion, due to Thomas' reaction to the disciples' report, resulting in disbelief. Thus, this setting in the house represents one of oscillating moods and experiences.

After Jesus had departed from among the disciples, Thomas came to the house where the disciples were gathered. Next, the author identifies Thomas as one of the twelve disciples called the Twin, and informs the reader of the fact that Thomas was not with the disciples when Jesus came among them. This statement functions to inform the reader of the rationale for Thomas' response to the disciples' report. Because Thomas was not present, the disciples reported to him that they had seen the Lord, consisting of the second Easter proclamation. Thomas, however, responds with a conditional statement that displays his apprehension and suspicion. He replied that he would not believe unless three things served as proof, evidence that would warrant his assent. The first of these conditions sought visual evidence of Jesus' hands, which had been pierced during his crucifixion—the nail marks. The second and third type of evidence that Thomas required for his believing consisted of physical and sensual proof of Jesus' crucifixion. That is, his demand required casting his fingers into the nail marks and his hand into the side of Jesus, which had been pierced with a sword to confirm Jesus' death (cf. 19:34).

The function of this scene is to advance the major complication of this episode. Thomas, like the disciples in scene five, would not be satisfied with a mere report. Thus, he requested and demanded his own visual and physical inspection of Jesus' wounds in order to believe.

Delineation of Scene Six

In scene six Thomas is introduced into a brief, self-contained scene, 20:24-25. Though brief in length, several factors suggest the differentiation of this scene from the previous and subsequent scenes. A narrator's aside at the beginning of this scene, suggesting that Thomas was not present in scene five, when Jesus had appeared among the disciples, indicates the change in the principal characters. The adversative conjunction, "but," (δὲ) and the temporal marker, "when," (ὅτε) both indicate the change in scene.

There is no specific temporal reference indicating when scene six occurred; however, the author provides sufficient temporal markers in scenes five, six, and seven for the reader to deduce that the temporal setting of scene five happened later during the evening. Scene five informs the reader that the events took place in the evening of the first day. The events of scene six occur sometime later that evening, on the same day that Jesus met with the disciples without Thomas present. The reader fills in the gap in the narrative with the temporal marker "when" (ὅτε, v. 24d). The meeting between the disciples and Thomas, therefore, happened much later in the evening, after Jesus departed and when Thomas arrived, presumably at the place where the disciples were gathered, which is not indicated in the narrative.

This spatial-setting, "the house where the disciples gathered," is implied in two references in the narrative: (1) This location served as a central meeting place (cf. vv. 2, 10, 18, 19, and 26); (2) in 20:26 the author notes that "the disciples were again (πάλιν) in the house, and Thomas was with them," which suggests that Thomas met with the disciples, who were again in the house eight days later. Thomas, however, was not at the house when Jesus appeared, but would be present eight days later. Further, this temporal marker in v. 26 indicates the period of Jesus' second appearance before the disciples, which was eight days after his initial appearance to the male disciples. Here, the author seems to be counting from the first day of the week for the period of scene seven, and hence the meeting with Thomas took place later that evening of the first day of the week. Thus, the meeting with the disciples and Thomas possibly took place in this same site. As such, 20:24-25 will be examined as a self-contained scene, with a change in characters and in the temporal-setting.

Temporal Process of Reading Scene Six

The reader is first informed that Thomas was not present with the disciples when Jesus appeared among them (20:24). In this transition scene (20:24), Thomas is featured as one of the main characters in the narrative. The two epitaphs for Thomas "one of the Twelve" and "the Twin," inform the reader not to confuse Thomas with some other character and to provide an initial characterization of him. Thomas is identified as "one of the Twelve" disciples and he is called "the twin" because he has a twin.

The author re-introduces Thomas into the narrative by identifying his place among the other disciples, as one of the Twelve, and provides the epitaph "the Twin." The author further informs the reader that Thomas was not present when Jesus first appeared to the other disciples. With this introduction, the author establishes the setting in which Thomas will be portrayed to the reader. First, Thomas is a disciple, and for some unspecified reason, he was not present among the disciples when Jesus met with them. Second, the appellation "the Twin" suggests Thomas' character in brief, as one who would require additional information in order to believe.

The reader receives direct discourse in 20:25a-b from the disciples as a group concerning their meeting with Jesus. This report was brief, bringing glad tidings regarding a matter that was of a central concern of the resurrection narrative, the resurrection appearance of Jesus to them. The disciples declare their visual experience of seeing the Lord, which represents the fourth report that was made at this point in the narrative. Thus, the reports and reactions of the disciples regarding Jesus' resurrection represent one of the themes to this point in the narrative.

Scene six appears to be merely a report of the meeting between Jesus and the disciples, which could be attached to scene five. The author includes direct discourse of the disciples for the first time in the resurrection narrative, which is necessitated because of Thomas' absence in scene five. This scene, however, is much more than a report; rather, it is an exchange that ensues after the disciples proclaim their Easter experience to Thomas.

In this scene the disciples proclaim the Easter formula: "We have seen the Lord" (v. 25b). This is the first time in the resurrection narrative that the author employs direct discourse from the disciples. Their voice is unified, but not unanimously, because Thomas, who is also a disciple (one of the Twelve), had presented the dissenting voice. The disciples' report, however, is not enough evidence to convince Thomas of their Easter experience. The author does not narrate specifically what Jesus told them and does not mention the fact that Jesus showed them his hands and his side. Further, the disciples' report omits other essential aspects of their experience, namely, their reception of the Holy Spirit, along with the authority to forgive or retain sins. Nevertheless, with this minimal direct discourse, the disciples fail to convince Thomas of their Easter experience.

In scene five the disciples are slow to react, but when they saw the hands and side of Jesus, they respond with gladness. In light of this scene, the reader anticipates how Thomas would react or respond to the disciples' report. On the one hand, the reader expects Thomas to respond negatively based on the disciples' delayed responses, which occurs for the most part throughout the resurrection narrative. On the other hand, the reader expects a positive response from Thomas because this report from the disciples is in accord with the report made by Mary in scene four. The reader anticipates that the disciples' collective report would be sufficient for Thomas to respond positively (20:25c-g). The reader is surprised and dismayed by Thomas' requirements for believing and sees a pattern in the clues and the corresponding types of responses recorded by the author.

In scene six Thomas goes much further by suggesting the physical and visual evidence that he required. The reader identifies Thomas' request as similar to but also exceeding the reader's needs to believe. Thus, the reader's response to Thomas' demand is unanticipated but expected, because Thomas' request calls for a display of Jesus that is both inhumane and unnecessary for belief—a report alone should be sufficient, if not mere visual proof. However, Thomas has to feel and see in order to believe.

When the disciples pass on their Easter experience to Thomas, he rebuts with a conditional statement, listing the condition to be met before giving his ascent. He required both visual and physical evidence, of a somewhat morbid and inhuman nature. Thomas' request was morbid in that he requested to see the wounds of Jesus, left by the crucifixion, and inhuman in that he wanted to thrust his fingers into Jesus' nail marks and his hand into Jesus' side. This morbid and inhumane notion suggests to the reader that what Thomas requested in order to ascertain the status of Jesus was extreme. Yet, Thomas' requests are representative of the disciples' requirement for a sign, but these requirements are not explicitly presented in the narrative.

In the end, Thomas' requirements are not just extreme in the sense of doubt and suspicion, but these requirements also represent a lack of response and voice, which are absent from the disciples as a whole. In other words, if the disciples as a whole could voice their doubt concerning Jesus' resurrection, these comments would be similar to Thomas' concerns as outlined in this scene.

Conclusion

The author employs minimal narrative and direct discourse in this scene to present the difficulty of the disciples in general, and Thomas in particular, in order to believe. The author opens this scene with an aside to re-introduce Thomas into the narrative. This transition scene provides the rationale for an additional appearance of Jesus to Thomas and the other disciples.

The reason for the following appearance, in scene seven, is that Thomas was missing when Jesus had first appeared to the disciples. Though Jesus verifies his resurrection to the disciples and gives them the Holy Spirit with authority, the evidence for Thomas to believe the second appearance is in doubt because he was not present. Further, the author includes this scene to allow the reader to detect further grounds and requirements for Jesus' post-resurrection appearance, which in this scene provides criteria that should conclusively prove that Jesus had in fact risen from the dead.

In this scene the author includes the first instance of direct discourse of the disciples in the resurrection narrative. The first direct discourse is a collective report from the disciple to Thomas, which, however, serves as the grounds for the third appearance.

The second direct discourse also functions to show how vulgar Thomas' requirements were, and hence, what the disciples required for accepting and believing in Jesus' resurrection, despite the previous reports and their previous experiences. In other words, Thomas' response serves as a foil for the disciples, displaying the disciples' delayed response and difficulties in accepting and accounting for the fact that Jesus had survived the crucifixion and burial.

This scene, as a whole, is designed and presented by the author as a conditional, transitory scene to reveal and reflect the disciples' difficulty and resistance to believe in the resurrection. Coupled with the previous scenes, where Mary and the two disciples searched for Jesus without results and finally with Mary's confirmation of Jesus' resurrection, this scene furthers the resurrection narrative's suspense by offering a conflict, consisting of Thomas' condition in order to believe.

This transition scene functions to prepare the reader for scene seven, which follows; but more importantly, it provides information for the reader to assess a characterization of Thomas and the disciples.

If the reader considers the place where the disciples met as the second major setting in the resurrection narrative, then this setting's atmosphere contributes to the story. The house's atmosphere, however, plays a significant role in scene six. For example, in considering the various events that occur in this house, the reader recalls:

(1) Mary's report to Peter and the Beloved Disciple (20:2) brings surprise and a situation necessitating immediate action; thus, the setting initially entails an atmosphere of doubt and concern, which leads the two disciples to investigate further.

(2) When the disciples return home from their trip to the tomb (20:10), no resolution is reached regarding the state and location of Jesus' body. The disciples, though apparently returning to their separate homes, eventually return to the meeting place of the other disciples, apparently without sharing their finding with the others. These factors, however, are not narrated, and thus they consist of pure speculation; this gap is not a part of the narrative world, but the reader can supply it.

(3) The atmosphere of the house radically changes with Mary's second report to the disciples, which is again not narrated. Her report brings glad tidings and good news about her encounter with Jesus, resulting in Mary's proclamation of the Easter event. The reader would expect the disciples to respond with a positive and joyous reaction to this news, yet the author does not narrate their reactions.

(4) In scene five the author reports that the disciples, without Thomas, were shut-in behind closed doors due to their fear of the Jews (20:19). Nonetheless, after Jesus shows the disciples his hands and side, they respond with gladness (20:20).

(5) In scene six, though the disciples proclaim their experience of the living Lord, Thomas responds with doubt and suspicion, refusing to believe until he himself physically and visually experiences Jesus.

(6) In anticipation of the spatial-setting in scene seven, the disciples, with Thomas present, are still behind closed doors when Jesus appears among them for the second time. After Jesus requests Thomas to confirm his doubts, Thomas makes a high Christological statement regarding his belief.

(7) At the end of scene seven, Jesus responds with a proverb or a beatitude that characterizes not only Thomas, who fails to believe without seeing, but also others who fail to recognize Jesus without seeing.

Thus, this setting functions as an atmosphere of ambivalence regarding the disciples' failure to come to terms with the fact of Jesus' resurrection. This spatial-setting also functions to display the mood and atmosphere of the disciples throughout the resurrection narrative in chapter 20 and to a certain extent in chapter 21. Therefore, the setting of scene six serves to confirm for the reader that the doubt and suspicion of Thomas are not too much different from those of the disciples as a whole, who failed to voice their apprehension and requirement for believing (cf. 20:20).

The function of this scene, therefore, is to serve as a transition scene between Jesus' first and second appearance to the male disciples. The first appearance, in scene five, confirms to the disciples, without Thomas present, that Jesus is now alive. Jesus' second appearance occurs in scene seven, wherein Jesus appears to Thomas, this time with the disciples lurking in the background. Thus, this scene also functions as a bridge scene to explain the need for a second appearance of Jesus to the male disciples in order to challenge Thomas' demand for further proof of Jesus' resurrection.[2] As such, this scene sets the conditions for and causes of the following scene, explaining the fact that Thomas was not present during the first appearance and that he would not believe unless his visual and physical conditions were met.

Scene Seven: Jesus' Second Appearance to Thomas with the Disciples Present: Jesus' Challenge to Thomas' Conditions; Thomas' High Christological Response; and Jesus' Reply; Narrative Summary of Chapter 20: The Purpose of the Resurrection Signs in the Presence of the Disciples, 20:26-31

Translation of John 20:26-31
26. And after eight days, his disciples were inside again, and Thomas was with them, the doors were shut, but Jesus came and stood among them and said, "Peace be with you." 27. Then, he said to Thomas, "Put your fingers here and see my hands and put out your hands, and put it in my side and do not be faithless, but believing. 28. Thomas answered and said to him, "My Lord and my God." 29. Jesus said to him, "Have you believed because you have seen me? Blessed are the ones who have not seen and yet believe." 30. Now, Jesus did many other signs before his disciples that are not written in this book. 31.

2   For bridge passages, see, e.g., Mlakuzhyil, *Christocentric Literary*, 104-106.

> But, these things are written that you may continue to believe that Jesus is the
> Christ, the Son of God, and that believing you may have life in his name.

Introduction

Scene seven commences eight days after Jesus first met with the disciples in scene five, after the disciples had reported to Thomas in scene six. The disciples are still behind closed doors, but this time Thomas is present with them. Again, as in scene five, Jesus appears in the same manner among the disciples and issues words of comfort, "Peace be with you." This is the third repetition of these words. The first repetition occurred in 20:19f, before the disciples had recognized Jesus. Jesus repeats these words again, without variation in 20:26, just before the commissioning of the disciples. Before Jesus confronted Thomas, Jesus renders these words of comfort, again without variation, to the disciples. Thus, these words not only served as a formal greeting to the disciples, but these words also function to comfort and to bring glad tidings to the distressed disciples, who remain shut-up behind closed doors.

Without any further preliminaries, Jesus proceeds to challenge Thomas' demands with physical and visual evidence of his resurrection. Jesus invites Thomas to put his finger into his nail marks and to view the marks in his hands; next, he invites Thomas to place his hand into his side. These challenges replicate Thomas' requirement for believing, which were narrated in scene six. Obviously, the author portrays the omniscience of the narrator and Jesus, who knew what had transpired in scene six, which narrated Thomas' requirements without Jesus being present. In the end, Jesus issues a gentle rebuke, instructing Thomas not to be "faithless," but rather "believing," and Jesus renders a beatitude commending those who could believe without seeing.

Delineation of Scene Seven

Scene seven is differentiated from the previous scene with a change in characters, with a change in the temporal-setting, and with a slight change in the events. Scene seven includes 20:26-31, representing the last scene of episode number two. Occurring eight days after scene six, in a self-contained scene, Jesus and Thomas serve as the principal characters, with the disciples as a group serving as a silent audience to this event. The spatial-setting, as argued in scene six remains the same, in the house where the disciples were gathered.

First, there is a slight alteration in this scene in comparison to what is not reported in scene six. In scene six the author does not mention that the door is shut. In scene seven, as in scene five, the doors are again closed shut.

Second, there is also a slight change in the theme in scene seven, as viewed in light of scenes five and six, where the focus was upon the appearance, response, and a commission of the disciples. In scene seven, Jesus comes again to the disciples to appear for the second time; however, this time he comes specifically to prove his resurrection in the way in which Thomas had requested. Scene five ends with Jesus' commissioning of the disciples with the Holy Spirit and authority, but here Jesus gently criticizes Thomas and the disciples for not believing without seeing and blesses those who believe without having to see Jesus physically.

The temporal-setting locates this event eight days after the previous scene. This change in time constitutes a new scene, along with a change in characters. The scene closes with Jesus' beatitude in 20:29. Verses 30-31 constitute the author's summary of this chapter, with a statement on the purpose of the signs. Thus, scene seven consist of vv. 26-31.

Temporal Process of Reading Scene Seven

The reader counts the temporal marker "eight days later" (v. 26a) from the Sabbath day when Mary first went to the tomb to a week and two days after the Sabbath. With this temporal marker, the reader expects some activity on the part of the disciples with their new authority and another appearance from Jesus to address Thomas' unbelief and requests. The author notes, "His disciples were again in the house," which comes as a surprise to the reader because the disciples are still inactive behind closed doors, just as they were when Jesus first appeared to them. Therefore, the reader is dismayed by this bit of information and still expects some sort of report on the disciples' activity, since Jesus' first appearance. The narrator's aside, "And, Thomas was with them" (v. 26b), focuses the reader more specifically on their second expectation, namely for Jesus to address Thomas' demands.

In 20:19 several statements evoke a respond in the reader. First, the reader's evaluation of the disciples' progress is confirmed by the clause: "the doors were shut" (v. 19c). This spatial-setting functions as a symbol of fear or doubt. This situation replicates the condition in which the disciples were eight days before this scene. The only element missing here is the phrase, "for the fear of the Jews" (20:19d). This situation causes the reader to question the effectiveness of Jesus' first appearance. Although Jesus commissioned the disciples, imparted the Holy Spirit upon them, and gave them the authority to remit or forgive sins of any person, eight days later the disciples were still in the house with the doors shut, possibly still because they feared the Jews.

Second, in 20:26e the reader is again informed, with variation, of the circumstances of Jesus' manner of appearing among the disciples. In 20:19 a phrase is inserted between the statements concerning the doors being shut and the notion that "Jesus came and stood among them." Thus, in 20:19 it was not clear to the reader that Jesus had come through shut doors. In 20:26 the reader is informed of the fact that the doors were shut, yet Jesus still came and stood among them. The author makes it clear to the reader that despite the doors being shut; Jesus appeared among the disciples without entering through the doors.

Finally, the repetition of the words "Peace be with you" again suggests words of greeting and comfort (cf. vv. 19 and 21). Obviously, this setting in the house with closed doors had warranted this kind of greeting. The reader would suspect, from this setting alone, that the disciples were in need of encouraging words, considering the events that had transpired several days before this scene. Perhaps, these words also function in scene seven to precede a purpose that Jesus had in mind in scene five (cf. 20:20, 22), namely, to breath the Holy Spirit on Thomas and give him authority to remit or forgive sins. The reader's speculations and expectations, however, are smashed and subverted by the next few verses.

In 20:27 the reader witnesses Jesus' challenge to Thomas, which is a repetition with slight variation of Thomas' demands in 20:25 and proceeds without delay to each of Thomas' requirements in order for him to believe and with a gentle rebuke, which suggests that Jesus was frustrated with Thomas for doubting and not believing Mary's and the disciples' Easter proclamation. In the final part of Jesus' challenge to

Thomas, he says to Thomas "do not be faithless, but believing" (v. 27g), which suggests the purpose of Jesus' meeting with Thomas: despite the ridiculous requirements and demands, his desire is to dispel all of Thomas' doubts. The reader recognizes Jesus' omniscient repetition of Thomas' requests, which were made when Thomas met with the disciples.

In 20:28 the reader is impressed at Thomas' high Christological statement because it places the epitaph of "God" upon Jesus as well as that of "Lord." This the first time in the Fourth Gospel narrative that Jesus is referred to with the high Christological title, "God." Like Thomas, the reader does not see the need to perform the demands that Thomas had made, even though Jesus was not present when Thomas made such request. In other words, Thomas did not have to test his demands in order to believe; the reader fills in the gaps in the narration, which suggests that visual sight alone was sufficient and convincing enough to dispel Thomas' doubt and cause him to believe.

The reader senses that Jesus' reply to Thomas' statement functions to minimize Thomas' proclamation, in that Jesus' rhetorical question criticizes Thomas' response, while at the same time Jesus' beatitude commends those whose faith did not require visual proof. The reader notices that Jesus does not praise Thomas for his response because what Thomas requires for faith did not correspond to the highest example of faith; rather, Thomas' requirements represented his doubt.

These last two remarks—a rhetorical question and beatitude—function, for the reader, to provide the overall theme of the chapter, the ultimate point of the narrative. That is, Jesus affirms and approves the kind of faith that happens without visual or physical proof. In other words, ideally, the reader acknowledges that Jesus desires the kind of faith that requires as little evidence as possible. This theme will be focused on in what follows.

The author's summary statement in vv. 30-31 functions both as a summary to scene seven—Jesus' meeting and appearance to Thomas— and as a summary of chapter 20. Though the author refers to the book as a whole in vv. 30-31 (see especially, the relative clause in 20:30b), these verses, as a whole, continue the preceding scene, summarizing the events so that the reader does not miss the point of the various signs presented in this chapter in particular. Because of the summary-like nature of the author's comments, these verses are included onto the end of scene seven, as a part of the analysis of scene seven.

The central and revolving theme of chapter 20, perhaps also in chapter 21, will be considered and examined when episode number three is examined. Indeed, the author provides a continuum of evidence for the resurrection of Jesus in chapter 20 and in chapter 21.

The first piece of evidence is the tomb site from where the body of Jesus is removed, witnessed by Mary Magdalene in the early morning, while it was still dark. The author presents this as the weakest evidence, yet as a sufficient sign for belief in the resurrection event.

In scene two the clothing itself provides the second piece of evidence for the resurrection event. The arrangement of the clothing neatly placed where Jesus had lain was apparently sufficient proof for the Beloved Disciple to believe. This piece of evidence by nature slightly exceeds that which is presented in scene one. From the appearance of an empty tomb to the inspection and discovery of clothing neatly wrapped and placed in their respective locations, the Beloved Disciple's belief still represents a faith without an understanding of the Scriptures.

The third piece of evidence is found by Mary, who stoops to look into the tomb and sees the two angels sitting where Jesus had lain. This piece of evidence offers supernatural or other worldly proof of the resurrection by two angels. Here again, the author presents evidence that moves from the appearance of an empty tomb to the inspection of the tomb with clothing inside and to two angels dressed in white robes as supernatural evidence for the resurrection of Jesus.

The fourth sign presented, as evidence of Jesus' resurrection in chapter 20, Jesus himself, whom Mary fails to recognize at first but who seeks to grasp him when he calls her by her name. Still again, this sign offers Jesus along with verbal proof for the resurrection. Thus, in scene four Jesus himself, in terms of both visual and verbal evidence, functions as evidence for faith in Jesus' resurrection.

In scene five Jesus offers to the disciples' verbal and visual proof. The author provides minimal amount of information concerning Jesus' hands and side, without specific mention of the scars that resulted from his crucifixion; the reader has to supply this information. What the disciples observed regarding Jesus' hands and side served as sufficient evidence to produce a response of gladness, without further proof. This act demonstrated to the disciples that Jesus was alive.

In scene six Thomas refused to believe the disciples' report as proof that Jesus survived the cross. The author does not provide a report from the disciples regarding the marks on Jesus' body, nor any other pertinent information about their meeting with Jesus, yet Thomas proceeds to make unnecessary demands, which would serve, for him, as sufficient proof for his assent to Jesus' resurrection. The disciples' report is the second report at this point in the narrative. Finally, in scene seven Jesus meets Thomas' demand by providing an opportunity for him to believe based on visual and physical evidence. This appearance would be easily accepted since the crucified and risen Jesus supplies a direct challenge.

Interestingly, corresponding to each sign there is a respective faith or lack thereof, and a reaction to each sign is offered as evidence for the resurrection. In other words, the responses to the signs are increasingly more or less what is expected for the type of faith that is called for.

In short, the author presents a dual theme in chapter 20. On the one hand, the author presents several signs of an increasingly concrete nature as evidence for Jesus' resurrection. On the other hand, the author employs characters as foils, which succeed or fail to respond conclusively in order to advance and develop the theme of the confirmation of Jesus' resurrection; characters are portrayed, for the most part, as believers or doubters to the increasing levels of evidence.

In closing, the author has stated reasons for such signs or evidence "in the presence of the disciples" was so that the reader "might continue to believe that Jesus is the Messiah, the Son of God" (v. 30). Moreover, not only would the reader be convinced of the resurrection and nature of Jesus, but also the reader would "have life in his name." In other words, all of the signs presented in this chapter in the presence of the disciples were presented so that the reader would continue to believe in the resurrection and authority of Jesus, the Son of God.[3]

---

[3] For the narrator's or implied author's intention to increase the faith of the disciples, see A. Hopkins, "A Narratological Approach to the Development of Faith in the Gospel of John." (Ph.D. dissertation, The Southern Baptist Theological Seminary, Texas, 1993) 191-235.

Conclusion

In this final scene of episode number two, the author develops for the reader a portrayal of Jesus in his post-resurrection state. Now, at this point in the narrative, the reader can construct an image of Jesus in this state and describe the roles that Jesus, the disciples, and Thomas played throughout the second episode of the resurrection narrative.

Regarding a portrayal of Jesus' nature at this point, the reader first encounters with him in scene four. In this scene Jesus forbids Mary from touching him because he had not ascended to the Father. No reference is made here to the marks of his crucifixion. Employing direct discourse, the author informs the reader that Jesus had not yet ascended to the Father; and therefore, Mary should not hold onto him.

In scene five the reader is told for the first time that Jesus appeared and stood among the disciples. Here, the reader is to assume that Jesus came to the disciples, passing through the shut doors; in other words, Jesus merely appears among the disciples, which illustrates Jesus' ability to become immaterial or quasi-physical. In addition, in scene five, Jesus showed the disciples his hands and his side. When Jesus refers to "his hands and side," the reader is aware of the fact that Jesus is pointing to his crucifixion experience.

In scene six Thomas' reply to the disciples' Easter proclamation indicated that he required seeing in order to believe. This episode suggests that a specific identification of Jesus' crucifixion experience was needed to evoke belief in Thomas.

Finally, in scene seven Jesus appears among the disciples and challenges Thomas' demands. Here, Jesus directly addresses Thomas' requirements in the way in which Thomas has stated in scene six. Thus, these spatial references to Jesus' body not only advance the narrative by revealing Jesus to Mary, the disciples, and Thomas, but also progressively provide more evidence for the physical, bodily resurrection of Jesus.

Regarding a portrayal of the disciples in scene seven, who are mentioned in the opening lines of this scene, they essentially remain in the background, while Jesus and Thomas interact. What is interesting, however, is the fact that they are still gathered behind closed doors as they were in scene five. This spatial setting indicates that, after their meeting with Thomas, the disciples remain inactive, despite their newly granted authority. Their inactivity implies that they had relapsed since their initial encounter with Jesus in scene five. Other than reporting and proclaiming their Easter experience with Thomas, they are still in seclusion. The author does not develop the disciples explicitly in this scene; they merely serve as a foil for the meeting between Jesus and Thomas.

In 20:29 there is an implicit reference to the disciples and an explicit reference to Thomas. In such the discourse between Jesus and Thomas could also be relevant to the disciples as a group, with the exclusion of the Beloved Disciple, who is not treated separately from the other disciples at this point in the resurrection narrative (cf. chapter 21).

In this episode the author portrayed the disciples with various techniques. The author, allowing the disciples as a group to proclaim their experience to Thomas, also presents the voice of the disciples. Even though the disciples are referred to several times in the episodes one and two, this scene represents the first occurrence where the author gives them a voice or allows them direct discourse. Interestingly, this direct discourse is presented by way of the group, rather than from a single individual, like Mary who is developed with direct discourse throughout the resurrection narrative up to 20:18. Thus, this use of direct discourse by the author functions to reveal the fact that the disciples are serving as foils in the narrative, pointing towards some other function. In other words, they are presented in the narrative with a collective voice to reveal the demands of Thomas. Thus, their collective voice allows the narrative to flow and move to its ultimate purpose.

Finally, concerning a portrayal of Thomas in episode number two, the author employs three scenes (scenes five, six, and seven) to develop his character. In scene five, Jesus meets with the disciples without Thomas present. His absence at this point in the narrative is necessary to develop the major complication of this episode. In scene six the author employs direct discourse so that Thomas can render his own unreasonable and unnecessary demands to believe that Jesus had survived the crucifixion. In scene seven Thomas receives his wishes, but he confirms Jesus as his God and his Lord without touching and feeling. The reader has to assume that Jesus' appearance was alone sufficient evidence for Thomas to believe in the resurrection. In other words, like the disciples, the sight of Jesus' scars was enough for Thomas to give a positive response to Jesus' appearance.

Although Thomas seems to respond to Jesus with reverence and respect, the author presents direct dialogue from Jesus with a rhetorical question to allow the reader to appraise Jesus' authority and thus the author's evaluation of Thomas' response. In other words, Jesus, as the protagonist of the story, offers a characterization of Thomas, which in the end represents criticism instead of praise. Thus, Thomas, and others like him, was not to be praised for this type of response because he only believed because he had seen Jesus.

In the end, the author presents a narrative summary to situate the signs in episodes number one and two with the purpose of continuing the faith of the reader, so that the reader may continue to believe that Jesus is the Christ, the Son of God. This summary points to the signs of the resurrection of Jesus, representing the various levels of faith that the reader can possess to have life in Jesus' name. The final appearance to Thomas ends with the highest level of faith, which includes a blessing for those who believe without seeing. This passage also serves as a transitional summary to prepare the reader for another sign as an example of the many other signs—the great catch of 153 fish, which Jesus also performed in the presence of the disciples. It serves to point out that Jesus, in his post-resurrection state, continues to provide signs for the disciples so that they may continue to believe in the resurrected Jesus. This final sign proves that without Jesus the disciples can do nothing. It also explains why they remain inactive after Jesus commissions them in scene five. In the next episode, the author continues this theme and addresses other unresolved matters in the Gospel and resurrection narrative.

CHAPTER FOUR

Episode Number Three:
On and Around the Sea of Tiberias—
Jesus' Third and Final Appearance to the
Male Disciples, John 21:1-25

Introduction

In this last and final episode, Jesus manifests himself to the male disciples for the third and final time in the Fourth Gospel's resurrection narrative.[1] The spatial-setting of this episode is situated on and around the Sea of Tiberias, in Galilee; the first two appearances take place in Jerusalem. Though the temporal-setting is reported with a vague Johannine expression, the period of this episode occurs during an unspecified period after episode number two.

The implied author's development of the major complication in this episode is to prove that, without Jesus, the disciples cannot accomplish anything and to further the theme of providing additional evidence for Jesus' post-resurrected status and relationship with the male disciples, especially by way of the reinstatement of Peter. In such, the author focuses on Jesus and Peter, along with the other disciples, who are lurking again in the background (cf. scene six, 20:26-29), with the

---

[1] See below, where I will argue that this count was because this is the third post-resurrection appearance of Jesus to the male disciples. Perhaps, Mary was omitted because Jesus had not yet ascended to the Father.

exception of the Beloved Disciple. The intent of this third appearance to the male disciples further advances Jesus' mission established in the previous episodes.

Episode number three continues to portray Jesus as one who seeks to encourage Peter, one of the principal characters in this episode, toward an effective ministry (cf. 20:21-23; 21:15-23). This episode contains five self-contained scenes.

Scene eight represents an introductory scene to vv. 1-14. It specifies the temporal- and spatial-settings, the purpose of scenes eight through ten, the seven disciples present during this episode, and the major complication of this episode—the disciples' unsuccessful fishing endeavor, vv. 1-3.

Scene nine is both a nature miracle and another recognition scene, in which Jesus appears to the male disciples for the third time. It continues the major complication of the disciples' inability to do anything without Jesus' assistance and highlights Peter's willingness to meet Jesus, vv. 4-8.

Scene ten represents the final part of the recognition scene in this episode. It furnishes the details of the miracle that Jesus performs for the disciples, includes a meal (breakfast) scene, and indicates the way in which Jesus manifests himself to the male disciples for the third time, vv. 9-14.

In scene eleven the disciples finish their meal with Jesus, and Jesus engages Peter in a question-and-answer dialogue, seeking to accomplish two objectives: to reinstate Peter after his denial and to commission him to care for his flock. The final part of the narrative includes Jesus' riddle, which predicts Peter's fate, vv. 15-19.

Finally, scene twelve is a dialogue between Jesus and Peter on the fate of the Beloved Disciple. It seeks to clarify a rumor that spread concerning the Beloved Disciple being alive before the *Parousia*. This final scene is the conclusion to the resurrection narrative and the entire Gospel; it includes the author's identification of himself as the Beloved Disciple and a hyperbole, vv. 20-25.

Outline of Episode Number Three

IV. Episode Number Three on and Around the Sea of Tiberias: Jesus' Third and Final Appearance to the Male Disciples, John 21:1-25.

    A.   Scene Eight: The Disciples' Go Fishing at Peter's Suggestion; No Success Fishing during the Night, 21:1-3.

    B.   Scene Nine: Jesus' Third Appearance to the Male Disciples: Jesus' Fishing Instruction to the Disciples; A Great Catch of Fish; The Beloved Disciple's Recognition of Jesus and Peter's Reaction, 21:4-8.

    C.   Scene Ten: Jesus Prepares Breakfast; The Great Catch of Fish; The Disciples' Apprehensive Recognition of Jesus; and Jesus Serves Breakfast, 21:9-14.

    D.   Scene Eleven: Jesus' Dialogue with Peter; Jesus' Prediction of Peter's Fate; and Jesus' First Command to Peter to Follow Him, 21:15-19.

    E.   Scene Twelve: Peter's Concern Regarding the Fate of the Beloved Disciple; Jesus' Reply; and Jesus' Second Command to Peter to Follow Him; Final Conclusion to the Fourth Gospel's Resurrection Narrative: The Identity and Witness of the Implied Author; and a Final Declaration Concerning the Things which Jesus Did, 21:20-25.

Delineation of Episode Number Three

The differentiation of episode three from the previous episodes is evident with a major change in locations, from Jerusalem to the Sea of Tiberias, and with the temporal marker, Μετὰ ταῦτα. Though episode number three is connected to the previous episodes of chapter 20, its purpose and theme consist of completing the portrayals of Peter and the Beloved Disciple. As such, this final episode concludes the entire Gospel and the resurrection narrative (chapters 20-21). In 20:30-31 the author provides a summary of episodes number one and two (chapter 20), stating the purpose of the signs that Jesus performed in the presence of the disciples. In 21:24-25 the author identifies himself as the Beloved Disciple and states a hyperbole. Thus, episode number three, 21:1-25, forms an unified narrative, which is connected to the previous episodes because it narrates the third resurrection appearance of Jesus and offers a final portrayal of the disciples, especially that of Peter and the Beloved Disciple. It is distinct from that which precedes it, because it seeks to establish the authority of the faith community, viz., Peter and the Beloved Disciple.

Scene Eight: The Disciples Go Fishing at Peter's Suggestion; No Success Fishing during the Night, 21:1-3

Translation of John 21:1-3

1. After these things, Jesus manifested himself again to the disciples by the Sea of Tiberias, and he manifested himself in this way. 2. Simon Peter, Thomas, the one called the twin, Nathanael, the one from Cana of Galilee, the sons of Zebedee, and two others of his disciples were together. 3. Simon Peter said to them, "I am going fishing." They said to him, "We are also coming with you." And during that night, they caught nothing.

Introduction

The third and final appearance of Jesus to the disciples begins in scene eight on and by the Sea of Tiberias. Scene eight establishes the setting of the third and final appearance to the male disciples, the disciples' fishing experience (vv. 1-14). The Sea of Tiberias is inserted as a narrator's aside in v. 14, reporting that Jesus appeared again to the disciples for the third time.

This introductory scene serves three purposes: (1) to establish the settings (temporal and spatial) of Jesus' third appearance to the male disciples; (2) to cite the seven disciples present, placing Peter first because he will be, along with Jesus, one of the central characters in this final episode; (3) to narrate the disciples' unsuccessful fishing experience after Jesus' last appearance in episode number two.

Delineation of Scene Eight

This introductory scene is differentiated from the previous scene primarily with a major change in the temporal- and spatial-settings, a change in characters,[2] and a sudden change in the nature of the events. First, this scene is delineated from the previous scene with a change in the temporal-setting, "after these things" (v. 1a, Μετὰ ταῦτα). Scene eight also contains a spatial gap that the reader must fill-in to make sense of the change in location (see the temporal reading below). The change in location involves a move, which is not narrated, from the house where the disciples were gathered, in Jerusalem, to a new spatial-setting on and by the Sea of Tiberias, which is located in Galilee (v. 1b).

Further, scene eight represents a change in characters, where the seven disciples, at this point, are alone on the sea or lake, while in the next scene the disciples require Jesus' help to fish successfully. The author generally refers to the disciples as a group. Here, in scene eight the author informs the reader of the precise number of disciples present: the number of disciples present in scene seven seems to be eleven, whereas here in scene eight there are only seven disciples mentioned.

Scene eight is differentiated from the previous scene with a radical change in events. In scene seven the author summarizes the first two episodes and states the purpose of the graded signs, establishing the pre-, post-ascension, and post-resurrection status of Jesus (vv. 30-31). The primary event of scene seven, as mentioned above, consisted of Jesus' challenge to Thomas concerning his lack of faith and ultimately his reason for believing, and Jesus' beatitude on believing without seeing. In scene eight the disciples decide to go fishing in Galilee at Peter's request. Instead of responding to the two previous appearances and the commission of Jesus, this scene marks a radical change in events due to

---

[2]   Concerning the characters in scenes six through nine, the following inverted parallelism emerges: A-B-C-A'-B'-C', in scene five (A) Jesus appears first to some of the disciples, with Thomas absent; in scene six (B) all of the disciples are present, with Jesus absent; in scene seven (C) Jesus appears before all of the disciples to confront Thomas and comments generally on two classes of people (e.g., those who believe without seeing and those who believe without requiring a sign); in scene eight (A') all of the disciples are present without Jesus, fishing unsuccessfully during the night in the lake; in scene nine (B') Jesus appears for the third time to all of the disciples; and in scene ten (C') Jesus confronts Peter on his love and on feeding his sheep. This recurring pattern advances the theme of the disciples' troublesome response to Jesus' appearances and instructions to believe, of which more later. Thus, this scene confirms the unity of scene eight with the previous chapter.

the disciples' fishing endeavor.

Finally, this scene as a whole introduces the reader to the mood or atmosphere of the third appearance of Jesus to the male disciples, continuing the theme introduced in scene six—Jesus' commissioning of the disciples—and the unresolved issue from scene seven, namely the disciples' failure to exercise their gift of the Spirit and authority. That is, in scene seven the disciples still doubt and are in need of a visual sign in order to believe as evident in Jesus' discourse with Thomas. In other words, the disciples have not yet begun their work as Jesus had commanded them.

Scene eight, vv. 1-3, therefore, is differentiated from the subsequent scene with a change in theme, characters, and a major change in the temporal- and spatial-settings. The primary event of the scene changes from a failure to catch fish in scene eight to a successful catch of fish with the assistance of Jesus in scene nine.

Temporal Process of Reading Scene Eight

Scene eight commences with the author's introductory report, consisting of four items: (1) the nature of the following scenes eight through ten, vv. 1-14, as a recognition scene of Jesus' third appearance to the male disciples; (2) the temporal- and spatial-settings of the third episode; (3) an introduction of the seven disciples present; (4) the decision of the disciples to go fishing at Peter's request. This introductory report contains a temporal gap that connects scene seven to scene eight and unfolds how the third appearance of Jesus occurs before the male disciples. As such, this report includes a major change in spatial-setting, from Jerusalem to Galilee, specifically, from the house in Jerusalem where the disciples gathered to the Sea of Tiberias in Galilee. This spatial gap in the narrative occurs due to the lack of narration regarding the transition from Jerusalem to Galilee. This gap has to be filled by the reader. Even though the setting changes from inside to outside, it implicitly suggests to the reader the disciples' attempt to evade the Jews in Jerusalem by moving to a safer, more conducive environment. The details of the disciples' transition from Jerusalem to Galilee are not mentioned. The reader recalls the only other mention of the location of the Sea of Tiberias as the Lake of Galilee (cf. John 6:1). In Galilee, the disciples could be together openly as a group without being subjected to seclusion behind closed doors in fear of the Jews (cf. Scenes Five and Seven).

The temporal-setting of this scene is somewhat vague due to the temporal marker, Μετὰ ταῦτα, which is a typical Johannine expression (cf. 3:22; 5:1, 14; 6:1; 7:1; 19:38; 21:1).[3] Though this expression is vague and non-specific, it does locate this scene sometime after the second appearance to the male disciples.

Two temporal markers illustrate the mood of scene eight through scene ten (vv. 1-14). On the one hand, the temporal reference, Μετὰ ταῦτα, places this event some time after scene seven. On the other hand, in light of the narration and action presented in scene eight, this marker indicates a lack of resolution to the chief motivating objective of the resurrection narrative, namely the proper display of faith on the part of the disciples as a whole. The function of the resurrection appearances should have necessitated action, moving the disciples to carry out their commission (cf. 20:21-23).

Second, the lack of resolution is further marked by the temporal indicator at the end of the scene (v. 3), specifying the disciples' fishing endeavor during that night. This reference to night not only suggests the period of this event but also signals to the reader the mood of the setting. This marker recalls the setting of Mary's trip to the tomb, and as in scene one, it indicates both the time and the mood of the disciples' experience. Interestingly, both events—Mary's search for the body of Jesus and the disciples' failure to catch fish—were unsuccessful at first. These two markers together function to indicate the mood of the narrative, which is a lack of resolution and the initial lack of success on the part of the disciples. The temporal marker suggests that some period had elapsed before this scene commences.

Not all of the disciples' names are mentioned. With the exception of Peter and Thomas, three of the seven disciples' names are provided with descriptive information.[4] The three disciples with formal appellations consist of Peter, Thomas, and Nathanael; four disciples are cited with

---

[3] See, e.g., Morris, *John*, 186, n. 40.

[4] E.g., complete appellations, familiar epitaph (i.e., Twin), or place of origin (i.e., Cana of Galilee).

descriptions only, the two sons of Zebedee and two other disciples.

In scenes five, six, and seven only one of the disciples is named, namely Thomas who is called the Twin. Only one of the disciples named in this scene, however, is not specifically mentioned in chapter 20, Nathanael of Cana in Galilee. The other disciple who is specifically addressed in chapter 20 is Peter; here, he is addressed with the surname Simon. Peter is also mentioned at the beginning of the narrative in scene two with the Beloved Disciple, who is not specifically cited in this list of seven disciples, but whose role is significant in this third episode.

By listing Simon Peter first, the author indicates his primary role in the narrative as one of the leaders of the disciples. This narrative technique indicates the priority that he will receive in this third episode, resolving a complication mentioned in chapter 19 and instructing him on the role that he was to carry out in the faith community.

The action of this scene commences with a decision of Peter to go fishing (v. 3b), which places the major complication of this episode at the beginning, corresponding to the commission given by Jesus in scene five. The disciples, without questioning or rejecting Peter's suggestion—which could be supplied by the reader—immediately, agreed to join him. During the night, the disciples, however, fish without success. In other words, though the disciples embark on a task as a group, they realize failure during the night without Jesus' assistance. Thus, this scene functions to introduce a major complication in the narrative for the reader: the disciples' inactivity concerns their mission as a group and results in failure without Jesus. Consequently, this complication suggests implicitly the need for another appearance by Jesus, possibly to address and resolve an issue concerning Peter introduced in chapter 19.

In this new setting, the reader is surprised by Peter's suggestion and unusual decision to go fishing. While the disciples are still together as a group, no longer behind closed doors in a house in Jerusalem, they still are displaying a sense of inactivity; that is, they are engaged in an activity that is not anticipated by the reader.

Conclusion

For the implied reader scene eight represents two general issues: (1) the nature of Jesus' third appearance to the disciples, including the location and a list of the disciples present during this and subsequent scenes; (2) the primary events of this scene are also provided, situating the reader for subsequent scenes: the disciples' decision to go fishing and their failure to catch fish. The author uses this scene also to orient the reader to this new episode, differentiating it from the previous scenes with the disciples and providing the setting for the following scenes. Thus, this scene is designed to function both as a transitional scene and as an introductory scene. As a transitional scene, it serves to continue the theme of Jesus' appearances to the disciples, with this scene providing new temporal- and spatial-settings, a new list of the characters, and a brief description of the events.

Further, as an introductory scene, the author provides information on the major complication that will be developed and detailed as the narrative progresses concerning Jesus' third appearance, the recognition scene, and the fishing experience—the miracle scene.

In summary, the temporal- and spatial-settings of this scene reestablish the fearful situation of the disciples, which was established in the previous scene (20:26-29), and thus promise and present the necessity of a third appearance of Jesus. The disciples flee from Jerusalem to Galilee and fail at a fishing endeavor. As such, a third appearance by Jesus in Galilee is expected by the reader to resolve their failure and to effect their call and commission.

Scene Nine: Jesus' Third Appearance to the Male Disciples: Jesus' Fishing Instruction to the Disciples; A Great Catch of Fish; The Beloved Disciple's Recognition of Jesus and Peter's Reaction, 21:4-8

Translation of John 21:4-8

4. Now early morning, Jesus had already come and stood on the shore, however, the disciples did not realize that it was Jesus. 5. Therefore, Jesus said to them, "Children, have you any fish?" They answered and said to him, "No." 6. And he said to them, "Cast the net on the right side of the boat, and you will find (some)." And then they threw it and were not able to draw it, by reason of the multitude of the fish. 7. Then, the disciple, that one whom Jesus loved, said to Peter, "It is the Lord!" Then, when Simon Peter heard that it was the Lord, he tied around himself the outer garment, for he was unclothed, and he threw himself into the Sea. 8. But, the other disciples came in the boat, for they were

not far from the land, about two hundred cubits, dragging the net of fish.

Introduction

In scene nine during the morning Jesus came and stood on the shore, but again the disciples at this point in the narrative did not recognize him. To aid in the disciples' recognition, he asks them a rhetorical question "Children, have you any fish?" This question was designed to receive a negative response from the disciples. After the disciples responded accordingly, Jesus instructed them to cast the net on the right side of the boat to locate fish. Without hesitation, the disciples followed Jesus' instructions and were able to haul in the sizable catch of fish. It was after the disciples' successful catch of fish that the Beloved Disciple recognized the person on the shore, and he told Peter, "It is the Lord!" Upon hearing that it was the Lord, Peter clothed himself and jumped into the sea, and the other disciples came toward the shore, this was about a hundred yards (two hundred cubits) away, dragging the net full of fish.

The purpose of this scene is dual: first to narrate the way in which Jesus was recognized and to introduce the miracle of the great catch of fish. Both of these purposes serve to explicate to the reader the nature of the post-resurrected Jesus. Moreover, these purposes communicate to the reader the continued concern that Jesus demonstrated toward the disciples.

Delineation of Scene Nine

Scene nine is differentiated from scene eight primarily with the introduction of the protagonist, Jesus, and the temporal- and spatial-settings. In scene eight the disciples decide to go fishing at Peter's request. They fish during the night, and the scene ends with a negative report on their fishing trip. Scene nine occurs in the early morning, after the disciples' unsuccessful fishing endeavor. This temporal-marker places this scene in the same temporal context as the beginning of the resurrection narrative (cf. 20:1-2).

During this period, Jesus appears on the shore and inquires if the disciples had caught any fish. As in previous scenes, Jesus relates to the disciples as a group, but they, like Mary in scene four, did not know that it was Jesus speaking to them from the shore. Thus, the appearance of Jesus in the narrative indicates a change of scene.

There is also a slight change in the spatial setting of this scene in comparison to scene eight. In the previous scene the disciples leave the shore in a boat to fish during the night. In scene eight Jesus, who was merely referred to in scene eight, is now on the shore, and the disciples are unsuccessfully fishing on the lake. With this slight change in the spatial-setting, the author illustrates to the reader a change in the disciples' endeavor. Thus, the spatial-setting facilitates the continuation of the theme begun in scene eight—the disciples' fishing endeavor.

Therefore, scene nine is differentiated from scene eight with a change both in characters and in the temporal- and spatial-settings. Though there is a change in these narrative devices, the event introduced in scene eight is continued and developed in scene nine, which is differentiated from the following scene, after the disciples' arrival on the shore.

Temporal Process of Reading of Scene Nine

At the outset of this scene, the author causes the reader to reflect on a similar temporal marker in scene one (20:1), indicating a point of reference for a consistent pattern in the resurrection narrative. The temporal marker, "Just after daybreak (πρωΐας)," serves as the turning point in the disciples' dilemma, which had begun in scene eight. It informs the reader of the temporal setting of this scene, during daylight, after dawn. Here, the author identifies this setting as Jesus' final appearance to the disciples, which will be significant as the initial phase of the reader's and characters' "recognition scene," or better, for the different levels of recognizing Jesus.[5] This marker also causes the reader to reflect on events that occurred after Mary's report to the disciples, which also happened within a similar period, namely, from the time when the two disciples inspected the tomb to the period when Jesus finally appeared to Mary.

After orienting the reader with the temporal-setting of this scene, the author provides the reader with privileged information, concerning insider knowledge, of which the disciples or characters in the story do not possess, that is, that Jesus was already standing on the beach (v. 4b).

---

[5]   For recognition or the theme of *anagnorisis*, see, e.g., Stibbes, *John*, 210.

This information introduces Jesus into the third episode a second time: the first instance was merely a reference to Jesus' third appearance, in a narrative aside; and the second instance, also in a narrative aside, where the author informs the reader that Jesus is now present on the shore.

The characters in the story, however, are not given this information. This lack of knowledge on the part of the disciples signals the beginning of the recognition scene in the resurrection narrative, and as such it leads the reader to associate this scene with previous scenes, especially the scene wherein Jesus stood behind Mary, but she did not know that it was Jesus, until he called her by name. Additionally, this scene causes the reader to reflect on the scene wherein Jesus stood among the disciples and their reaction was delayed until Jesus had revealed the marks on his body. Thus, the reader could classify this scene along with other recognition scenes in the resurrection narrative.

The author initially persuades the reader of Jesus' post-resurrection appearance; thus, a pattern begins to emerge concerning the quasi-physical state in which Jesus appears before the disciples. Jesus' appearance on the shore suggests that the reader is an insider concerning the various appearances of Jesus. In v. 4c the reader is given inside, omniscient information concerning the disciples' inability to recognize Jesus on the shore. Like Mary in scene four, "the disciples did not know (ἤδεισαν) that it was Jesus."

As a whole, vv. 4-7 reflects the entire recognition scene, where Jesus appears, but he is not immediately recognized. The disciples do recognize that they are communicating with a person on the shore; however, the reader surmises that possibly due to the distance or the lack of adequate light or angle of vision, the disciples were not able to recognize Jesus. The text does not supply this information. What the author does imply in the narrative and what the reader may supply by way of speculation, based on previous information supplied by the narrative, is that for some reason the disciples' inability to recognize Jesus on the shore of the lake is possibly due in part to the fact that Jesus is not to be easily recognized. Thus, the reader has to assume that Jesus is in some sort of quasi-physical state.

Since light and distance are not provided as factors, the reader must assume, at this point, that Jesus, in some way, must make himself known to the disciples. In this instance, it is not by sight, but as in the appearance to Mary, by voice. The reader, however, wonders why, after two previous appearances to the disciples, Jesus is still unable to be recognized immediately by the disciples.

Therefore, the temporal- and spatial-settings—the time of day and the distance, respectively—do not factor into the situation, since Jesus' quasi-physical nature allows him the ability to conceal himself. The atmosphere, however, serves to establish the mood of the recognition scenes. It allows the reader to recognize previous scenes, especially scene four, the first appearance of Jesus.

In v. 5 Jesus reveals himself in part with a term of endearment, παιδία.[6] Obviously, this form of address, Jesus' instruction to the disciples on where to throw the net, and the great catch of fish (ἀπὸ τοῦ πλήθους τῶν ἰχθύων, v. 6) represent sufficient information for the Beloved Disciple to recognize Jesus. Before the Beloved Disciple's recognition, the disciples follow the instruction of the stranger on the shore. First, Jesus addresses them as "children" or "lads," and inquires if they had caught any fish, employing the Greek particle μή τι, which expects a negative response. Accordingly, the disciples, as a group, respond in the negative, οὔ. After Jesus passionately speaks to the disciples in v. 4c, then the Beloved Disciple, whom the author identifies as the one whom Jesus loved (ἠγάπα—imperfect active), recognizes that it is the Lord speaking. This recognition occurs after the great catch of fish.

The stranger instructs them to fish on the right side of the boat because there they will find some fish. Immediately, the reader surmises that the disciples are unable to do anything without Jesus' assistance. According to this pattern of recognition, Peter responds by putting on his outer garment and by jumping into the sea, exhibiting a sense of excitement. The other disciples came hauling the great catch of fish. In v. 8 the author provides additional information on the distance of the disciples from the land, being a hundred yards from the shore, which

---

6   See, Barrett, *St. John*, 579. Here, Barrett notes that this term is not used in this sense, as a form of address, elsewhere in the Fourth Gospel. He believes that it is used in Modern Greek to address adults. He notes also that *Teknia* is commonly used in Johannine writings, cf. 4:49; 16:21; I Jn 2:14-18; 3:17.

could explain why Jesus was not immediately recognizable.

Peter's actions read in light of the denial scene, however, could indicate some other sort of motive, possibly guilt? It is therefore not surprising to the reader that Peter does not recognize Jesus immediately, because Jesus is partly responsible for the others' ability to recognize him. Yet, the order of the recognition fills a gap and continues to illuminate a pattern for the reader, namely the response of the Beloved Disciple and the reaction of Peter, which are both similar to their responses in scene two.

In this scene Peter only responds after he "heard" from the Beloved Disciple that it was the Lord on the shore. This information suggests, on the one hand, for the reader, that Peter needed to hear another person's report in order to respond. On the other hand, the reader is informed that the Beloved Disciple is the first to witness certain events and to reach a point of believing with minimum evidence. This priority seems to become more established as the narrative progresses.

Peter's manner of responding is worth noting because he seems to be portrayed as the one is willing to respond to Jesus without fully understanding the implications of his action, and as such, Peter is portrayed by the author as one that is willing to respond and act on the report of others, yet in this sense he provides leadership (cf. 20:3). In short, rather than the author's portrayal of these two disciples being one of contrast or comparison, it seems that the author is seeking to portray these two disciples as fulfilling two different roles: the Beloved Disciple's ability to recognize and believe with little evidence; and Peter as one that is willing to act and respond to various reports without fully understanding his actions or without a clear rationale for his reactions.

Conclusion

The third appearance of Jesus to the male disciples happens according to the pattern of previous appearances of Jesus, similar to the appearance scenes in chapter 20, especially in Jesus' appearance to Mary and in particular in his appearance to the disciples in scene five. The author provides several clues to the reader that the lack of recognition is not to be attributed to the disciples as a whole, but that this lack of recognition, like the ones in episodes one and two, is due to the quasi-physical nature of the post-resurrection Jesus.

The reader equipped with privileged information, surmises that Jesus is the one responsible, not only for the disciples' ability to recognize Jesus but also for the success of the disciples when he appears on the shore. The disciples' ability to recognize Jesus is not to be seen as based on the temporal-setting, after dawn, nor is it to be attributed to the disciples' distance from the shore where Jesus is standing, but it is solely based on Jesus' willingness to reveal himself.

Peter's response to the report of the Beloved Disciple causes him to put on his outer garment and jump into the sea to swim ahead of the disciples. His willingness to act is not based on his recognition but is to be attributed to his reaction to the report of the Beloved Disciple. As in scene eight, Peter takes the initiative, jumping into the sea and leading the disciples to the shore to meet Jesus. The reader could compare his action in this scene with his actions in a previous scene where he and the Beloved Disciple inspected the tomb. Here in scene eight, the reader could speculate that Peter's actions were motivated by guilt, resulting from his denial of Jesus earlier in the Passion narrative.

In short, this recognition scene confirms for the reader the quasi-physical nature of Jesus in the post-resurrection appearance scenes. The author, however, provides information to lead the reader with privileged information that it was not the inability of the disciples to recognize Jesus, but that the disciples needed Jesus to be successful in their fishing endeavor and to enable them to recognize him, which is based indeed on the level or degree of faith of the disciple (cf. 20:29).

Scene Ten: Jesus Prepares Breakfast; The Great Catch of Fish; The Disciples' Apprehensive Recognition of Jesus; and Jesus Serves Breakfast, 21:9-14

Translation of John 21:9-14

9. Then, when they arrived on to the land, they saw a charcoal fire with fish lying on it, and bread. 10. Jesus said to them, "Bring some of the fish that you have just caught." 11. Then, Simon Peter went up and dragged the net on to the land, full of large fish, a hundred and fifty-three (of them), and although there were so many, the net did not split. 12. Jesus said to them, "Come, eat breakfast." But, none of them dared to ask him, "Who are you?" Because they

knew that it was the Lord. 13. Jesus came and took the bread and gave it to
them and likewise the fish. 14. Now, this was the third time Jesus manifested
himself to the disciples, after he was raised from the dead.

Introduction

Scene ten commences when the disciples arrived on the shore, on
which they saw a fish and bread meal cooking on a charcoal fire. Jesus
instructed the disciples to bring some of the fish that they had caught,
and Peter went onto the boat and dragged the net full of one hundred and
fifty-three fish onto the shore; even though it contained such a large
amount of fish, the net did not tear. Jesus invited the disciples to
breakfast, and none of the disciples sought his identity because they
knew that it was the Lord. Jesus served them the fish and bread. The
author concludes this scene with a narrator's summary pointing to this
series of events as Jesus' third resurrection appearance to the male
disciples.

The function of scene ten is three-fold: (1) to prepare the reader for
the initial phase of the meal scene, the preparation of breakfast by Jesus;
(2) to add specificity to the miracle scene, which is sandwiched within
the meal scene and which describes in detail the extent of the miraculous
catch of fish; (3) to describe the mood of the final aspect of the meal
scene, which serves the purpose of concluding the recognition scene and
report on Jesus third appearance to the male disciples. Thus, scene ten
succeeds to prepare the reader with more details on Jesus' post-
resurrection status and relationship with the disciples.

Delineation of Scene Ten

Scene ten continues and advances the theme introduced in scene
eight and advanced in scene nine concerning the disciples' fishing
endeavor: the recognition scene that now concludes with a meal scene.
The theme of fishing is brought to a conclusion in this scene and is
identified with a subsequent and contemporaneous temporal-setting,
namely the subordinating conjunction, ὡς, and coordinating conjunction,
οὖν, which indicate not only the temporal aspect of this scene, referring
back to another scene, but also serve as a coordinating, transitional
phrase between scenes nine and ten.

The new spatial-setting of the disciples reaching the shore of the beach serves as the principle site for the remaining events of this episode. Thus, scenes ten through twelve occur in this vicinity, the shore of the sea.

That this scene brings closure to the events of the two previous scene is indicated by the *inclusio* between 21:1 and 21:14, which suggests the manner in which Jesus revealed himself to the male disciples for the third time and is also indicated by the conclusion of the disciples' fishing trip. In this scene the fish are brought to the land (εἰς τὴν γῆν), indicating a change in the spatial-setting of this scene. Thus, the disciples fishing experience is brought to a completion with their breakfast at the shore with Jesus.

Several events in this scene separate or distinguish this scene from the previous and subsequent scenes (nine through eleven): (1) the disciples arrive onto the land or shore (v. 9a); (2) a charcoal fire is already prepared, with fish and bread (v. 9b); (3) Jesus instructs the disciples to bring some of the fish that they had just caught (v. 10); (4) Peter hauls the large fish onto the shore from alongside the boat, numbering one hundred and fifty-three fish, without damaging the net (v. 11); (5) Jesus invites the disciples to come to breakfast (v. 12a-b); (6) a narrator's aside is provided on the disciples' refusal to inquire regarding Jesus' identity because "they knew that it was the Lord" (v. 12c-e); (7) Jesus shares with the disciples the bread and fish in a symbolic, ceremonial fashion (v. 13); and finally, a narrator's report on this being the third of Jesus' appearance to the disciples, "after he was raised from the dead," v.14.

Scene ten is differentiated from the previous scene with a change in the spatial-setting and with a change in the events, with the disciples' breakfast at shore with Jesus. Scene ten is also differentiated from scenes nine and eleven with a narrator's report and summary at the beginning and end of the scenes, vv. 9 and 14. Thus, scene ten (vv. 9-14) forms a complete, self-contained scene.

Temporal Process of Reading Scene Ten

After the disciples arrive at the shore, the author introduces a number of symbolic features into the narrative that cause the reader to reflect back to earlier scenes, involving other signs and significant events. These features not only prepare the reader for what is to come in the narrative but also direct the reader to connect symbolically the resurrection narrative to other events in the life of Jesus and the disciples. First, for example, when the disciples reach the shore, the author reintroduces the charcoal fire as a way to point back to the scene where Peter denied Jesus three times (cf. 18:18). This device prepares the reader for a symbolic revising of this dark moment in the life of Peter when he warmed himself by a charcoal fire outside the court where Jesus was being investigated. Second, the author points the reader back to another scene, involving the sign of the feeding of the multitude, wherein fish and bread are served as symbolic elements in the sign of multiplying the loaves and fish for the multitudes (cf. 6:9-11).

With the fish and bread now being placed alongside and associated with the charcoal fire and with these two signs being placed together, the reader is invited to reflect first on a negative experience in the life of Peter, recalling Peter's denial, which is unresolved to this point in the narrative, and second on a positive sign of the miraculous multiplying of fish and loaves. These two symbolic features place the two events into different spatial- and temporal-settings, and the meal and the miraculous catch of fish scenes. As such, these two signs together conclude the recognition scene and prepare the reader for the next scene, a conciliatory scene (see below).

The author then interrupts for a moment the presentation of these two signs—the allusions to the denial scene and the miraculous catch of fish—to include direct discourse from Jesus, who issues a request to the disciples, as a whole, to bring the fish that they had caught. This request of Jesus causes the reader to pause and reflect on the new context in which these two signs are now placed. Peter alone, however, responds to this request by dragging the fish onto the land.

The net was full of one hundred and fifty three large fish, and yet the net remained intact. The author does not provide any additional clues to the meaning of these two symbols: the significance of the number of fish and the notion of the net not being torn. Since there are apparently no clues in the Fourth Gospel text to facilitate the meaning or understanding of these signs, the meaning of this number is known only by the author and the reader of this Gospel. Otherwise, the author would have provided an explanation of these symbols to the reader. The reader could only know that 153 large fish were caught and the net remained intact.[7]

Concerning the symbolic meaning of the net not being torn, despite the number of fish being caught, the reader could only speculate on its specific meaning using the information provided by the text. Assuming some understanding of the fishing enterprise, the reader could infer that both the number of fish and the integrity of the net were both signs of Jesus' power or they could have had something to do with the mission of the disciples.

Even if these symbols are not explained in the text by the author, they nonetheless provide detailed information of the disciples' experience. As such, this detailed information makes the scene realistic and thus more reliable. With these details, the reader is convinced of the miraculous catch of fish and the events that followed.

When Jesus invites the disciples to eat breakfast, this represents the second time Jesus is portrayed as requesting something specific from the disciples; the first occurred in v. 10, wherein he asks them to bring some of the fish that they had just caught. This second request demonstrates Jesus' abiding concern and love for the disciples (cf. v. 12a-b). It also foreshadows Jesus' subsequent discussion with Peter regarding the feeding of and the tending to Jesus' sheep and lambs. The author, however, withholds this information from the reader at this point in the narrative. Thus, the author portrays Jesus as an example of how Peter should care for Jesus' sheep and lambs.

In 12c-e the author includes the thoughts of the disciples as a group in the form of direct discourse to the reader, regarding the fact that the disciples did not dare to ask Jesus, "Who are you?" First, this scene refers the reader back to the recognition scene in vv. 4-7: when the disciples were in the boat, only the Beloved Disciple recognized that it was Jesus who was speaking and providing instructions from the shore. The reader recalls that Peter had responded immediately to the report of the Beloved Disciple and Peter who jumped into the water, after he heard that it was the Lord. Second, the author presents the thoughts of the disciples to the reader to establish further the author's omniscient point

---

[7]   For recent proposals on the meaning of the 153 fish, see, e.g., Carson, *John*, 672-673.

of view in the narrative. The author not only informs the reader of what they refused to ask Jesus, but also the author informs the reader of the fact that they all knew that it was the Lord. Thus, the author's point of view establishes the reliability of the narrator and confirms for the reader that Jesus had risen from the dead (cf. v. 14).

The manner in which Jesus presents the bread and the fish to the disciples causes the reader to reflect back to the feeding sign in chapter 6. This event is ceremonial in that it reflects for the reader other events where Jesus presents a meal to the disciples and the crowd (cf. John 6:1-15).

The report of this being the third time that Jesus manifested (ἐφανερώθη) himself to the disciples forms an *inclusio* with v. 1 and confirms and summarizes Jesus' third appearance to the male disciples for the reader. The author seems to suggest to the reader that this was the way in which Jesus manifested himself to his disciples after he was raised from the dead. This third appearance of Jesus offers another report in a summary format to the reader of Jesus rising from the dead. This reports provides to the reader a statement of fact that Jesus indeed had manifested himself to the male disciples on three different occasions, recalling for the reader the two previous ways in which Jesus had appeared to the disciples—twice in Jerusalem in the house where the disciples were gathered and once in Galilee by the sea of Tiberias. The reader, however, notes that this is Jesus' fourth appearance in the resurrection narrative. This information represents a disagreement between what the author cites and what the reader actually knows, and as such, the reader has to supply the implications of this information, which refers only to the male disciples.

Conclusion

Scene ten brings to a conclusion the way in which Jesus manifested himself to the male disciples for the third time, concluding the recognition scenes and the fishing scenes. In scene nine Jesus gave the disciples instructions on where to fish. Scene ten provides the record on the number of fish that the disciples actually caught. Scene ten also brings to closure for the reader the disciples fishing endeavor, where in scene eight they fish all night unsuccessfully and in scenes nine and ten, with the assistance of Jesus, they were able to catch a large number of fish. This represents the last and final sign in the Fourth Gospel.

Scene ten further confirms to the reader the fact that all of the disciples present did not need to ask Jesus for his true identity because they knew that it was the Lord. Thus, scene ten functions to confirm to the reader the way in which the third appearance of Jesus happened before the disciples after he was raised from the dead.

The author presents a unified and coherent narrative at this point in the resurrection narrative to the reader. The author connects the initial scenes of episode number three with the previous episodes. In fact, the reader in scenes eight presupposes the first two episodes, nine, and ten: (1) the recognition scene, (2) the appearance motif, and (3) the mission of the disciples. In such the author persuades the reader with devices and details, which are connected to information presented earlier in the narrative.

Scene Eleven: Jesus' Dialogue with Peter; Jesus' Prediction of Peter's Fate; and Jesus' First Command to Peter to Follow Him, 21:15-19

Translation of John 21:15-19

15. When they had finished eating, Jesus said to Simon Peter, "Simon, son of John, do you love me more than these?" He said to him, "Yes, Lord; you know that I am fond of you." He said to him, "Feed my lambs." 16. He said to him the second time, "Simon, son of John, do you love me?" He said to him, "Yes, Lord; you know that I am fond of you." He said to him, "Tend my sheep." 17. He said to him the third time, "Simon, son of John, are you fond of me? Peter was grieved, because he said to him the third time, "Are you fond of me?" and he said to him, "Lord, you know all things; you know that I am fond of you." Jesus said to him, "Feed my sheep. 18. Truly, Truly, I say to you, when you were young, you girded yourself and walked where you would; but when you grow old, you will extend out your hands and another will gird you and carry you where you do not wish to go." 19. (Now, this he said to show by what death he was to glorify God.) And after he said this, he said to him, "Follow me."

Introduction

Scene eleven begins after the disciples complete their meal. Afterwards, Jesus engages Peter in a question-and-answer dialogue on his love for Jesus and commissions Peter to care for Jesus' flock. The first question is somewhat ambiguous because it is difficult to determine from the context what Jesus had meant by the phrase, "... more than these." Moreover, the author's shifting of terms for love (ἀγαπᾷς and φιλῶ) as well as for feeding/tending (Βόσκε / Ποίμαινε) and the author's selection of nouns for lamb, sheep, and little sheep (τὰ ἀρνία, τὰ πρόβατά), make it even more difficult to decipher Jesus' purpose and Peter's responses.[8] The difficulty lies in whether the reader would respond to these synonyms or would read them on different levels. Further, in the final question, Jesus uses the verb φιλῶ, and Peter, appealing to Jesus' knowledge, replies with the same verb that Jesus had last employed.

After this three-fold question and response, Jesus offers a riddle on the fate of Peter, and the narrator's aside provides the reader with an interpretation of such, saying that this is the way in which Peter's death would glorify God. Finally, at the end of this scene Jesus instructs Peter for the first time to follow him.

In scene eleven, after the disciples complete their meal with Jesus, a discussion and dialogue occur between Jesus and Peter. This discourse is of a question-and-answer nature, with Jesus leading the discussion and raising critical questions for Peter to address. Although Peter's name is mentioned in scene nine (v. 11), there he plays a secondary role in the narrative. In the previous scenes, the disciples function as a group, all of which participate in the catch of fish, but Peter is singled out as the one who hauls in the fish onto the shore at Jesus' instruction. In other words, whereas Peter plays this minor role in scene nine, in scene eleven he and Jesus are engaged and focused on by the author. Scene ten ends with a report on this event, being the third appearance of Jesus to the disciples. The adverbial clause at the beginning of scene eleven serves as a transitional clause into the subsequent dialogue between Jesus and Peter.

Delineation of Scene Eleven

An adverbial phrase marks the temporal succession of a new scene, scene eleven. After the disciples are finished with their meal, Jesus

---

[8]   For a discussion on these terms, see, e.g., Brown, *John*, 1102-1106.

commences immediately with a dialogue focusing on Peter's commitment, work, and faithfulness. Just as Peter denied Jesus three times, Jesus would question Peter three times concerning his love for him and regarding Peter's future tasks of caring for Jesus' flock.

In the previous scene Peter is the primary focus of the narrative because the author specifically refers to Peter several times up to this point in the narrative to prepare the reader for this scene. In fact, in all of the previous scenes in this third episode, Peter is placed in a central role, with the exception of the recognition scene, where the Beloved Disciple is the first to recognize Jesus. In scene eleven Peter's relationship and commitment to Jesus is the primary focus of the narrative and is placed into question, particularly Peter's love and devotion and his subsequent role and mission to follow Jesus. Thus, scene eleven is differentiated from the previous scene with the dialogue between Jesus and Peter.

Moreover, scene eleven is differentiated from the previous and subsequent scenes with four events: (1) a brief summary from the author, marking the end of the disciples' breakfast; (2) a subsequent conversation—a number of questions from Jesus and answers from Peter containing repetition with variation; The topic was Peter's love and commitment to Jesus and his subsequent role in the community; (3) a riddle concerning the way in which Peter was going to die and give glory to God; and lastly, (4) a summary by the author in the form of a narrator's aside, interpreting the meaning of the riddle for the reader. Obviously, the reader needed an explanation of this metaphor, whereas Peter, on the story-level, knew or probably sensed what Jesus meant, as seen in the following scene, scene twelve, where Peter shows some concern regarding the fate of the Beloved Disciple.

Concerning the differentiation of scene eleven from scene twelve— regarding where scene eleven precisely ends and scene twelve begins— v. 19 could be broken up into two parts: the first part includes the narrator's report to the reader and the second part contains a temporal clause and command to Peter, indicating the possible beginning of scene twelve. Since it concludes Jesus and Peter's brief conversation concerning the role and fate of Peter, scene eleven, however, includes the entire verse, v. 19.

In v. 20 the author begins the scene with Peter's concern about the fate of the Beloved Disciple as in scene three, where Mary turns and sees

Jesus behind her but did not know that it was Jesus. In fact, the author uses the same participle for turned, Ἐπιστραφεὶς, which functions to heighten the intensity of the scene with the brief transition between these two scenes (eleven and twelve).

Temporal Process of Reading Scene Eleven

The author presents to the reader a long anticipated event, namely how Jesus would deal with Peter after the latter denied him three times. The author portrays Jesus as patient and gentle in waiting for the right time to confront Peter regarding his role and commitment to him. So, it was after the disciples had fished all night, after Jesus had manifested himself to them, after the disciples had acquired a large caught of fish, after Peter had brought the fish ashore, after they had completely recognized that it was the Lord, and after they had finished eating, that Jesus begins to question Peter.

This scene commences with a brief temporal transition, and then the dialogue begins. Jesus engages Peter in a question-answer-command dialogue, concerning Peter's devotion and commitment to him and Peter's future role in the community. At this point, the author had mentioned Peter's name in the third episode several times. In scene eight Peter is listed first among the other disciples. In addition, in scene eight Peter suggests the fishing trip and the other disciples agreed to follow him.

In scene nine, after the Beloved Disciple recognizes Jesus on the shore and proclaims, "It is the Lord," Peter puts on his outer garment and jumps into the water and swims to the shore. Finally, in scene ten Peter drags in the net full of large fish at the request of Jesus. Thus, the reader suspects from the constant reference to Peter that he will play a major role to play in this episode.

In scene eleven the reader's suspicions come to fruition in Jesus' conversation with Peter. With the exception of the Beloved Disciple, Peter is the only disciple who acts or speaks in the third episode. Why does Jesus address Peter specifically? Peter is no doubt one of the leaders among the disciples, as evidenced by the author's constant references to him. The repetition of the question-and-answer dialogue can best be seen in a parallel structure, indicating the progressive repetition with variation.

The Structure of the Dialogue between Jesus and Peter: Jesus'
Questions and Commands; Peter's Responses. (1) Jesus: "Simon, son of
John, do you love (ἀγαπᾷς) me more than these?" (2) Peter: "Yes,
Lord; you know that I am fond (φιλῶ) of you." (3) Jesus: "Feed my
lambs (τὰ πρόβατά μου)." (4) Jesus: "Simon, son of John, do you
love (ἀγαπᾷς) me?" (5) Peter: "Yes, Lord; you know that I am fond
(φιλῶ) of you." (6) Jesus: "Tend (Ποίμαινε) my sheep." (7) Jesus:
"Simon, son of John, are you fond (φιλεῖς) of me? (8) Narrative aside:
Peter was grieved, because he said to him the third time, "Are you fond
(φιλεῖς) of me?" (9) Peter: "Lord, you know all things; you know that I
am fond (φιλῶ) of you." (10) Jesus: "Feed my sheep..."

Vv. 15-17 concerns the literary device of rhetorical questions raised
by Jesus. These verses employ repetition with slight variation. These
variations in the nouns and verbs employed by the author have an effect
on the reader, that is, the author uses these words precisely to
demonstrate Peter's lack of love and commitment concerning his mission
as one of the lead disciple. Indeed, the case can be made that the author
employs these synonyms for love and fondness concerning the Beloved
Disciple's appellations. Variations used here in vv. 15-17, however, have
a direct rhetorical effect, not only on Peter, as will be seen later, but also
on the reader.

In short, the variations employed by Jesus concerning the synonyms
for love suggest that Peter's true devotions for Jesus and his sheep/lambs
are lacking or are insufficient. For example, Jesus employs ἀγαπᾷς in
his first two questions (1 and 4, above), where Peter's response to these
questions uses the term φιλῶ (see, e.g., 2 and 5, above) a lesser degree
of love than Jesus or the reader would expect. Peter did not respond in
kind or with the same term that Jesus employed in his questions to him;
Peter simply sought to be truthful; he only had a friendly, causal love for
Jesus, as evidenced by his denial of Jesus on three different occasions.

In his last question to Peter, Jesus condescends to Peter's term, φιλῶ
(see, 7, above) and Peter becomes angry, not only due to the constant
repetition of the question, but also due to the variation of the question in
terms of what Peter was responding to in the two previous uses of the
term, φιλῶ. That is, Jesus was questioning the level of love that Peter

had displayed since the previous resurrection appearances. Peter acknowledges that Jesus knew all things, including the true level of his love. It seems as though Peter had loved fishing rather than carrying out the commission, which Jesus had given to all of the disciples.[9]

In v. 18a the reader encounters another "Amen, Amen..." statement. The reader recognizes this miracle formula, which introduces a dialogue with an "Amen, Amen..." statement, which is a Johannine formula or rhetorical device. This device functions to highlight a revelation of some sort.

Jesus reminds Peter and the reader of the condition of freedom that Peter had when he was young. Two such issues are commented upon briefly: (1) "you gird yourself," that is, Peter had put on his own clothes, and (2) "walked where you would," suggests that when Peter was young he once had the ability or freedom to go wherever he wished. This condition of freedom is contrasted with the second half of the riddle and is marked by an adversative conjunction "but," indicating Peter's condition or state of bondage and death, which is accompanied by three conditions: (1) "you will extend out your hands," which suggests that when Peter becomes old he will request help to lead him to crucifixion; (2) "another will gird you," namely, Peter will ask for help to be clothed and will need another to help him; (3) "and will carry you where you do not wish to go," this statement indicates that Peter will be carried to a place against his own will. The reader has to continue reading to receive an interpretation of this riddle by the author, viz., a narrator's aside. At this point, the reader grasps the essence of the contrast between Peter's youth and old age. For the reader knows that Peter's youth is a condition of freedom, and his older age is marked by some sort of helplessness and bondage, requiring another to assist him in some unsought endeavor.

V. 19 contains a narrator's aside to explain the riddle to the reader and a subsequent command from Jesus to Peter. The author employs an aside to assist the reader with an interpretation of this riddle. In essence, it explains to the reader that Jesus provides this riddle to reveal Peter's fate. The author supplies a clue for the reader to complete the intended meaning. That is, Peter, like Jesus, would be crucified; that is, this would

[9]   See, e.g., Carson, *John*, 676-678.

be the way in which Peter would die.

The reader can perceive in v. 19b Jesus' command, "follow me," in two ways: (1) In the immediate context it means to follow Jesus in death. Here Jesus is instructing Peter to follow him and not attempt to resist his fate. (2) As the following scene indicates, Jesus also meant for Peter to follow him literally, as Peter does in v. 20. The following scene will show that while Peter does follow Jesus, literally, Peter reluctantly accepts Jesus' pronouncement of his fate. Peter then shows concern about the other disciple's (the Beloved Disciple's) fate. The author makes it is clear to the reader in the riddle in v. 19a that Jesus was referring to Peter's death—that is, how Peter would be glorifying God— and in v. 19b Jesus issues another command to Peter, after the riddle was explained to the reader. Here, Peter seems to understand what Jesus meant (see v. 21 below).

Conclusion

In this scene the author seeks to restore and commission Peter and reveal to the reader Peter's fate by means of a riddle. The author places more emphasis on the commission than on a clear reference to Peter's denial, which is only alluded to with the charcoal fire and with the three-fold repetition of questions, which focuses on Peter's level of devotion. The dialogue between Jesus and Peter is perceived by the reader as a challenge to the level of Peter's love and commitment. Despite Peter's and the reader's degree of love and commitment, Jesus still commissions Peter and the reader to care for his flock.

Another central feature of this scene is Jesus' prediction of the death of Peter. The author employs a riddle to illustrate Peter's declining level of freedom to the point of death, to point out how Peter will glorify God, which is a glorification similar to the glorification that Jesus displayed in his crucifixion. The meaning of the riddle was explained to the reader as the way in which Peter in the end would glorify God.

The final emphasis of the author is placed on the first command issued by Jesus to Peter to follow him. Despite his fate, Peter is required to follow Jesus. The reader perceives this command as a statement to summarize Jesus' commission and prediction, but also it is to be taken literally.

**Scene Twelve: Peter's Concern Regarding the
Fate of the Beloved Disciple; Jesus' Reply; and
Jesus' Second Command to Peter to Follow Him;
Final Conclusion to the Fourth Gospel's
Resurrection Narrative: The Identity and
Witness of the Implied Author; and a
Final Declaration Concerning the
Things which Jesus Did, 21:20-25**

Translation of John 21:20-23

20. Peter turned and saw following them the other disciple, whom Jesus loved,
who also reclined on his breast during supper, and said to him, "Lord, who is it
that is going to betray you?" 21. When Peter saw him, he said to Jesus, "What
about this man?" 22. Jesus said to him, "If I want him to remain until I come,
what is it to you? You follow me!" 23. Therefore, this saying went out to the
brethren that this disciple would not die; yet Jesus did not say to him that he
would not die, but, "If I want him to remain until I come, what is that to you?"
24. This is the disciple who is testifying about these things, and the one who
wrote these things, and we know that his testimony is true. 25. But, there are
also many other things which Jesus did; which, if they were written one by one,
I suppose the world would not have room for the books that would be written.

Introduction

The scene quickly changes from when Peter turned around and saw
the Beloved Disciple following them. The narrator's aside at this point
identifies this disciple with an earlier scene in the Gospel regarding the
privileged information that Jesus gave to this disciple during supper
concerning the one whom was going to betray Jesus. Peter then asked
Jesus a question concerning the fate of this disciple. Jesus replied by
saying that if this disciple should remain until I come, what does it have
to do with you (Peter). The narrator's aside indicates that Jesus' saying
became a rumor that suggested that this disciple would not die before the
Parousia. The author's next comment is to seek to dispel this rumor by
reiterating what Jesus had actually said. Scene twelve, episode number
three, and the Gospel come to an end with a testimonial statement
revealing the author's identity as the Beloved Disciple. The Beloved
Disciple finally concludes with a hyperbole, which suggests that he
witnessed much more than he could write: in fact if all of the things that
Jesus did were written, then the world would not have enough room to

contain all the books that would be written.

In vv. 24-25 the reader senses the final conclusion to the resurrection narrative and the final conclusion to the Gospel. Like the first conclusion to the resurrection narrative, this conclusion briefly refers to the other things that Jesus did. It mentions the reliability of the author and identifies the author with the disciple in scene twelve. It affirms the truthfulness of the author's testimony, which is argued also in scene twelve. In short, this conclusion summarizes the Gospel by identifying the Beloved Disciple as the one responsible, in some fashion or another, with the writing of this testimony; it concludes with a hyperbole.

The function of this section for the reader is to bring final closure to the Gospel: to identify the person responsible for this revelatory testimony. It finally mentions the works incompleteness and incomprehensible nature.

Delineation of Scene Twelve

Scene twelve is primarily differentiated from scene eleven with a slight change both in the spatial-setting and in the theme of the discussion. At the end of scene eleven, Jesus instructs Peter "to follow," him, and here in scene twelve the reader notes that Peter was reluctantly carrying out these instructions (see below).

In the previous scenes, the spatial-setting indicates that Jesus and the disciples were sitting around a charcoal fire. Here, in this scene Jesus, Peter, and the Beloved Disciple are in transition, with Peter following Jesus and the Beloved Disciple following them. Thus, this slight change in the spatial location—from the location of the charcoal fire to Peter and the Beloved Disciple following Jesus—indicates a change in scenes.

Second, a slight change in the theme also indicates a new scene. First, though the characters do not change from scene eleven to scene twelve, where Jesus was in dialogue with Peter, the focus of the discussion between Jesus and Peter shifts to the Beloved Disciple; the Beloved Disciple has no direct discourse in this scene (see below). Second, although the content of the dialogue between Jesus and Peter shifts from a focus on Peter to that of the Beloved Disciple, the subject of the Beloved Disciple's death or fate is now the concern of Peter. As such, this slight change in the subject of the conversation, along with the indication of a transition occurring, represents a new scene to the reader.

Temporal Process of Reading Scene Twelve

In scene twelve, although Peter remains the principal dialogue partner with Jesus, the theme of this scene shifts to a focus on the Beloved Disciple and on the conclusion to both the resurrection narrative and the Gospel. The continuative conjunction "but" (δὲ) should be read in the text because it advances the theme of the scene and indicates to the reader the connection to the previous scene; that is, it is temporal and spatially connected to the events of the previous scenes in the third episode. Temporally, this scene occurs after the discussion between Jesus and Peter in scene eleven. In fact, the transition between scene eleven and twelve are narrated to the reader in "real" narrative time, that is to say, it is narrated in a fashion to resemble the actual time in which these events occurred, with no comments from the narrator to divide the two scenes.

Spatially, scene twelve's events occur while Jesus, Peter, and the Beloved Disciple are in transit. In fact, scene eleven ends with Jesus' command to Peter to follow him. In scene twelve this command is being carried out by Peter, albeit, reluctantly.

At the close of scene eleven, the author connects and bases Peter's subsequent actions and concerns regarding Jesus' prophetic saying regarding Peter's fate (vv. 18-19) and on the narrator's aside in v. 19. Here, in scene twelve the reader is placed again in a privileged position over against the characters in the story-world concerning the meaning and interpretation of Jesus' riddle, and as such the reader is allowed to experience both the riddle and its interpretation, along with Jesus' command to Peter to follow him. Accordingly, Peter reluctantly obeys Jesus' command and literally follows him. In so doing, however, Peter looks back and sees the Beloved Disciple following them. Thus, this conjunction (δὲ) indicates the relationship between scene eleven and scene twelve.

Peter's action in. v. 20 of turning and looking back behind at the Beloved Disciple functions as a transition between these two scenes and indicates Peter's reluctance to follow Jesus. Further, this transitional action of Peter recalls for the reader scene four wherein Mary Magdalene also "turns and looks behind" (v. 14b). Like the transition between scenes three and four in episode number one, where Mary turns from looking into the tomb in order to look behind, Peter, while following

Jesus, turns to look back at the other disciple who was following them. Both of these passages employ a similar Greek work for "turning..." ('Επιστραφείς), and as such, the reader senses this usage of the verbs in both contexts—namely, a lack of recognition and a desire for more information, respectively.

The participial phrase, "following them the other disciple, whom Jesus loves..." suggests to the reader that both Peter and the Beloved Disciple were following Jesus. Here, although Peter seems to be obeying Jesus' command to follow, Peter's concerns shift to focus on the fate of the Beloved Disciple. The two disciples following Jesus is not intended to mean or imply a contrast between them. Though the reader might notice this contrast initially, the central purpose of this scene is to dispel a rumor about the fate of the Beloved Disciple.

Before the reader can focus on the fate of the Beloved Disciple, the author inserts a narrator's aside concerning the Beloved Disciple. Here, the Beloved Disciple is identified in three statements or clauses. First, he is again identified as the disciple whom Jesus loves. The function of this first statement is to reorient the reader with the relationship between Jesus and this disciple and hence to provide an appellation to his character that the reader can identify with in earlier narrative scenes. This appellation identifies him as a paradigmatic character that possesses certain actions to emulate. Interestingly, in the previous scene the author places Peter and Jesus in dialogue regarding caring for Jesus' flock. Here, in scene twelve the author focuses on the personal, close relationship that existed between Jesus and the Beloved Disciple.

Second, the author inserts a flashback into the Gospel narrative to a scene regarding the Last Supper scene (13:21-30, esp. v. 23). In this supper scene the author also focuses on the close, spatial distance between Jesus and the Beloved Disciple, who "was reclining next to him" (v. 23). In other words, this is the second instance where the author draws on the events surrounding the supper scene to provide evidence on the close relationship between Jesus and the Beloved Disciple. In other words, this second instance modifies and explains the meaning of the appellation of the Beloved Disciple.

Third, the author draws from the same supper scene, but this time the Beloved Disciple's direct discourse from that scene is repeated in a different context with the use of indirect discourse by the author to support further the meaning of the Beloved Disciple's appellation. The discourse itself, during the supper scene, as well as in the present context, illustrates the Beloved Disciple's privileged position concerning certain insider information that the other disciples do not possess, including Peter.

In short, after the command in v. 19, Peter follows Jesus somewhat mechanically—at least it appears this way to the reader. Peter looks back and sees the Beloved Disciple following them, and then the author interjects a brief commentary concerning the identity of the Beloved Disciple. As his title affirms, Jesus loved this disciple.

Upon seeing this disciple following them, Peter raises a question of concern regarding the fate of this disciple. Possibly, due to the surprise of his fate, Peter now seeks to shift the focus of the conversation to this other disciple. The reader, however, does not sense a controversy between these two disciples, but the function of this scene is introduced by Peter's question, namely the rumor that spread about the fate of this disciple. Jesus indirectly responds by saying, "If I want him to remain until I come, what is that to you." This is to say it is Jesus' prerogative to determine the fate of those who follow me; therefore, his fate should not concern you. Jesus' rhetorical question, which is in the form of a first class conditional statement, requires no response from Peter.

As in the case of the Beloved Disciple, this rhetorical question indicates the privilege of Jesus to comment and raise questions concerning the fate of the disciples.[10] The rumor itself was taken to mean that the Beloved Disciple would not die but would remain until Jesus comes. The author, however, interprets Jesus' saying not to refer to the death of the Beloved Disciple but to restate rhetorically the conditional statement itself. The repetition by the author of this rumor reinforces the original direct discourse of Jesus in response to Peter's concern, which functions to seek information regarding the fate of the Beloved Disciple.

---

[10] It is the Beloved Disciple's privileged position because of his role as the recorder and witness of Jesus and the disciples, and it is Jesus' privilege alone to predict or foretell the fate of others because he is Lord. The author explains and clarifies the saying or rumor, concerning not the fate of the Beloved Disciple, but what Jesus was not saying, that is what he meant, for a specific reason, which was quite bluntly to put Peter in his rightful place and predetermine role, as shepherd of Jesus' flock.

In short, the author makes clear that Jesus was not predicting the fate of the Beloved Disciple but was addressing Peter's concerns. As such, the author's rhetorical device functions to correct and dispel a false rumor.

Vv. 24-25 represents the conclusion to the resurrection narrative and to the Gospel as a whole, where in a narrator's footnote the author identifies himself as the author of the Gospel. The structure of these final two verses is in chiastic parallelism with the first conclusion to the resurrection narrative (20:20-31). Both conclusions refer to the additional works of Jesus, his signs, and to the fact that not all of Jesus' signs or works could be recorded; and both conclusions refer to the reliability of the testimony as written in this Gospel.

The differences lie in the focus of each conclusion. Vv. 30-31 point out that Jesus did many more signs in the presence of his disciples, which serves the purpose of deepening the disciples' and reader's belief in Jesus, and thus this deeper belief would produce a more productive life. Further, the conclusion to chapter 20, vv. 30-31 summarizes the various levels of faith, for the reader, as revealed in Jesus' appearances in episodes number one and two.

In 21:24 the identity of the author is revealed to the reader, this is made explicit for the first time in the Gospel narrative.[11] It also affirms the reliability and testimony of the author as a witness to these events. Thus, the differences lie in the function of these conclusions. Although each conclusion refers to similar events, the first conclusion identifies the intent of Jesus' signs, while the second conclusion identifies the author and refers to the incompleteness of this testimony.

The relative pronoun "this" refers the reader back to the antecedent, who is the Beloved Disciple, the one whom Jesus loved—the one who sat at supper and inquired of Jesus concerning the one who was to betray Jesus. This one was identified as the one who testifies (ὁ μαρτυρῶν) about "these things," which brings the reader back to the sayings and deeds of Jesus in the Fourth Gospel. The reader now knows who is providing this testimony and further identifies the Beloved Disciple as the one who wrote these things. Moreover, the reader can trust this

---

[11] See 19:35. This verse also affirms the reliability of the implied author's testimony, but it does not explicitly identify this person at this point of the Gospel narrative.

testimony and witness because it is true. Since the one who testifies is reliable, then it follows that the Beloved Disciple's testimony will also be true and reliable.

Finally, the author informs the reader of the fact that there is far more information regarding the signs of Jesus mentioned in the first conclusion to the Gospel in 20:30-31, of which this final episode illustrates. Here, in conclusion, after the author delineates the role of the Beloved Disciple, introducing the Beloved Disciple as the one with special privileges in the narrative world of the Fourth Gospel, the Beloved Disciple is finally identified as the author, the one responsible for writing the testimony of Jesus.

Conclusion

In scene twelve the author's focus remains on Peter and Jesus; the Beloved Disciple is brought into the scene indirectly with a flashback to the supper scene to further identify to the reader an example to be emulated and to dispel a rumor regarding his fate. In the end, the reader does not detect any conflict between Peter and the Beloved Disciple. The evidence indicates that Peter's fate was revealed in scene eleven, and then he became concerned about the fate of the Beloved Disciple. In addition, the author's insertion of the supper scene seems to suggest further that the Beloved Disciple had a privileged role in the narrative as a whole, which is identified in the conclusion to the Gospel (21:24-25). The reader, however, understands Peter's concern, and the author's insertion of the supper scene serves as a foil to dispel the rumor about the fate of the Beloved Disciple. In other words, the reader grasps the function of this scene as a disclaimer concerning the rumor about the fate of the Beloved Disciple.

V. 24 concerns the person who was both a witness to these events and responsible for recording these words. From a literary-rhetorical perspective, this concern is not on the actual flesh-and-blood author, but it focuses on what this text reveals about the identity of the implied author in the text.

Like the first conclusion, the reader is also informed here of the incompleteness of this work, given that there are many more things not included, which leads the reader to bring forward the information in 20:31, which indicates, along with 21:24, the notion that more information about Jesus is available to convince future readers of the significance of Jesus' work. As such, the second and final conclusion bears a similar form as the conclusion to chapter 20, not as mere repetition, replicating the style of 20:30-31, but with variation causing the reader to infer information from both conclusions to ascertain the author's identity, the purpose of the Gospel as a whole and the resurrection narrative in particular (cf. 20:30-31), and the inexhaustible nature and works of Jesus. In short, the world could never exhaust the significance of Jesus the Christ, the essence of the Gospel, and the subject of this testimony of God to the world.

CHAPTER FIVE

Conclusion

This literary-rhetorical reading shows that the Fourth Gospel's resurrection narrative as it now stands is a coherent, unified narrative text on its terms. This study proposed a temporal process of reading John 20-21 from the perspectives of the implied author and the implied reader, paying particular attention to the responses of the implied reader. It also suggests that the implied author employs various narrative techniques and devices, persuading the reader of the fact and nature of Jesus' resurrection. The temporal process reading of John 20-21 also demonstrates—from the perspective of the implied reader—the implied author's success at informing and convincing the implied reader of the resurrection overall purpose and mission.

The first chapter of this work reviewed the history of scholarship and proposed a methodology for reading the resurrection narrative from a literary-rhetorical perspective. After presenting the thesis of the study, chapter 1 presented the objective and rationale for this literary-rhetorical method, which was to read John 20-21 on its own terms and as it now stands because little attention has been given to this section of the Gospel as a coherent, unified narrative text—as shown in the history of scholarship section. The next section of chapter 1 outlined the methodology: (1) a literary, text-centered type of narrative criticism, (2) a rhetorical or reader-response approach, focusing on the implied reader in the text during a temporal process of reading. The final section of chapter 1 delineated the structure of John 20-21 into three episodes and twelve scenes, illustrating the unity between the parts (episodes) and sections (scenes).

Each subsequent chapter (2-4) has offered cumulative conclusions.

Each conclusion summarizes the findings of the present chapter in light of the findings in the previous sections and chapters. This final chapter supplements the overall findings by suggesting some integrative observations about the strategic designs of the implied author with the corresponding responses of the implied reader. Several observations can be made concerning the resurrection narrative of the Fourth Gospel as it now stands and on its own terms.

The first observation is that the Synoptic Gospels and the Fourth Gospel present different versions of the empty tomb and of Jesus' appearances, possibly by different implied authors and possibly to different implied readers. This work illustrates the benefit of reading the Fourth Gospel on its own terms in order to take seriously the unified message of the Fourth Gospel—the narrative of the implied author directed to the implied reader in this text.

The second observation is that although there appears to be on the surface a clear conclusion at the end of chapter 20 (vv. 30-31), this work advances a reading of the Fourth Gospel as it now stands as the necessary first step toward comprehending the entire message of the implied author and the various responses of the implied reader. Concerning the question of whether we are dealing with a document that is unified as a whole or one that reflects its original order, this work argues that there is no text-critical evidence to suggest that the Fourth Gospel ever circulated without chapter 21. The alleged conclusion in 20:30-31 was read as a conclusion to the events and episodes in chapter 20, and thus, serves as a summary from the vantage point of the implied reader, who builds consistency during the temporal or sequential process of reading (see below). Besides, several scenes in the Fourth Gospel— especially those in episodes number one and two—presuppose the existence of chapter 21, without which the Fourth Gospel would not represent a coherent narrative text. This work illustrates the unity of these two chapters by considering, for example, the denial scene of Peter, the identity of the Beloved Disciple, the role of Peter among the disciples, and the faith and mission of the disciples.

The third observation is that the so-called aporias or gaps in the text represented information in the narrative that the implied reader understands and fills during the process of reading. This work demonstrates that the implied author inserted these gaps and omitted information as rhetorical devices that the implied reader can comprehend even in cases where the real reader can only speculate (cf. 153 fish and the net that remained intact).

The fourth observation is that in scene eleven Jesus is portrayed as dispelling a rumor concerning the fate of the Beloved Disciple. Indeed, it seemed that the former possibly was included as a foil for the latter in order to explain or defend a conditional statement made by Jesus regarding the Second Coming in light of the alleged death of the Beloved Disciple. These mysteries are generated primarily due to historical-critical concerns: (1) the addition of the final chapter, (2) the person(s) responsible for this addition to the Gospel, (3) the nature of the composition and redaction, (4) the Beloved Disciple's death—historical-critical scholars believed that this rumor was an actual record of the Beloved Disciple's death, which was narrated outside the story-world of the characters in the narrative. What these investigations fail to do is to read the text as it now stands. To read the text as it now stands, one has to take seriously the riddle and the rumor at face value, following the clues of each to determine how the implied author is seeking to persuade the implied reader toward some sort of deeper belief or action. In other words, one must ask: What does the implied author seek to communicate to the implied reader in the text? Rather than asking: What type of history does the text provide in terms of the fate of this disciple? Indeed, the approach of historical-critical scholars primarily have not been concerned with a reading of the text in as much as they have been concerned with a historical-critical readings of the history behind the text.

The fifth observation is that the purpose of the narrative can be determined during the temporal process of reading in terms from the vantage point of the implied reader. From this point of view, this work argues that the implied author employed several strategies and devices to cause the implied reader to identify with certain characters (e.g., the Beloved Disciple) and to remain at a distance from others (e.g., Thomas, Jewish leaders, and Peter). Within this point of view, the implied author illustrates several levels of faith to the implied reader, elevating the kind of faith that does not require "seeing" in order to believe in the resurrection of Jesus (cf. 20:29). In short, the implied author expects the implied reader's faith to emulate the faith of the Beloved Disciple, who in the end is identified as the implied author of the Fourth Gospel.

During the temporal process of reading the three episodes and twelve scenes, the implied reader's faith is challenged and transformed by the four primary strategies of the implied author. First, in episode number one the implied reader is informed and confronted with the missing corpse of Jesus. At this point in the narrative, the implied reader remained in suspense until scene four regarding the whereabouts of Jesus' body. Yet, in scenes one, three, and four the implied reader identified with Mary Magdalene's plight as portrayed through the temporal- and spatial-settings, which illustrated—viz., the symbolism of darkness and the empty tomb—the mood and atmosphere of Mary's experience at the tomb.

Second, in scene three the implied reader's faith is supplied with additional evidence regarding the experience of the two disciples at the empty tomb. Although the two disciples react differently to the clothes in the tomb, the implied reader identifies with the faith-reaction of the Beloved Disciple. The implied reader is confronted for the first time in the resurrection narrative with a notion of belief without seeing and as such is expected to identify with the Beloved Disciple.

Third, in episode number two the implied reader does not identify with the disciples' reaction to the risen Jesus. As in the case of the Beloved Disciple's faith in scene two, the implied reader is informed of the type of faith expected by the implied author. The doubting of Thomas and the disciples as a whole (not including the Beloved Disciple) is designed to confront and challenge the faith of the implied reader. In v. 29 the implied reader received a narrative aside from the implied author that suggests an ideal faith, which consists of seeing without believing. In v. 31 the implied author suggests the purpose of the signs given in chapter 20, which suggested that there exist many levels of faith and the purpose of this chapter, and thus, the Gospel as a whole was designed to strengthen the faith of the implied reader.

Finally, in episode number three the implied reader is confronted first with the inactivity of the disciples' faith and mission. The implied reader's faith is developed further in vv. 1-14 because without Jesus the disciples—and consequently, the implied reader—cannot have a successful mission. The symbolism of the 153 fish and the net that remained intact suggested to the implied reader information perhaps regarding the mission of the disciples; the real reader is not informed of the meaning of these two symbols. During Jesus' conversation with Peter concerning his level of love/devotion, the implied reader's faith is developed to even a higher level—from faith without seeing to the necessity of Jesus' presence for a successful mission to the ministry of feeding/tending the sheep/lambs of Jesus, despite the level of love/devotion of Peter and the implied reader. In the final scene of episode number one, the implied reader's faith is now situated to follow Jesus by not identifying with Peter's fate. In v. 24 the implied author is revealed to the implied reader as the Beloved Disciple and the testimony of this disciple is confirmed to the implied reader regarding the veracity of this Gospel. Thus, the strategy of the implied author was designed to strengthen and develop the faith of the implied reader.

The sixth observation is that the implied author seeks to establish the certainty of the resurrection of Jesus—viz., the four appearances of Jesus in John 20-21. During each of the resurrection appearances, the implied author provided a detailed narrative of the nature of Jesus' body so that the implied reader could observe and identify with certain characterizations of Jesus in the narrative. Although the resurrection event proper was not narrated, the implied author records details concerning Jesus' death, burial, and four appearances to strengthen the faith of the implied reader, and thus, argues convincingly the fact of Jesus' resurrection.

The seventh observation is that the unity of the text can be established by differentiating each episode and scene from the one that precedes and follows it. This study differentiated the episodes and scenes based on literary criteria regarding changes in one or more of the following: the temporal-, spatial-settings, the characters, the events, and the theme or purpose.

Finally, the eighth observation is that each episode in the resurrection narrative has its major complication. The first episode has the missing body of Jesus, evoking faith on several levels, but it calls for faith on the highest level—faith without seeing. Episode number two's major complication is that will the disciples as a whole exhibit their faith in the resurrected Jesus. This complication seeks to demonstrate the quasi-physical nature of the post-resurrected Jesus and focuses on the corresponding faith-response and responsibility of the disciples. Lastly, the major complication of episode number three is to prove to the disciples and to the implied reader that without Jesus they can do nothing. It further seeks to reestablish the relationship between Jesus and Peter and predict Peter's fate, and to some extent, it seeks to dispel the rumor regarding the fate of the Beloved Disciple. The central complication of the narrative, from 19:38-42 through chapter 21, is to prove to the implied reader that *in fact* Jesus was raised from the dead.

In closing, rather than focusing on the backside of the tangled web of history behind John 20-21, this work provides a reading on the artistic, front side of the tapestry of the Fourth Gospel's resurrection narrative. Indeed, this work presents a unified, coherent reading of the narrative as it stands and on its own term. In the end, this finely woven tapestry convinces the implied reader of Jesus' resurrection and strengthens the faith and mission of the disciples as well as its implied reader. Such observations and conclusions, therefore, provide insight into the narrative unity of the Fourth Gospel's resurrection narrative and into the implied author's strategies and implied reader's responses, thus presenting a coherent, unified reading of the Fourth Gospel's resurrection narrative. This work, therefore, highlights the need for future literary-rhetorical research of other resurrection narrative texts to ascertain what these texts have to say for themselves as they now stand and on their on terms, providing temporal process of reading the Synoptic Gospels' resurrection tapestries.

BIBLIOGRAPHY

Abbott, Edwin A. *Johannine Grammar*. London: Adam and Charles Black, 1906.

_____. *Johannine Vocabulary: A Comparison of the Words of the Fourth Gospel with those of the Three*. London: Adam and Charles Black, 1905.

Abrams, M. H. *The Mirror and the Lamp: Romantic Theory and the Critical Tradition*. New York: Oxford University Press, 1953.

Agourides, S. "Peter and John in the Fourth Gospel," in *Papers presented to the Third International Congress on New Testament Studies held at Christ Church, Oxford*, 1965, Part I: New Testament Scriptures, ed. by F. L. Cross, *SE*, vol. IV, 3-7, Berlin: Akademie-Verlag, 1968.

Alsup, John E. *The Post-Resurrection Appearance Stories of the Gospel Tradition: A History-of-Tradition Analysis with Text-Synopsis*. Stuttgart: Calwer Verlag, 1975.

Alter, Robert. *The Art of Biblical Narrative*. New York: Basic Books, Inc., 1981.

_____. *The World of Biblical Literature*. New York: Basic Books, 1991.

Anderson, Janice C. and Stephen D. Moore, eds. *Mark and Method: New Approaches in Biblical Studies*. Minneapolis: Fortress Press, 1992.

Aland, Kurt, Matthew Black, Carlo Martini, Bruce Metzger, and Alan Wikgren, eds. *Novum Testamentum Graece*. 27th ed. Stuttgart: Deutsche Bibelstiftung, 1993.

Appold, M. *The Oneness Motif in the Fourth Gospel: Motif Analysis and Exegetical Probe into the Theology of John*. WUNT 2. Tubingen: Mohr-Siebeck, 1976.

Ashton, John, ed. *The Interpretation of John*. IRT 9. Philadelphia: Fortress Press, 1986.

_____. *Understanding the Fourth Gospel*. Oxford: Clarendon Press, 1991.

Auerbach, E. *Mimesis: The Representation of Reality in Western Literature*. Princeton: Princeton University Press, 1953.

Aune, David E. *The New Testament in its Literary Environment*. Library of Early Christianity 8. Edited by Wayne A. Meeks. Philadelphia: The Westminster Press, 1987.

Bacon, Benjamin W. *The Gospel of the Hellenists*. ed. by Carl H. Kraeling. New York: Henry Holt and Company, 1933.

_____. *The Fourth Gospel in Research and Debate: A Series of Essays on Problems Concerning the Origin and Value of the Anonymous Writings Attributed to the Apostle John*. New Haven: Yale University Press, 1908.

Bailey, J. A. and Lyle D. Vander Broek. *Literary Forms in the New Testament: A Handbook*. Louisville: Westminster/John Knox Press, 1992.

_____. *The Traditions Common to the Gospels of Luke and John*. SNT 7. Leiden: Brill, 1963.

Bal, Mieke. *Narratology: Introduction to the Theory of Narrative.* Toronto: University of Toronto Press, 1985.

_____. "The Laughing Mice, or: On Focalization." *PoT* 2 (1981): 202-210.

Bar-Efrat, S. "Some Observations on the Analysis of Structure in Biblical Narrative." *VT* 30 (1980): 154-173.

Barnhart, Bruno. *The Good Wine: Reading John from the Center.* New York: Paulist Press, 1993.

Barrett, C. K. "John and the Synoptic Gospels." *ExpTim* 85, 8 (1974): 228-233.

_____. *The Gospel According to St. John: Introduction with Commentary and Notes on the Greek Text.* 2d ed. London: SPCK, 1978.

_____. *The Gospel of John and Judaism.* Philadelphia: Fortress, 1975.

Bartholomew, Gilbert L. "Feed my Lambs: John 21:15-19 as Oral Gospel." *Semeia* 39 (1987): 69-96.

Bashford, Bruce. "The Rhetorical Method in Literary Criticism." *Ph& Rh* 9 (1976): 133-146.

Bauckham, Richard. "The Beloved Disciple as Ideal Author." *JSNT* 49 (1993): 21-44.

Beardslee, W. *Literary Criticism of the New Testament.* Philadelphia: Fortress Press, 1970.

Beck, David Richard. "Readers and Anonymous Characters in the Fourth Gospel: The Discipleship Paradigm." Ph.D. dissertation, Duke University, North Carolina, 1995.

Berkenkotter, Carol. "Understanding a Writer's Awareness of Audience." *CCC* 32 (1981): 388-399.

Berlin, Adele. *Poetics and Interpretation of Biblical Narrative*. B&LS 9. Sheffield: The Almond Press, 1983.

Best, E. *Mark: The Gospel as Story*. Edinburgh: T. & T. Clark, 1983.

Bible and Culture Collective. *The Postmodern Bible*. Ed. by Elizabeth A. Castelli, Stephen D. Moore, Gary A. Phillips, and Regina M. Schwartz. New Haven: Yale University Press, 1995.

Bloom, Edward, ed. "In Defense of Authors and Readers." *Nov* 11 (1977): 5-25.

Boomershine, Thomas E. *Mark, The Storyteller: A Rhetorical-Critical Investigation of Mark's Passion and Resurrection Narrative*. New York: Union Theological Seminary, 1974.

Booth, Wayne C. *The Rhetoric of Fiction*, 2d ed. Chicago: The University of Chicago Press, 1983.

Borchert, Gerald L. "John," in *Mercer Commentary on the Bible*, ed. by Watson E. Mills and Richard F. Wilson, 1043-1082. Macon: Mercer University Press, 1995.

Botha, E. "The Case of Johannine Irony Reopened I: Suggestions, Alternative Approaches." *Neotest* 25, 2 (1991b): 221-232.

_____. "The Case of Johannine Irony Reopened II: The Problematic Current Situation." *Neotest* 25, 2 (1991a): 209-220.

Bowen, C. "The Fourth Gospel as Dramatic Material." *JBL* 49 (1930): 292-305.

Bradley, Mark A. "The Function of Questions in the Fourth Gospel: A Narrative-Critical Inquiry (John)." Ph.D. dissertation, Golden Gate Theological Seminary, California, 1995.

Bratcher, R. "'The Jews' in the Gospel of John." *BT* 26, 4 (1975): 401-409.

Braun, Willi. "Resisting John: Ambivalent Redactor and Defensive Reader of the Fourth Gospel." *SR* 19 (1990): 59-71.

Bremond, C. "The Narrative Message." *Semeia* 10 (1978): 5-56.

Briggs, Robert C. *Interpreting the New Testament Today: An Introduction to Methods and Issues in the Study of the New Testament*, 2d ed. Nashville: Abingdon Press, 1973.

Brodie, Thomas L. *The Gospel According to John: A Literary and Theological Commentary*. New York: Oxford University Press, 1993.

_____. *The Quest for the Origin of John's Gospel: A Source-Oriented Approach*. New York: Oxford University Press, 1993.

Bronzwaer, W. "Implied Author, Extradiegetic Narrator and Public Reader." *Neophil* 62 (1978): 1-18.

_____. "Mieke Bal's Concept of Focalization: A Critical Note." *PoT* 2, 2 (1981): 193-201.

Brown, Raymond E. *The Gospel According to John*. ABS vols. 29-29A. Garden City: Doubleday & Co., 1966 and 1970.

_____. "Roles of Women in the Fourth Gospel." *TS* 36 (1975): 688-699.

Brown, Schuyler. "John and the Resistant Reader: The Fourth Gospel after Nicea and the Holocaust." *JLS* 5 (1989): 252-61.

_____. "Reader Response: Demythologizing the Text." *NTS* 34 (1988): 232-237.

Bruns, J. E. *The Art and Thought of John*. New York: Herder and Herder, 1969.

_____. "The Use of Time in the Fourth Gospel." *NTS* 13 (1967): 285-290.

Bultmann, R. *History of the Synoptic Tradition*, rev ed. Translated by John Marsh. Peabody: Hendrickson Publishers, 1963.

_____. *Primitive Christianity in Its Contemporary Setting*. New York: Meridian, 1956.

_____. "Rudolf Bultmann's Review of C. H. Dodd: The Interpretation of the Fourth Gospel." Translated by W. G. Robinson, reprinted from *HDB* 27, 2 (1963): 9-22.

_____. *The Gospel of John: A Commentary*. Translated by G. R. Beasley-Murray, R. W. N. Hoare, and J. K. Riches. Philadelphia: Westminster Press, 1971.

Burge, Gary M. *Interpreting the Gospel of John*. Guides to New Testament Exegesis. Grand Rapids: Baker Book House, 1992.

Burnett, Fred W. "Postmodern Biblical Exegesis: The Eve of Historical Criticism." *Semeia* 51 (1990): 51-80.

Buse, I. "St. John and the Marcan Passion Narrative." *NTS* 4 (1957): 215-19.

Buttrick, David G. *The Mystery and the Passion: A Homiletic Reading of the Gospel Traditions*. Minneapolis: Fortress Press, 1992.

Calinescu, Matei. *Rereading*. New Haven: Yale University Press, 1993.

Carson, D. A. "Current Source Criticism of the Fourth Gospel: Some Methodological Questions." *JBL* 97, 3 (1978): 411-429.

_____. *The Gospel According to John*. Grand Rapids: William B. Eerdmans Publishing Company, 1991.

_____. "Selected Recent Studies of the Fourth Gospel." *Themelios* 14 (January-February 1989): 57-64.

_____. "Understanding Misunderstanding in the Fourth Gospel." *TB* 33 (1982): 59-91.

Cassian, A. "John XXI." *NTS* 3 (1956-57): 132-136.

Cassidy, Richard J. *John's Gospel in New Perspective: Christology and the Realities of Roman Power*. Maryknoll: Orbis Books, 1992.

Chambers, Ross. "Commentary in Literary Texts." *CI* 5 (1975): 323-337.

Chatman, Seymour. *Story and Discourse: Narrative Structure in Fiction and Film*. Ithaca: Cornell University Press, 1978.

Cline, David J. A., David M. Gunn, and Alan J. Hauser. *Art and Meaning: Rhetoric in Biblical Literature*. JSOTSup 19. Sheffield: JSOT Press, 1982.

Collins, Adela Y. "New Testament Perspectives: The Gospel of John." *JSOT* 22 (1982): 47-53.

Collins, J. C. "The Rediscovery of Biblical Narrative." *CS* 21 (1981): 45-58.

Collins, Raymond F. *Introduction to the New Testament*. Garden City: Doubleday & Company, 1983.

_____. "The Representative Figures in the Fourth Gospel." *DoR* 94 (1976): 118-132.

_____. *These Things Have Been Written: Studies on the Fourth Gospel*. Louvain: Eerdmans, 1990.

Connick, M. "The Dramatic Character of the Fourth Gospel." *JBL* 67 (1948): 159-69.

Countryman, Louis William. *The Mystical Way in the Fourth Gospel: Crossing Over into God*. Rev ed. Valley Forge: Trinity Press International, 1995.

Craig, William L. *Assessing the New Testament Evidence for the Historicity of the Resurrection of Jesus*. Lewiston: E. Mellen Press, 1989.

Cribbs, F. L. "A Study of the Contacts That Exists between St. Luke and St. John." SBLSP, 2:1-93. Cambridge: SBL, 1973.

Crosman, Inge. "Reference and the Reader." *PoT* 4, 1 (1983): 89-97.

Crosman, Robert. "How Readers Make Meaning." *ColLit* 9 (1982): 207-215.

Crossan, John D. "Waking the Bible: Biblical Hermeneutic and Literary Imagination." *Int* 32 (1978): 269-285.

Cullmann, Oscar. *The Johannine Circle*. Translated by J. Bowden. London: SCM Press, 1976.

Culpepper, R. Alan. *Anatomy of the Fourth Gospel: A Study in Literary Design*. Philadelphia: Fortress Press, 1983.

Daniel, Elinor Perkins. "A Rhetorical Analysis of the Resurrection Appearance Narrative in the Christian Gospels." Ph.D. dissertation, Georgia State University, Georgia, 1995.

Davies, Margaret. *Rhetoric and Reference in the Fourth Gospel*. JSNTSup 69. Sheffield: JSOT Press, 1992.

Davis, Robert C. and Ronald Schleifer. *Contemporary Literary Criticism: Literary and Cultural Studies*. Rev. ed. New York: Longman, 1989.

de Boer, M. "Narrative Criticism, Historical Criticism, and the Gospel of John." *JSNT* 47 (1992): 35-48.

de Jonge, M. "The Beloved Disciple and Date of the Gospel of John," in *Text and Interpretation*, ed. by F. S. M. Black, E. Best, and R. Mcl. Wilson, 99-114. Cambridge: University Press, 1979.

_____. "Jesus as Prophet and King in the Fourth Gospel." *ELT* 49, 1 (1973): 161-177.

de La Potterie, Ignace. *The Hour of Jesus: The Passion and Resurrection of Jesus According to John: Text and Spirit*. London: St. Paul Publications, 1989.

Deeks, David. "The Structure of the Fourth Gospel." *NTS* (1968-69): 107-128.

Detweiler, Robert. "After the New Criticism: Contemporary Methods of Literary Interpretation," in *Orientation by Disorientation: Studies in Literary Criticism and Biblical Literary Criticism in Honor of William A. Beardslee*, ed. by Richard A. Spencer, 1-23. PTMS 35. Pittsburgh: Pickwick, 1980.

Devenish, Philip E. "The So-called Resurrection of Jesus and Explicit Christian Faith: Wittgenstein's Philosophy and Marxsen's Exegesis as Linguistic Therapy." *JAAR* 51, 2 (1983): 171-190.

Dodd, C. H. *About the Gospels*. Cambridge: Cambridge University Press, 1950.

_____. *Historical Tradition in the Fourth Gospel*. Cambridge: Cambridge University Press, 1963.

_____. *The Interpretation of the Fourth Gospel*. Cambridge: Cambridge University Press, 1953.

Dods, M. *The Gospel of John*. London: Hodder & Stoughton, 1903.

Dolezel, Lubomir. "Eco and His Model Reader." *PoT* 2 (1980): 181-188.

_____. "Extensional and Intensional Narrative Worlds." *Poetics* 8 (1979): 193-221.

_____. "Narrative Modalities." *JLS* 5 (1976): 5-15.

Doty, William G. "Fundamental Questions about Literary-Critical Methodology: A Review Article." *JAAR* 40 (1972): 521-527.

Duke, Paul D. *Irony in the Fourth Gospel*. Atlanta: John Knox Press, 1985.

Dunn, J. D. G. "Let John be John," in *Das Evangelium und die Evangelien*, ed. by P. Stuhlmacher, 309-39. WUNT 28. Mohr: Tübingen, 1983.

Eagleton, Terry. *Literary Theory: An Introduction*. Minneapolis: University of Minnesota Press, 1983.

Eco, Umberto. *The Role of the Reader*. Bloomington: Indiana University Press, 1979.

_____. "The Theory of Signs and the Role of the Reader." *BMMLA* 14 (1981): 35-55.

Ede, Lisa and Andrea Lunsford. "Audience Addressed/Audience Invoked: The Role of Audience in Composition Theory and Pedagogy." *CCC* 35 (1984): 140-154.

Edwards, H. E. *The Disciple Who Wrote These Things*. London: Clarke, 1953.

Egan, Kieran. "What is a Plot?" *NLH* 9 (1978): 455-473.

Eller, V. *The Beloved Disciple*. Grand Rapids: Eerdmans, 1987.

Ellis, Peter F. *The Genius of John. A Composition-Critical Commentary on the Fourth Gospel*. Collegeville: Liturgical Press, 1984.

Eslinger, Lyle. "The Wooing of the Woman at the Well: Jesus, The Reader and Reader-Response Criticism." *JLit&Th* 1, 2 (September 1987): 167-183.

Evans, C. F. *Resurrection and the New Testament*. Naperville: Alec R. Allenson, Inc., 1970.

Felder, Cain Hope., ed. *Stony the Road We Trod: African American Biblical Interpretation*. Minneapolis: Fortress Press, 1991.

Filson, F. "Who was the Beloved Disciple?" *JBL* 68 (1949): 83-8.

Fiore, B. "N. T. Rhetoric and Rhetorical Criticism." *ABD* 5 (1992): 715-719.

Fiorenza, Elisabeth S. *Bread Not Stone: The Challenge of Feminist Biblical Interpretation*. Boston: Beacon Press, 1984.

Fish, Stanley E. *Is There a Text in This Class?: The Authority of Interpretive Communities*. Cambridge: Harvard University Press, 1980.

_____. *Text and Texture: Close Readings of Selected Biblical Texts*. New York: Schoken, 1979.

Fishbane, Michael. "Recent Work on Biblical Narrative." *Prooftexts* 1 (1981): 91-104.

Flanagan, Neil. "The Gospel of John as Drama." *BibTo* 19 (1981): 264-70.

Forestell, J. T. *The Word of the Cross: Salvation as Revelation in the Fourth Gospel*. AB 57. Rome: Biblical Institute, 1974.

Forster, E. M. *Aspects of the Novel*. New York: Penguin Books, 1962.

Fortna, R. *The Fourth Gospel and its Predecessor*. Edinburgh: T. & T. Clark, 1989.

_____. *The Gospel of Signs: A Reconstruction of the Narrative Source Underlying the Fourth Gospel*. SNTSMS 11. Cambridge: Cambridge University Press, 1970.

Fowler, R. S. "Who is the 'Reader' in Reader-Response Criticism." *Semeia* 31 (1985): 5-23.

Fowler, Robert M. *Let the Reader Understand: Reader-Response Criticism and the Gospel of Mark*. Minneapolis: Fortress Press, 1991.

_____. "Reading Matthew Reading Mark: Observing the First Step toward Meaning-as-Reference in the Synoptic Gospels," in K. H. Richards, ed., SBLSP, 1-16. Atlanta: Scholars Press, 1986.

France, R. T. and David Wenham, eds. *Gospel Perspectives: Studies of History and Tradition in the Four Gospels*. Vols. I and II. JSNTSup 32. Sheffield: JSOT Press, 1980, 1981, and 1983.

Freed, E. D. *Old Testament Quotations in the Gospel of John*. SNT 11. Leiden: Brill, 1965.

_____. "The Son of Man in the Fourth Gospel." *JBL* 86, 4 (1967): 402-409.

Freedman, William. "The Literary Motif: A Definition and Evaluation." *Nov* 4 (1971): 123-131.

Freud, Elizabeth. *The Return of the Reader: Reader-Response Criticism.* New Accents. London and New York: Methuen, 1987.

Friedman, Norman. "Forms of the Plot," in *The Theory of the Novel*, ed. by Philip Stevick, 91-94. New York: The Free Press, 1967.

Frye, N. *Anatomy of Criticism.* Princeton: Princeton University Press, 1971.

Frye, Roland M. "A Literary Perspective for the Criticism of the Gospels," in *Jesus and Man's Hope: Essays from the Pittsburgh Festival on the Gospel*, vol. 2, ed. by Donald G. Miller and Dikran Y. Hadidian, 193-221. Pittsburgh: Pittsburgh, Theological Seminary, 1971.

_____. "Literary Criticism and Gospel Criticism." *TToday* 36 (1979): 207-219.

Fuller, Reginald H. *The Formation of the Resurrection Narratives.* New York: Macmillan, 1971.

_____. "The Passion, Death and Resurrection of Jesus According to St. John." *CS* 25 (1, 1986): 51-63.

Funk, Robert W. *The Poetics of Biblical Narrative.* Sonoma: Polebridge Press, 1989.

Gaffney, J. "Believing and Knowing in the Fourth Gospel." *TS* 26, 2 (1965): 215-241.

Garvie, Alfred E. *The Beloved Disciple: Studies of the Fourth Gospel.* London: Hodder and Stroughton Limited, 1922.

Garvin, Harry R., ed. *Rhetoric, Literature and Interpretation.* Bucknell Review 28 no. 1. Lewisburg: Bucknell University Press, 1983.

Genette, Gérard. *Narrative Discourse: An Essay in Method.* Translated by Jane E. Lewin. New York: Cornell University Press, 1980.

Gerhart, Mary. "The Restoration of Biblical Narrative." *Semeia* 46 (1989): 13-29.

Giblin C. H. "Suggestion, Negative Response and Positive Action in St. John's Portrayal of Jesus." *NTS* 26 (1980): 197-211.

_____. "The Tripartite Narrative Structure of John's Gospel." *Bib* 72 (1991): 449-468.

Givin, C. H. "Suggestion, Negative Response and Positive Action." *NTS* 26 (1979-80): 191-211.

Grant, Robert M. and David Tracy. *A Short History of the Interpretation of the Bible.* Rev. ed. Minneapolis: Fortress Press, 1984.

Green, Joel B., ed. *Hearing the New Testament: Strategies for Interpretation.* Grand Rapids: William B. Eerdmans Publishing Company, 1995.

Guthrie, Donald. *New Testament Introduction,* rev. ed. Leicester: Apollos and Downers Grove: InterVarsity Press, 1990.

Haenchen, E. *A Commentary on the Gospel of John,* 2 vols. Translated by R. W. Funk. Philadelphia: Fortress Press, 1984.

_____. "History and Interpretation in the Johannine Passion Narrative." *Int* 24 (1970): 198-219.

Hagg, Thomas. *The Novel in Antiquity.* Berkeley: University of California Press, 1983.

Hanson, Anthony T. *The Prophetic Gospel: A Study of John and the Old Testament.* Edinburgh: T & T Clark, 1991.

Harner, P. *The "I Am" of the Fourth Gospel*. FBBS 26. Philadelphia: Fortress, 1970.

Harris, Wendell V. *Dictionary of Concepts in Literary Criticism and Theory*. New York: Greenwood Press, 1992.

Hartman, Lars. "An Attempt at a Text-Centered Exegesis of John 21." *ST* 38 (1984): 29-45.

_____ and Birger Olsson, eds. *Aspects on the Johannine Literature: Papers Presented at a Conference of Scandinavian New Testament Exegetes at Uppsala, June 16-19, 1986*. ConBNT 18. Uppsala: Almqvist and Wiksell International, 1987.

Harvey, Van Austin. *The Historian and the Believer: The Morality of Historical Knowledge and Christian Belief*. New York: Macmillan, 1966.

Hawkin, David J. "The Function of the Beloved Disciple Motif in the Johannine Redaction." *LTP* 33 (1977): 135-150.

Heil, John Paul. *The Gospel of Mark as a Model for Action: A Reader-Response Commentary*. Mahwah: Paulist Press, 1992.

Hellenga, Robert R. "What is a Literary Experience Like?" *NLH* 14 (1982): 105-115.

Hernadi, Paul, ed. *What is Literature?* Bloomington: Indiana University Press, 1981.

Hirsch, E. D. *The Aims of Interpretation*. Chicago: University of Chicago Press, 1976.

_____. *Validity in Interpretation*. New Haven: Yale University Press, 1967.

Holman, C. Hugh and William Harmon. *A Handbook to Literature*. 5th ed. New York: Macmillan Publishing Company, 1986.

Hopkins, Anthony Dennis. "A Narratological Approach to the Development of Faith in the Gospel of John." Ph.D. dissertation, The Southern Baptist Theological Seminary, Texas, 1993.

Hoskyns, E. C. *The Fourth Gospel*. 2d ed, London: Faber and Faber, 1947.

Howard, J. K. "Passover and Eucharist in the Fourth Gospel." *SJT* 20. (1967): 330-37.

Howard, W. F. *The Fourth Gospel in Recent Criticism and Interpretation*. Revised by C. K. Barrett. London: Epworth, 1955.

Hunter, A. M. *According to John*. Philadelphia: Westminster, 1968.

Iser, Wolfgang. *Aesthetic Experience and Literary Hermeneutics: Theory and History of Literature*, vol. 3. Translated by Michael Shaw. Minneapolis: University of Minnesota Press, 1982.

_____. *The Act of Reading: A Theory of Aesthetic Response*. Baltimore: Johns Hopkins University Press, 1978.

Jeremias, Joachim. *The Eucharistic Words of Jesus*. Rev. ed. Philadelphia: Trinity Press International, 1990.

Johnson, N. E. "The Beloved Disciple of the Fourth Gospel." *CQR* 167, 364 (1966): 278-291.

Johnston, G. *The Spirit-Paraclete in the Gospel of John*. SNTSMS 12. Cambridge: University, 1970.

Johnston, Robert K. "Interpreting Scripture: Literary Criticism and Evangelical Hermeneutics." *C&L* 22 (1982): 33-48.

Kawin, Bruce F. *Telling it Again and Again: Repetition in Literature and Film*. Ithaca: Cornell University Press, 1972.

Keener, Craig S. *The IVP Bible Background Commentary: New Testament*. Downers Grove: InterVarsity Press, 1993.

Kelber, Werner H. "Narrative and Disclosure: Mechanisms of Concealing, Revealing, and Revealing." *Semeia* 43 (1988): 1-20.

_____. *Mark's Story of Jesus*. Philadelphia: Fortress Press, 1979.

_____. *The Oral and Written Gospel*. Philadelphia: Fortress Press, 1983.

Kennedy, George. *Classical Rhetoric and Its Christian and Secular Tradition from Ancient to Modern Times*. Chapel Hill: University of North Carolina Press, 1980.

_____. *New Testament Interpretation through Rhetorical Criticism*. Chapel Hill: University of North Carolina Press, 1984.

Kermode, F. "John," in *The Literary Guide to the Bible*, ed. by F. Kermode and R. Alter, 440-466. Cambridge: The Belknap Press of Harvard University Press, 1987.

_____. *The Genesis of Secrecy: On the Interpretation of Narrative*. Cambridge: Harvard University Press, 1979.

Kikawada, Isaac M. "Some Proposals for the Definition of Rhetorical Criticism." *Sem* 5 (1977): 67-90.

Kilgallen, John J. *A Brief Commentary on the Gospel of John*. Lewiston: Mellen Biblical Press, 1992.

Kingsbury, J. D. *Matthew as Story*. Philadelphia: Fortress Press, 1986.

Kinniburgh, E. "The Johannine 'Son of Man'." *SE* 4 (1965): 64-71.

Kopas, Jane. "Jesus and Women: John's Gospel." *TToday* 41 (1984): 201-205.

Kort, Wesley A. *Story, Text, and Scripture: Literary Interests in Biblical Narrative*. University Park: The Pennsylvania State University Press, 1987.

Kostenberger, Andreas Johannes. "The Mission of Jesus and the Disciples According to the Fourth Gospel: With Implications for the Fourth Gospel's Purpose and the Mission of the Contemporary Church (John)." Ph.D. dissertation, Trinity Evangelical Divinity School, Illinois, 1994.

Koster, H. "One Jesus and Four Primitive Gospels." *HTR* 61, 2 (1968): 203-247.

Köster, Craig R. *Symbolism in the Fourth Gospel: Meaning, Mystery, Community*. Minneapolis: Fortress Press, 1995.

Kotze, P. "John and Reader's Response." *Neotest* 19 (1985): 50-63.

Kugel, James. "On the Bible and Literary Criticism." *Prooftexts* 1 (1981): 217-236.

Kurz, William S. "The Beloved Disciple and Implied Reader." *BTB* 19, 3 (1989): 100-107.

_____. *Reading Luke-Acts: Dynamics of Biblical Narrative*. Louisville: Westminster/John Knox Press, 1993.

Kuyper, L. J. "Grace and Truth. An Old Testament Description of God and Its Use in the Johannine Gospel." *Int* 18, 1 (1964): 3-19.

Kysar, Robert. "Community and Gospel: Vectors in Fourth Gospel Criticism." *Int* 21, 4 (1977): 355-366.

_____. *John's Story of Jesus*. Philadelphia: Fortress Press, 1984.

_____. *The Fourth Evangelist and His Gospel: An Examination of Contemporary Scholarship*. Minneapolis: Augsburg, 1975.

_____. "The Fourth Gospel: A Report on Recent Research," in *ANRW*; *Geschichte und Kultur*, II 25.3, 2389-2480, 1972.

_____. "The Source Analysis of the Fourth Gospel. A Growing Consensus?" *NTS* 15, 2 (1973): 134-152.

Lanser, Susan. *The Narrative Act: Point of View in Prose Fiction*. Princeton: Princeton University Press, 1981.

Lategan, B. J. "Introduction: Coming to Grips with the Reader in Biblical Literature." *Semeia* 49 (1989): 3-20.

Lee, Dorothy A. *The Symbolic Narratives of the Fourth Gospel: The Interplay of Form and Meaning*. JSNTSup 95. Sheffield: Sheffield Academic Press, 1994.

Leitch, Vincent B. *American Literary Criticism from the Thirties to the Eighties*. New York: Columbia University Press, 1988.

Lemmer, H. "A Possible Understanding by the Implied Reader, of Some of the *Coming-Going-Being-Sent* Pronouncements, in the Johannine Farewell Discourses." *Neotest* 25, 2 (1991): 289-310.

Lentricchia, Frank. *After the New Criticism*. Chicago: University of Chicago Press, 1980.

Leon-Dufour, Xavier. "Towards a Symbolic Reading of the Fourth Gospel." *NTS* 27 (1981): 439-456.

Liebert, E. "That you may Believe: The Fourth Gospel and Structural Development." *BTB* 4 (1984): 67-73.

Lightfoot, R. H. *Saint John's Gospel*. Edited by C. F. Evans. London: Oxford University Press, 1956.

Lindars, B. "The Composition of John XX." *NTS* 7 (1960): 142-147.

_____. *Behind the Fourth Gospel*. Studies in Creative Criticism 3. London: SPCK, 1971.

_____. *John*. New Testament Guides. Sheffield: Sheffield Academic Press, 1990.

_____. *The Gospel of John*. London: Oliphants, 1972.

Linnemann, Eta. *Historical Criticism of the Bible: Methodology or Ideology?* Grand Rapids: Baker Book House, 1990.

Lorenzen, Thorwald. *Resurrection and Discipleship: Interpretive Models, Biblical Reflections, Theological Consequences*. Maryknoll: Orbis Books, 1995.

Lotman, J. M. "Point of View in a Text." *NLH* 6 (1975): 339-352.

_____. "The Text and the Structure of Its Audience." Translated by Ann Shukman. *NLH* 14 (1982): 81-87.

Louis, R. R. Gross, with James S. Ackerman and Thayer S. Warshaw, eds. *Literary Interpretations of Biblical Narratives*. Vols. I and II. Nashville: Abingdon, 1974 and 1982.

Lüdemann, Gerd. *The Resurrection of Jesus: History, Experience, Theology*. Minneapolis: Fortress Press, 1994.

Maddox, R. *The Purpose of Luke-Acts*. Edinburgh: T. & T. Clark, 1982.

Magness, J. Lee. *Sense and Absence: Structure and Suspension in the Ending of Mark's Gospel*. Atlanta: Scholars Press, 1986.

Mahoney, Robert. *Two Disciples at the Tomb: The Background and Message of John 20.1-10*. Frankfurt: Herbert Lang Bern, 1974.

Mailloux, Steven. "How to be Persuasive in Literary Theory: The Case of Wolfgang Iser." *Cent* 1 (1981): 65-73.

_____. *Interpretive Conventions: The Reader in the Study of American Fiction.* Ithaca: Cornell University Press, 1982.

_____. *Rhetorical Power.* Ithaca: Cornell University Press, 1989.

Malbon, E. S. "Galilee and Jerusalem: History and Literature in Markan Interpretation." *CBQ* 44 (1982): 242-55.

_____ and Adele Berlin, eds. *Characterization in Biblical Literature. Semeia* 63, *SBL*, gen ed. Daniel Patte. Atlanta: Scholars Press, 1993.

Malherbe, Abraham J. *Ancient Epistolary Theorists.* Atlanta: Scholars Press, 1988.

Mandelbaum, M. "A Note on History as Narrative." *H&T* 6 (1967): 416-17.

Marsh, J. *Saint John.* Harmondsworth: Penguin, 1968.

Martin, Wallace. *Recent Theories of Narrative.* Ithaca and London: Cornell University Press, 1986.

Martyn, J. Louis. *History and Theology in the Fourth Gospel,* rev ed. Nashville: Abingdon Press, 1979.

Marxsen, Willi. *Jesus and Easter: Did God Raise the Historical Jesus from the Dead?* Translated by Victor P. Furnish. Nashville: Abingdon Press, 1990.

_____. *The Resurrection of Jesus of Nazareth.* Translated by Margaret Kohl. Philadelphia: Fortress Press, 1970.

Mattill, A. J. "Johannine Communities behind the Fourth Gospel: George Richter's Analysis." *TS* 38, 2 (1977): 294-315.

Maynard, A. H. "The Role of Peter in the Fourth Gospel." *NTS* 20 (1984): 531-48.

McConnell, Frank, ed. *The Bible and the Narrative Tradition.* New York and Oxford: Oxford University Press, 1986.

McDonald, James I. H. *The Resurrection: Narrative and Belief.* London: SPCK, 1989.

McKnight, Edgar V. and Elizabeth S. Malbon. *The New Literary Criticism and the New Testament.* Valley Forge: Trinity Press, 1994.

_____. *Meaning in Texts.* Philadelphia: Fortress Press, 1979.

_____. *Postmodern use of the Bible: The Emergence of Reader-Oriented Criticism.* Nashville: Abingdon Press, 1988.

_____. *The Bible and the Reader: An Introduction to Literary Criticism.* Philadelphia: Fortress Press, 1985.

McNamara, M. "The Ascension and the Exaltation of Christ in the Fourth Gospel." *SC* 19, 47 (1967): 65-73.

McPolin, J. "Mission in the Fourth Gospel." *ITQ* 36, 2 (1969): 113- 122.

Meeks, Wayne A. "Galilee and Judea in the Fourth Gospel." *JBL* 85 (1966): 159-169.

_____. "Galilee and Judea in the Fourth Gospel." *JBL* 85, 2 (1966): 159-169.

Menken, M. J. J. *Numerical Literary Techniques in John: The Fourth Evangelist's Use of Numbers of Words and Syllables.* Leiden: E. J. Brill, 1985.

Metzger, Bruce M. *A Textual Commentary on the Greek New Testament*, 3rd ed.; London: United Bible Societies, 1971.

_____. *The Text of the New Testament: Its Transmission, Correction and Restoration.* Rev. ed. New York; Oxford, 1968.

Meyer, Ben F. "The Challenges of Text and Reader to Historical-Critical Method," in *The Bible and Its Readers*, ed. by Wm. Beuken, Sean Freyne, and Anton Weiler, 3-12. Philadelphia: Trinity Press, 1991.

Minear, Paul S. "'We Don't Know Where…' John 20:2." *Int* 30 (1976): 115-139.

_____. "The Audience of the Fourth Evangelist." *Int* 31 (1977): 339-354.

_____. "The Original Function of Jn. 21." *JBL* 102 (1983): 85-98.

Miranda, Jose P. *Being and the Messiah: The Message of St. John.* Maryknoll: Orbis, 1977.

Mlakuzhyil, George. *The Christocentric Literary Structure of the Fourth Gospel.* AnBib 117. Roma: Editrice Pontificio Istituto Biblico, 1987.

Moeller, H. "Wisdom Motifs and John's Gospel." *BEST* 6, 3 (1963): 93-98.

Moloney, Francis J. "Who is 'the Reader' in/of the Fourth Gospel?" *ABR* 40 (1992): 20-33.

_____. *Belief in the Word. Reading the Fourth Gospel: John 1-4.* Minneapolis: Fortress Press, 1993.

_____. *Glory not Dishonor: Reading John 13-21.* Minneapolis: Fortress Press, 1998.

_____. *The Gospel of John.* Collegeville: The Liturgical Press, 1998.

Moore, Robert R. "Soteriology and Structure: An Evangelical Study of the Relation between the Soteriology and the Present Literary

Structure of the Fourth Gospel." Ph.D. dissertation, Emory University, Georgia, 1981.

Moore, Stephen D. "Rifts in (a reading of) the Fourth Gospel, or: Does Johannine Irony still Collapse in a Reading that Draws Attention to Itself?" *Neotest* 23, 1 (1989): 5-17.

_____. "Are the Gospels Unified Narratives?" in SBLSP, ed. by K. H. Richards, 443-458. Atlanta: Scholars Press, 1987.

_____. *Literary Criticism and the Gospels: The Theoretical Challenges.* New Haven: Yale University Press, 1989.

_____. *Mark and Luke in Poststructuralist Perspectives: Jesus Begins to Write.* New Haven: Yale University Press, 1992.

_____. "Negative Hermeneutics, Insubstantial Texts: Stanley Fish and the Biblical Interpreter." *JAAR* 54 (Winter 1986): 707-19.

Morgenthaler, Robert. *Statistik des Neutestamentlichen Worrschatzes.* Zürick: Gotthelf-Verlag, 1958 and 1982.

Morris, L. *Studies in the Fourth Gospel.* Grand Rapids: Eerdmans, 1969.

_____. *The Gospel According to John: The New International Commentary on the New Testament.* Rev. ed. Grand Rapids: Eerdmans, 1995.

Morton, A. Q. and J. McLeman. *The Genesis of John.* Edinburgh: The Saint Andrews Press, 1990.

Mosher, Harold F. "A New Synthesis of Narratology." *PT* 1 (1980): 171-186.

Moule, C. F. D. "The Individualism of the Fourth Gospel." *NovT* 5 (1962): 171-190.

Muilenburg, J. "Literary Form in the Fourth Gospel." *JBL* 51 (1932): 40-53.

Myers, Ched. *Binding the Strong Man. A Political Reading of Mark's Story of Jesus*. New York: Orbis Books, 1990.

Neirynck, F. "John 21." *NTS* 36 (1990): 321-336.

_____. *Jean et les synoptiques: Examen critique de l'exegese de M. E. Boismard*. BETL 49. Louvain: Louvain University Press, 1979.

_____. "John and the Synoptics: The Empty Tomb Stories." *NTS* 30 (1984): 161-187.

Newman, Barclay M. "Some Observations Regarding the Argument, Structure and Literary Characteristics of the Gospel of John." *BT* 26 (1975): 234-239.

_____. and Eugene A. Nida. *A Translator's Handbook on the Gospel of John*. New York: United Bible Society, 1980.

Newsom, Carol A. and Sharon H. Ringe, eds. *The Women's Bible Commentary*. Louisville: Westminster/John Knox Press, 1992.

Neyrey, Jerome H. *The Resurrection Stories*. Wilmington: Del. M. Glazier, 1988.

Nicholson, G. *Death as Departure: The Johannine Descent-Ascent Schema*. SBLDS 63. Chico: Scholars Press, 1983.

Nicol, W. "The History of Johannine Research during the Past Century." *Neotest* 6 (1972): 8-18.

_____. *The Semeia in the Fourth Gospel*. SNT 32. Leiden: Brill, 1972.

Niebuhr, Richard R. *Resurrection and Historical Reason: A Study of Theological Method*. New York: Charles Scribner's Sons, 1957.

O'Collins, Gerald. *Interpreting the Resurrection: Examining the Major Problems in the Stories of Jesus' Resurrection*. New York: Paulist Press, 1988.

_____. *Jesus Risen: An Historical, Fundamental and Systematic Examination of Christ's Resurrection*. New York: Paulist Press, 1987.

_____. *The Resurrection of Jesus Christ*. Valley Forge: Judson Press, 1973.

_____. *What are They Saying about the Resurrection?* New York: Paulist Press, 1978.

O'Day, Gail R. "John," in *The Women's Bible Commentary*, ed. C. Newsom and S. Ringe, 293-304. London: SPCK and Louisville: Westminster/John Knox Press, 1992.

_____. "Narrative Mode and Theological Claim: A Study in the Fourth Gospel." *JBL* 105, 4 (1986): 657-668.

_____. *Revelation in the Fourth Gospel*. Philadelphia: Fortress Press, 1986.

O'Rourke, John J. "Asides in the Gospel of John." *NT* 21 (1979): 210-219.

_____. "*Eis* and *en* in John." *BT* 25 (1974): 139-142.

_____. "The Historical Present in the Gospel of John." *JBL* 93 (1974): 585-590.

Odeberg, H. *The Fourth Gospel Interpreted in its Relation to Contemporaneous Religious Currents in Palestine and the Hellenistic-Oriental World*. Uppsala: Almquist and Wiksells, 1927.

Olsson, Birger. *Structure and Meaning in the Fourth Gospel: A Text Linguistic Analysis of John 2:1-11 and 4:1-42*. Translated by Jean Gray. ConBNT 6. Lund: Gleerup, 1974.

Ong, Walter J. *Orality and Literacy: The Technologizing of the Word*. London: Methuen Co., 1982.

Osborne, Grant R. *The Resurrection Narratives: A Redactional Study*. Grand Rapids: Baker Book House, 1984.

Ostenstad, Gunnar. "The Structure of the Fourth Gospel: Can it be Defined Objectively?" *ST* 45, 1 (1991): 33-55.

Painter, John. "Johannine Symbols: A Case Study in Epistemology." *JThSoAfrica* 27 (1979): 26-41.

Pamment, M. "Focus in the Fourth Gospel." *ExpTim* 97 (1985): 71-75.

_____. "The Meaning of '*dokas*' in the Fourth Gospel." *ZNW* 74 (1983): 12-16.

Pancaro, S. "'People of God' in St. John's Gospel." *NTS* 16, 2 (1970): 114-129.

_____. *The Law in the Fourth Gospel: The Torah and the Gospel, Moses and Jesus, Judaism and Christianity According to John*. NovTSup 42. Leiden: E. J. Brill, 1975.

_____. "The Relationship of the Church to Israel in the Gospel of John." *NTS* 21, 3 (1975): 396-405.

Parker, Pierson. "Two Editions of John." *JBL* 75 (1956): 304-314.

Parsons, Mikeal C. *The Departure of Jesus in Luke-Acts: The Ascension Narratives in Context*. Sheffield: JSOT Press, 1987.

Patte, Daniel. *Ethics of Biblical Interpretation: A Reevaluation.* Louisville: Westminster John Knox Press, 1995.

_____. *The Gospel According to Matthew: A Structural Commentary on Matthew's Faith.* Philadelphia: Fortress Press, 1978.

_____. *The Religious Dimensions of Biblical Texts: Greimas's Structural Semiotics and Biblical Exegesis.* Atlanta: Scholars Press, 1990.

_____ and Patte, A. *Structural Exegesis: From Theory to Practice.* Philadelphia: Fortress Press, 1978.

Perelman, Chaim. *The Realm of Rhetoric.* Translated by Wm. Kluback. Notre Dame: University of Notre Dame Press, 1982.

Perkins, Pheme. *Resurrection: New Testament Witness and Contemporary Reflection.* Garden City: Doubleday, 1984.

Perrin, Norman. *The Resurrection: According to Matthew, Mark, and Luke.* Philadelphia: Fortress Press, 1977.

Perry, Charles Austin. *The Resurrection Promise: An Interpretation of the Easter Narratives.* Grand Rapids: W. B. Eerdmans Pub. Co., 1986.

Perry, John Michael. *Exploring the Resurrection of Jesus.* Kansas, City: Sheed & Ward, 1993.

Petersen, Norman R. "Literary Criticism in Biblical Studies," in *Orientation by Disorientation: Studies in Literary Criticism and Biblical Literary Criticism in Honor of William A. Beardslee*, ed. by Richard A. Spencer, 25-50. PTMS 35. Pittsburgh: Pickwick, 1980.

_____. "The Reader in the Gospel." *Neotest* 18 (1984): 38-51.

_____. *Literary Criticism for New Testament Critics.* Philadelphia: Fortress Press, 1978.

_____. "Point of view in Mark's Narrative." *Semeia* 12 (1978): 110-113.

_____. "When is the End not the End? Literary Reflections on the Ending of Mark's Narrative." *Int* 34 (1980): 157-166.

Peterson, Robert A. *Getting to Know John's Gospel: A Fresh Look at Its Main Ideas.* Phillipsburg: Presbyterian and Reformed Publishing Company and Great Commission Publication, 1989.

Pfitzner, V. C. "They knew it was the Lord: The Place and Function of John 21.1-14 in the Gospel of John." *LuthThJ* 20, 2-3 (1986): 64-75.

Phillips, G. "This is a Hard Saying. Who can be a Listener to it?": Creating a Reader in John 6." *Semeia* 26 (1983): 23-56.

Piwowarczyk, May Ann. "The Narratee and the Situation of Enunciation: A Reconsideration of Prince's Theory." *Genre* 9 (1976): 161-177.

Polzin, Robert M. "Literary and Historical Criticism of the Bible: A Crisis in Scholarship," in *Orientation by Disorientation: Studies in Literary Criticism and Biblical Literary Criticism in Honor of William A. Beardslee*, ed. by Richard A. Spencer, 99-114. PTMS 35. Pittsburgh: Pickwick, 1980.

Porter, J. R. "Who Was the Beloved Disciple?" *ExpTim* 77, 7 (1966): 213-214.

Porter, Stanley. "Reader-Response Criticism and New Testament Study: A Response to A. C. Thiselton's *New Horizon in Hermeneutics*." *JLit&Th* 8 (1994): 94-102.

_____. "Why Hasn't Reader-Response Criticism Caught on in New Testament Studies." *JLit&Th* 4 (1990): 278-92.

Powell, Mark A. *What is Narrative Criticism?* Guides to Biblical
Scholarship. Minneapolis: Fortress Press, 1990.

_____, Cecile G. Gray, and Melissa C. Curtis. *The Bible and Modern
Literary Criticism: A Critical Assessment and Annotated
Bibliography.* Westport: Greenwood Press, 1992.

_____. "Toward a Narrative-Critical Understanding of Mark." *Int* 47
(1993): 341-346.

_____. "Types of Readers and Their Relevance for Biblical
Hermeneutics." *TSR* 12 (Fall 1990): 67-76.

Priest, James E. (ed.). *Johannine Studies: Essays in Honor of Frank
Pack.* Malibu: Pepperdine University Press, 1989.

Prince, Gerald. *A Dictionary of Narratology.* Lincoln and London:
University of Nebraska, 1987.

_____. *Narratology: The Form and Functioning of Narrative.* Janua
Liguarum. Studia Memoriae Nicolai van Wijk Dedicata. Series
Maior 108. New York: Mouton Publishers, 1982.

_____. "On Readers and Listeners in Narrative." *Neophil* 55 (1971): 117-
122.

Quast, Kevin. *Peter and the Beloved Disciple: Figures for a Community
in Crisis.* JSNTSup 32. Sheffield: JSOT Press, 1989.

_____. *Reading the Gospel of John: An Introduction.* Mahwah: Paulist
Press, 1991.

Rabinowitz, Peter J. *Before Reading: Narrative Conventions and the
Politics of Interpretation.* Ithaca: Cornell University Press, 1987.

_____. "Truth in Fiction: A Reexamination of Audiences." *CI* 4 (1977):
121-141.

Reed, Walter L. "A Poetics of the Bible: Problems and Possibilities." *JLit&Th* 1, 2 (September 1987): 154-166.

Reinhartz, Adele. "Jesus as Prophet: Predictive Prolepses in the Fourth Gospel." *JSNT* 36 (1989b): 3-16.

_____. "The Narrative Structure of the Fourth Gospel." Ph.D. dissertation, McMaster University, 1981.

_____. *The Word in the World: The Cosmological Tale in the Fourth Gospel.* SBLMS 45. E. F. Campbell, ed. Atlanta: Scholars Press, 1992.
_____. "The New Testament and Anti-Judaism: A Literary Critical Approach." *JES* 25, 4 (1988): 524-37.

Resseguie, James L. "Reader Response Criticism and the Synoptic Gospels." *JAAR* 52 (1984): 307-324.

Rhoads, David. "Narrative Criticism and the Gospel of Mark." *JAAR* 50 (1982): 411-434.

_____ and D. Michie. *Mark as Story: An Introduction to the Narrative of a Gospel.* Philadelphia: Fortress Press, 1982.

Ricci, Carla. *Mary Magdalene and Many Others: Women who Followed Jesus.* Translated from the Italian by Paul Burns. Minneapolis: Fortress Press, 1994.

Richter, David H. "Reader as Ironic Victim." *Nov* 14 (1981): 135-151.

Ricoeur, Paul. *Time and Narrative.* 3 vols. Chicago: Chicago University Press, 1984, 1986, and 1988.

_____. "The Narrative Function." *Semeia* 13 (1978): 177-202.

Ridderbos, H. "The Structure and Scope of the Prologue to the Fourth Gospel." *NovT* 8 (1966): 180-201.

Riley, W. "Situating Biblical Narrative: Poetics and the Transmission of Community Values." *ProcJrBibAssoc* 9 (1985): 38-52.

Rimmon-Kenan, Shlomith. *Narrative Fiction: Contemporary Poetics.* London: Methuen, 1983.

Robinson, J. A. T. "The Relationship of the Prologue to the Gospel of John." *NTS* 9 (1962-3): 120-129.

_____. *The Priority of John.* London: SCM Press, 1985.

Robinson, J. M. "Recent Research in the Fourth Gospel." *JBL* 78, 3 (1959): 242-252.

Russell, D. A., and M. Winterbottom, eds. *Ancient Literary Criticism: The Principal Texts in New Translations.* Oxford: Claredon Press, 1972.

Ruthrof, H. G. "Aspects of a Phenomenological View of Narrative." *JNT* 4 (1974): 87-99.

Ryken, Leland, ed. *The New Testament in Literary Criticism.* A Library of Literary Criticism. New York: Fredrick Ungar Publishing Co., 1984.

Sanders, Joseph N. and B. A. Mastin. *A Commentary on the Gospel According to St. John.* New York: Harper and Row Publishers, 1968.

Schenk, Wolfgang. "The Roles of the Readers or the Myth of the Reader." *Semeia* 48 (1989): 55-80.

Schnackenburg, Rudolf. *The Gospel According to St. John.* 3 vols., vol. 1 translated by Kevin Smyth; vol. 2 translated by Cecily Hastings, Francis McDonagh, David Smith, and Richard Foley; and vol. 3 translated by David Smith and G. A. Kon. New York: Seabury Press, 1980.

Schneidau, Herbert N. "Let the Reader Understand." *Semeia* 39 (1987): 135-145.

Schneiders, Sandra M. "John 21:1-14." *Int* 43 (1989): 70-75.

_____. "Women in the Fourth Gospel." *BTB* 12 (1982): 25-45.

_____. "Reflections on Commitment in the Fourth Gospel." *BTB* 6 (1976): 258-263.

_____. "Symbolism and the Sacramental Principle in the Fourth Gospel," in *Segnie sacramenti nel Vangelo diGiovanni*, ed. by Pius-Ramon Tragan, 221-235. Studia Anselmiana, 66. Rome: Editrice Anselmiana, 1977.

Scholes, Robert. "Cognition and the Implied Reader." *Diacritics* 5 (1975): 13-15.

_____. *The Nature of Narrative*. New York: Oxford University Press, 1966.

_____ and R. Kellogg. "Plot in Narrative." in *Perspectives on Fiction*, ed. by J. Calderwood and H. Toliver, 277-302. London: Oxford University Press, 1968.

Segovia, Fernando F. "The Final Farewell of Jesus: A Reading of John 20:30-21:25." *Semeia* 53 (1991): 167-190.

_____. "Toward a New Direction in Johannine Scholarship: The Fourth Gospel from a Literary Perspective." *Semeia* 53 (1991): 1-22.

_____. *The Farewell of the Word: The Johannine Call to Abide*. Minneapolis: Fortress Press, 1991.

_____, ed. *"What is John?": Readers and Readings of the Fourth Gospel*. SBL Symposium Series. Atlanta: Scholars Press, 1996.

_____ and Mary Ann Tolbert, eds. *Reading from this Place: Social Location and Biblical Interpretation in the United States*. Vol. 1 and 2. Minneapolis, Fortress Press, 1995.

Senior, Donald. *The Passion of Jesus in the Gospel of John*. Collegeville: The Liturgical Press, 1991.

Shaw, A. "Image and Symbol in John 21." *ExpTim* 86, 10 (1975): 3111.

Sheeley, Steven. "The Narrator in the Gospels: Developing a Model." *PerRelSt* 16 (Fall 1989): 213-223.

Silberman, Lou H. "Listening to the Text." *JBL* 102 (1983): 3-26.

Sloyan, Gerard S. *John*. Atlanta: John Knox Press, 1988.

_____. *What Are They Saying About John?* Mahwah: Paulist Press, 1991.

Smalley, Stephen S. "The Signs in John XXI." *NTS* 20 (1974): 275-288.

_____. *John: Evangelist and Interpreter*. Exeter: Paternoster Press, 1978.

_____. "The Johannine Son of Man Sayings." *NTS* 15, 3 (1969): 278-301.

_____. "Keeping up with Recent Studies; Part 12 St John's Gospel." *ExpTim* 97, 4 (1986): 102-108.

Smith, D. Moody. "The Presentation of Jesus in the Fourth Gospel." *Int* 31, 4 (1977): 367-378.

_____ "Johannine Studies," in *The New Testament and Its Modern Interpreters*, ed. by E. J. Epps and G. W. McRae, 271-296, Philadelphia: Fortress Press, 1989.

_____. *The Composition and Order of the Fourth Gospel: Bultmann's Literary Theory*. New Haven: Yale University Press, 1965.

Solages, Mgr de. *Jean et les Synoptiques*. Leiden: Brill, 1979.

Staley, Jeffrey L. "Subversive Narrator/Victimized Reader: A Reader Response Assessment of a Text-Critical Problem, John 18.12-24." *JSNT* 51 (1993): 79-98.

_____. *Reading with a Passion: Rhetoric, Autobiography, and the American West in the Gospel of John*. New York: Continuum, 1995.

_____. *The Print's First Kiss: A Rhetorical Investigation of the Implied Reader in the Fourth Gospel*. SBLDS 82. Atlanta: Scholars Press, 1988.

Stanzel, Franz K. "Teller-Characters and Reflector-Characters in Narrative Theory." *PT* 2, 2 (1981): 5-15.

Stein, Richard L. "Historical Fiction and the Implied Reader: Scott and Iser." *Nov* 14 (1981): 213-231.

Stephens, John and Ruth Waterhouse. "Authorial Revision and Constraints on the Role of the Reader: Some Examples from Wilfred Owen." *PT* 8, 1 (1987): 65-83.

Sternberg, Meir. *The Poetics of Biblical Narrative*. Bloomington: Indiana University Press, 1985.

_____. *Expositional Modes and Temporal Ordering in Fiction*. Baltimore and London: Johns Hopkins University, 1978.

Stibbe, Mark. "A Tomb with a view: John 11:1-44 in Narrative Critical Focus." *NTS* 40 (1994): 38-54.

_____. *John's Gospel*. New Testament Readings. London and New York: Routledge, 1994.

_____. *John as Storyteller: Narrative Criticism and the Fourth Gospel*. Cambridge: Cambridge University Press, 1992.

_____. *John*. England: JSOT Press, 1993.

_____, ed. *The Gospel of John as Literature: An Anthology of Twentieth-Century Perspectives*. Leiden: E. J. Brill, 1993.

Strachan, R. H. *The Fourth Evangelist: Dramatist or Historian?* London, 1925.

Stroup, G. W. *The Promise of Narrative Theology: Recovering the Gospel in the Church*. Atlanta: John Knox Press, 1981.

Stuhlmacher, Paul, ed. *The Gospel and the Gospels*. Grand Rapids: William B. Eerdmans Publishing Company, 1991.

Stuhlmacher, Peter. *Historical Criticism and Theological Interpretation of Scripture: Toward a Hermeneutics of Consent*. Translated with an Introduction by Roy A. Harrisville. Philadelphia: Fortress Press, 1977.

Suleiman, Susan R. "Of Readers and Narratees: The Experience of 'Pamela.'" *L'Esprit* 21 (1981): 89-97.

_____ and Inge Crosman, eds. *The Reader in the Text: Essays on Audience and Interpretation*. Princeton: Princeton University Press, 1980.

Swidler, Leonard. *Biblical Affirmation of Women*. Philadelphia: The Westminster Press, 1979.

Talbert, Charles H. *Reading John: A Literary and Theological Commentary on the Fourth Gospel and the Johannine Epistles*. New York: Crossroad, 1992.

_____. *Reading Luke*. New York: Crossroad, 1982.

_____. "The Myth of a Descending-Ascending Redeemer in Mediterranean Antiquity." *NTS* 22, 4 (1976): 418-439.

_____. "The Disciples in Mark: The Function of a Narrative Role." *JR* 57 (1977): 386-405.

_____. "The Gospel of Mark as Narrative Christology." *Semeia* 16 (1979): 57-97.

_____. *The Narrative Unity of Luke-Acts*. Vol. I, Philadelphia: Fortress Press, 1986.

Taylor, Michael J., ed. *A Companion to John: Readings in Johannine Theology (John's Gospel and Epistles)*. New York: Alba House, 1977.

Taylor, Vincent. *The Gospel According to St. Mark*. Rev. ed. Grand Rapids: Baker Book House, 1981.

Teeple, H. *The Literary Origin of the Gospel of John*. Evanston: Religion and Ethics Institute, 1974.

Temple, William. *Readings in John's Gospel*. First and Second Series. London: Macmillan and Co., 1953.

Tew, Grady Timothy. "The Pneumatology of John as Seen in the Fourth Gospel (Spirit Texts)." Ph.D. dissertation, New Orleans Baptist Theological Seminary, Louisiana, 1993.

Thiselton, A. C. "Structuralism and Biblical Studies." *ExpTim* 89 (1978): 329-35.

Thompson, Marianne M. *The Humanity of Jesus in the Fourth Gospel*. Philadelphia: Fortress Press, 1988.

Tolbert, Mary Ann. "How the Gospel of Mark Builds Character." *Int* 47 (1993): 347-357.

_____, ed. *The Bible and Feminist Hermeneutics. Semeia* 28. Chico: Scholars Press, 1983.

_____. *Sowing the Gospel: Mark's World in Literary-Historical Perspective*. Minneapolis: Fortress Press, 1989.

Tompkins, Jane P. *Reader-Response Criticism: From Formalism to Post-Structuralism*. Baltimore: Johns Hopkins University Press, 1980.

Trudinger, L. P. "Subtle Wordplays in the Gospel of John and the Problem of Chapter 21." *JRT* 28 (1971-72): 27-31.

Uspensky, Boris. *A Poetics of Composition: The Structure of the Artistic Text and Typology of a Compositional Form*. Translated by Valentina Zavarin and Susan Wittig. Berkeley: University of California Press, 1973.

van Belle, Gilbert, ed. *Johannine Bibliography 1966-1985: A Cumulative Bibliography on the Fourth Gospel*. Lueven: University Press, 1988.

van Iersel, Bastiaan. *Reading Mark*. Translated by W. H. Bisscheroux. Collegeville: The Liturgical Press, 1988.

van Segbroeck, F. C., M. Tuckett, G. Van Belle, and J. Verheyden, eds. *The Four Gospels 1992: Festschrift Frans Neirynck*, vol. III. Lueven: University Press, 1992.

van Tilborg, S. "The Gospel of John: Communicative Processes in a Narrative Text." *Neotest* 23 (1989): 19-27.

Verdaasdonk, Hugo. "Some Fallacies about the Reading Process." *Poetics* 10 (1981): 91-107.

von Wahlde, Urban C. "Literary Structure and Theological Argument in Three Discourses with the Jews in the Fourth Gospel." *JBL* 103, 4 (1984): 575-584.

_____. *The Earliest Version of John's Gospel*. Wilmington: Michael Glazier, 1989.

Vorster, Willem S. "The Reader in the Text: Narrative Material." *Semeia* 48 (1989): 21-39.

Waetjen, Herman C. *A Reordering of Power: A Socio-Political Reading of Mark's Gospel.* Minneapolis: Fortress Press, 1989.

Wagner, Günter, ed. *An Exegetical Bibliography of the New Testament: John and 1, 2, 3 John.* Vol. 3. Macon: Mercer University Press, 1983.

Ward, Patricia A. "Revolutionary Strategies of Reading: A Review Article." *C&L* 33 (1983): 9-18.

Warner, Martin, ed. *The Bible as Rhetoric: Studies in Biblical Persuasion and Credibility.* Warwick Studies in Philosophy and Literature. London and New York: Routledge, 1989.

Wead, David W. "Johannine Irony as a Key to the Author-Audience Relationship in John's Gospel," in *JAAR*, Section on Biblical Literature, ed. by Fred O. Francis, 33-50. Missoula: Scholars Press, 1974.

_____. "The Johannine Double Meaning." *RQ* 13 (1970): 106-120.

_____. *The Literary Devices in John's Gospel.* Theologischen Dissertationen. Vol. 4. Basel: Friedrich Reinhart Kommissionsverlag, 1970.

Webster, E. C. "Pattern in the Fourth Gospel," in *Art and Meaning: Rhetoric in Biblical Literature*, ed. by D. Clines and D. Gunn, 230-257. JSOTSup 19. Sheffield: Almond Press, 1982.

Wellhausen, J. *Das Evangelium Johannis.* Berlin: G. Reimer, 1908.

Westcott, B. F. *The Gospel According to St. John.* Vol. 2. London: John Murray, 1982.

White H. "The Value of Narrativity in the Representation of Reality." *CI* 7 (1980): 5-27.

Wiarda, T. "John 21:1-23: Narrative Unity and its Implication." *JSNT* 46 (1992): 53-71.

Wicker, B. *The Story-Shaped World: Fiction and Metaphysics*. London: Athlone Press, 1975.

Wilder, Amos N. *Early Christian Rhetoric: The Language of the Gospel*. London: SCM Press, 1964.

_____. *The Bible and the Literary Critic*. Minneapolis: Fortress Press, 1991.

Witherington, Ben, III. *John's Wisdom: A Commentary on the Fourth Gospel*. Louisville: Westminster John Knox Press, 1995.

Wuellner, Wilhelm. "Is There an Encoded Reader Fallacy?" *Semeia* 48 (1989): 40-54.

_____. "Putting Life Back into the Lazarus Story and Its Reading: The Narrative Rhetoric of John 11 as the Narration of Faith." *Semeia* 53 (1991): 113-132.

Yacobi, Tamar. "Narrative Structure and Fictional Mediation." *PT* 8, 2 (1987): 355-372.

INDEX

Studies in Biblical Literature

This series invites manuscripts from scholars in any area of biblical literature. Both established and innovative methodologies, covering general and particular areas in biblical study, are welcome. The series seeks to make available studies that will make a significant contribution to the ongoing biblical discourse. Scholars who have interests in gender and sociocultural hermeneutics are particularly encouraged to consider this series.

For further information about the series and for the submission of manuscripts, contact:

Hemchand Gossai
Department of Religion
Muhlenberg College
2400 Chew Street
Allentown, PA 18104-5586

To order other books in this series, please contact our Customer Service Department:

(800) 770-LANG (within the U.S.)
(212) 647-7706 (outside the U.S.)
(212) 647-7707 FAX

or browse online by series at:

WWW.PETERLANG.COM